Palgrave Studies in Islamic Banking, Finance, and Economics

Series Editors
Mehmet Asutay
Business School
Durham University
Durham, UK

Zamir Iqbal
Islamic Development Bank
Jeddah, Saudi Arabia

Jahangir Sultan
Bentley University
Boston, MA, USA

The aim of this series is to explore the various disciplines and sub-disciplines of Islamic banking, finance and economics through the lens of theoretical, practical, and empirical research. Monographs and edited collections in this series will focus on key developments in the Islamic financial industry as well as relevant contributions made to moral economy, innovations in instruments, regulatory and supervisory issues, risk management, insurance, and asset management. The scope of these books will set this series apart from the competition by offering in-depth critical analyses of conceptual, institutional, operational, and instrumental aspects of this emerging field. This series is expected to attract focused theoretical studies, in-depth surveys of current practices, trends, and standards, and cutting-edge empirical research.

More information about this series at
http://www.palgrave.com/gp/series/14618

Amadou Thierno Diallo ·
Ahmet Suayb Gundogdu

Sustainable Development and Infrastructure

An Islamic Finance Perspective

palgrave
macmillan

Amadou Thierno Diallo
Islamic Development Bank
Jeddah, Saudi Arabia

Ahmet Suayb Gundogdu
Islamic Development Bank
Jeddah, Saudi Arabia

ISSN 2662-5121   ISSN 2662-513X (electronic)
Palgrave Studies in Islamic Banking, Finance, and Economics
ISBN 978-3-030-67093-1   ISBN 978-3-030-67094-8 (eBook)
https://doi.org/10.1007/978-3-030-67094-8

This Palgrave Macmillan imprint is published by the registered company Springer Nature
Switzerland AG
The registered company address is: Gewerbestrasse 11, 6330 Cham, Switzerland

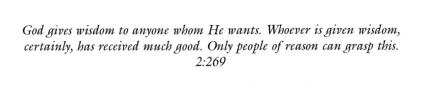

God gives wisdom to anyone whom He wants. Whoever is given wisdom, certainly, has received much good. Only people of reason can grasp this.
2:269

PREFACE

Most books on Islamic finance and development issues are written from an academic perspective. Although academic reflection is key for future direction, dissatisfaction with development efforts, as evidenced from failure of sustainable development efforts, suggests the need for a different look. Development work has many details and a folded approach would not lead to cogent resolution of protracted issues. Each intervention area requires specific elaboration for meaningful impact. What is perfectly correct for one sector might be detrimental for another.

Millennium development goals (MDGs) were a good start in framing sustainable development with clear objectives to interlink different areas of development work in pursuit of poverty alleviation, income inequality, and hunger. Their successor sustainable development goals (SDGs) built on lessons learned from MDGs. The major obstacle to achieving SDGs is very often stipulated as the need for massive resource mobilization to carry out interventions. The effectiveness of interventions, however, is never questioned. Since interventions are stunted so are efforts for resource mobilization: no one wants to waste resources for abortive projects. The general impression is that the resources allocated are wasted with the unfair enrichment of the few in the process of carrying out barren projects. Historical focus has been on project outputs in the form of project assets, assuming that any infrastructure development would provide an enabling environment for growth. The assumption has been that the economic growth will happen by itself through the trickling-down effect for employ-ment, poverty alleviation, income inequality, and hunger. Regardless of a string of economic growth years, however, the issues are still there and this leads to the questioning of the validity of assumptions. An economic growth approach for sustainable development does not work. The idea of inclusive growth emerges to address the missing link. However, even this inclusiveness idea alone, despite its ability to touching upon an important missing link, is not enough. A more holistic approach is needed to under-stand the role of finance in sustainable development and infrastructure projects. More importantly, focus should be on outcomes: a link between project outputs and desired sustainable development outcome needs to be established during project formulation. In order to achieve the desired outcome for sustainable development, financing is an important tool. It should be utilized subtly and skillfully vis-à-vis infrastructure projects.

Islamic finance, with its strict Riba restrictions, rules, and other checks and balances, is a very good fit for infrastructure development in pursuit of sustainable development. When it comes to sustainable development, Islamic finance has enough tools to intervene for impact. However, the success of developmental projects is not only related to Islamic finance—where more policy discourse is needed—but also requires guidance from the principles of Islamic economics. This book intends to elaborate on a different aspect of infrastructure development vis-à-vis sustainable devel-opment, drawn from decades of real-life development banking experience, and to propose impactful intervention methods based on wisdom from both Islamic economics and finance.

Jeddah, Saudi Arabia   Amadou Thierno Diallo
Jeddah, Saudi Arabia   Ahmet Suayb Gundogdu

CONTENTS

About the Authors

Amadou Thierno Diallo is the Acting Director General of Global Practices, and Director of the Economic and Social Infrastructure Department, at the Islamic Development Bank, where he has been employed since 2011. He supervises the Bank's activities to support the socio-economic development efforts of its 57 member countries through the identification and prioritization of investment projects and programs as well as the development and implementation of policies and strategies. His previous roles at the IsDB have been as Acting Director of the Agriculture and Rural Development Department and Director of the Office of the Vice President Operations.

Before joining the IsDB, he held several positions at the African Development Bank, including as Resident Representative Mali and as a Manager of the Energy and ICT sectors. He also has 10 years' experience in the mining sector in Guinea as well as in the private sector in the USA.

He holds a BS in Mining Engineering from the University of Conakry, Guinea, an MS in Mineral Economics from the University of Montana, an MBA in Finance, and a Master's in Public and International Affairs from the University of Pittsburgh. He is bestowed by the President of Mali with the Officer of the Order of Merit of the Republic of Mali for services rendered for the development of the country.

Ahmet Suayb Gundogdu is the Senior Technical Specialist for the Director General of Global Practices and Chief Economist at the Islamic

Development Bank, where he has been employed since 2008. Before joining the bank, he was pursuing his PhD in Economics at Virginia Tech, USA.

He holds a BA in International Trade from Bogazici University and an MA in International Development from the International University of Japan. He completed his PhD in Islamic Finance at Durham University, UK. Gundogdu has held several positions within the IDB Group: he served as a Senior Program Manager at Islamic Solidarity Fund for Development and managed a portfolio of approximately $1 billion at the International. He also has early career experience in industries, commercial banking, business consulting, and international business.

LIST OF FIGURES

LIST OF TABLES

CHAPTER 1

Islamic Finance for Sustainable Development Goals

Islamic finance practitioners and scholars are drawn toward the sustainable development goals (SDGs) of the United Nations because the goals are perfectly aligned with the philosophy of Islamic finance. Scholars reflect on the role of Islamic finance as a reemerging financial alternative in the context of SDGs. Often the profit–loss sharing arrangement of Islamic finance, its solidarity-based feature for poverty alleviation, and its use of *Sukuk* for resource mobilization to finance infrastructure development are highlighted.[1] In the context of SDGs, it is key to link Islamic financial institutions and capital markets to address the vulnerability of the poor, financial stability, and development. The critical component for achieving SDGs is resource mobilization, and this is a key focus of the developmental agenda for 2015–2030. The SDG programs to achieve the given targets require unprecedented resource mobilization compared with their predecessors, the programs of the millennium development goals (MDGs), which focused on a limited number of targets.[2] Therefore it is vitally important that we examine the potential role that Islamic finance can play in the effort to support the resource mobilization for SDGs. If we examine the academic research in this area, we see that it offers

[1] Zarrouk (2015).

[2] Ahmed et al. (2015).

© The Author(s), under exclusive license to Springer Nature Switzerland AG 2021
A. T. Diallo and A. S. Gundogdu, *Sustainable Development and Infrastructure*, Palgrave Studies in Islamic Banking, Finance, and Economics, https://doi.org/10.1007/978-3-030-67094-8_1

1

only limited insights. This is because there has been little opportunity for scholars to obtain hands-on experience of the practice of Islamic developmental finance as there is still a gap to be bridged between academic research and hands-on real-life practice.

The conventional understanding of economics and finance with SDGs is now converging to that of Islamic as finance is not instrumental anymore, but a means to achieving sustainable development. What differs in Islamic finance is related to the underlying financing contracts but more importantly with the wider economic perspective. Finance is a tool that can be used to achieve *Maqasid Al Shariah* in Islam. Although there are key differences between sustainable development goals and the classical definition of *Maqasid Al Shariah*, the philosophical convergence toward Islamic conventions encourages the need for a joint effort. However, there still exist major underlying distinctions: (1) the Islamic definition of poverty is net worth-based while SDGs assume an income approach. From an SDG viewpoint, a person with high levels of debt is not categorized as poor as long as such debt generates income. During the cycle of loan growth that feeds accelerated economic activity, poverty statistics substantially improve. However, once the circle is broken, in a very short period poverty numbers will explode as income depends on uninterrupted economic activity while debt is outstanding; (2) Islamic philosophy stands for fairness and harmony among humans. Every person is created with particular attributes to form a harmonious human collective. In Islam, everybody is equally valuable, yet unique and different; (3) the Islamic approach proposes matching noninterest-based financial products, in lending and resource mobilization, to address the peculiarities of intervention areas: there is no one-size-fits-all product.

The practice of Islamic development suggests the key success factor as the ability to harness the right blend of resource mobilization tools – namely grants, concessional loans, and commercially priced loans – with the most effective programs. It is most important to match development programs with the correct resource mobilization methods and platforms. Many of the proposals for the harnessing of *Zakat*, *Waqf*, and *Qard Hasan* fail to consider real-life implications. In many instances these tools are proposed for intervention areas interchangeably.[3] Contemporary hands-on approaches and appropriate Islamic resource mobilization interventions for SDG programs are shown in Table 1.1.

The essence of the Islamic poverty alleviation approach is to provide a blend of resources to encourage cooperation among the active poor as opposed to competition in a zero-sum game. The aim is to generate added value within the value chains to tackle the issue of poverty in rural areas before the poverty migrates to urban areas. Once poverty is transformed into urban areas, it is much more difficult to manage: migrants may not develop the skills that are needed quickly enough to add value to an urban economy. Hence, experience shows that if a microfinance program is designed properly in terms of profit–loss sharing with Islamic finance products, it can tackle the original issue: rural poverty.[4] In particular, the group purchase of raw materials and the sale of products as a group give substantial bargaining power to farmers and microfinance institutions. It is then possible to achieve high profit margins. In such cases, an economic empowerment fund can help to alleviate poverty.

In the following three sections we shall examine the three interventions for resource mobilization (in Table 1.1) in relation to Islamic finance.

1.1 COMMERCIAL RESOURCES FOR ISLAMIC MICROFINANCE AND ECONOMIC INFRASTRUCTURE DEVELOPMENT

With commercially priced loans (see Table 1.1), the funds returned to fund providers by beneficiaries/borrowers consist of the principals plus the market markups. The purpose of such loans is to create an enabling environment through financial inclusion. Some scholars have proposed offering interest-free loans (*Qard Hasan*) to the poor; however, the returns of commercially priced loans are based on market rates to ensure value addition for the investments.[5] Further, as a finance strategy to generate economic activity, grants and concessional loans mislead an economy and allocate resources to inefficient transactions. In order to assure value addition, such programs should be used with market rates.

---

[3] Gundogdu (2019).

[4] Wilson (2007).

[5] Elgari, M. A. (n.d.) The Qard Hasan Bank. Mimeo.

Table 1.1 Development programs, SDGs, and resource mobilization.

Islamic resource mobilization	SDGs	Programs
1. **Commercially priced loans**: Islamic finance modes (funds returned from beneficiaries of finance, principals plus market markups, to fund providers)	Economic empowerment funds Developmental *Waqf*	Economic Empowerment Program: Islamic Microfinance in value chain
	1. Investment *Sukuk*	1. Public–private partnership
	2. Two-step *Murabaha/Musharaka*	2. Small and medium-sized enterprise line of financing
	SDG #1: No poverty	
	SDG #7: Affordable and clean energy	
	SDG #9: Industry innovation, and infrastructure	
	SDG #8: Decent work and economic growth	
2. **Grants**: *Zakat* (direct transfer of funds from the rich to the poor; neither principals nor markups go back to fund providers)	*Zakat* platform	1. Support for microfinance beneficiaries to eradicate hunger
	SDG #2: Zero hunger	2. Wealth distribution programs as opposed to social transfer, food stamps, and social security systems
	SDG #5: Gender equality	
	SDG #10: Reduced inequalities within and between countries	

Islamic resource mobilization		SDGs	Programs
3. **Concessional loans:** *Qard Hasan* (funds returned with principals plus market markups; markups spent on programs for beneficiaries, with the principals returned to the fund providers)	Complementary Currency Cash *Waqf*/Cash *Waqf Sukuk*	SDG #3: Good health and well-being SDG #4: Quality education SDG #6: Clean water and sanitation SDG #11: Sustainable cities and communities	Flagship programs related to social investment

Source Based on Gundogdu (2018)

Contrary to the commonly held belief, poor people can be a source of sustainable economic growth if they are endowed with an enabling environment. Economic empowerment is an integrated approach of Islamic finance that excludes no one. Its purpose is to invest with the poor and undertake economic activities, using Islamic financing formats, with low-income marginalized groups, unemployed youth, and productive families.

The concept of economic empowerment has been applied in several countries and has yielded some very encouraging results.[6] It is more profitable and less risky for all parties: fund providers, fund users, and communities. It is very effective at combatting poverty and achieving social security and development because its economic projects are more stable and resistant. The basis of the concept is that fundamental barriers exist that must be lifted to help eradicate poverty and integrate the poor into value chains so that they can achieve self-sustenance. Accordingly, economic empowerment through Islamic microfinance assumes that the essential needs of the poor are multidimensional. In other words, poverty has several facets and financing is just one of them. Poverty has more to do with the inability to take advantage of certain enabling factors: project opportunities, economies of scale to compete with large producers, networks for market access, fair price formation, and, most importantly, supportive infrastructures.[7]

Economic empowerment is indeed an Islamic microfinance program; however, for several reasons, it is not called Islamic microfinance as such. The philosophy behind the concept of economic empowerment is to address problematic issues with microfinance, whether such finance is Islamic or conventional. Unfortunately, though, microfinance lending programs very often defeat their purpose. Poor people become worse off because microfinance institutions (MFIs) run businesses for profit once the system proves that they are viable. MFIs prey on the poor by lending

---

[6] The Islamic Development Bank's results have been impressive for Palestine, Sudan, Yemen, Kazakhstan, and Benin.

[7] A supportive infrastructure involves the creation and supply of economic zones, industrial zones, warehouses, generators, water purification units, incubators, packaging centers, laboratories, and other projects that cannot be provided by one initiative but can be achieved within the framework of unions, cooperatives, and solidarity groups. One of the objectives of these supportive projects is to ensure that initiatives for the economic empowerment of the poor have the same chance of success as large and medium enterprises in the private sector.

money without considering value addition in enterprises and by fueling competition in communities. In some instances, MFIs charge up to 200 percent interest by subtle deceit. For example, they ask for US$1 return per day, compounding such a repayment until it reaches 200 percent interest per annum. The financially illiterate poor do not understand such a calculation.[8]

In order to generate value addition for the poor, the economic empowerment concept focuses on value chains and encourages group cooperation rather than competition. Experience shows that the agricultural sector supports value addition; however, the informal urban employment sector, which fuels zero-sum game competition, does not. MFIs adopt microfinance beneficiaries as business partners, buy agricultural input goods for all farmers at a discounted price, and act as offtakers during harvests in order to sell the farmers' produce in bulk for higher prices. Such an approach can generate a 20 percent margin for input purchases and a 20 percent margin for the sale of harvests. The farmers are no longer susceptible to exploitation because of such intervention. For this reason, by participating in microfinance programs, farmers are better off. Even after paying a 15 percent markup on financing, they still have a 25 percent margin. Besides, the concept has ancillary benefits such as group training and bulk storage. Indeed, this model can be expanded to other supportive infrastructures in order to support value chains. Further, microfinance programs can be supported by *Zakat* to avoid the use of microfinance loans by farmers for food. The use of loans for food is one of the main reasons why microfinance interventions fail. The poor very often spend microfinance loans on food out of desperation. Thus, the poor default on their loans and are punished for the rest of their lives by financial institutions refusing them further access to funds. With the concept of economic empowerment, such drawbacks are addressed with *Zakat* money, if needed, in order to ensure that farmers can have food; thus, the farmers use their loans solely for their enterprises. However, unlike the proposal by some scholars to use *Zakat* to lend *Qard Hasan* to farmers, *Zakat* must be used in its traditional context and not for insuring farmers or bailing them out.[9] Experience has shown that after farmers become aware that the origin of their resources is *Zakat*, or there

---

[8] Sinclair (2012).
[9] Kahf (2004).

is a possibility of a bailout with *Zakat* money, they tend to default or present a default case.[10]

An economic empowerment fund represents resource mobilization in a cash *Waqf* format. Advice for use of cash *Waqf* concept is not a novelty.[11] More specifically, Haneef et al. developed an integrated *Waqf*-based Islamic microfinance design in Bangladesh as a means to alleviate poverty.[12] Resources mobilized under an economic empowerment fund are invested in microfinance but with a commercial return. The purpose is to create a snowball effect that enables the poor to access finance, with ring-fencing through discounted input prices, fair harvest prices, and micro *Takaful*. Ultimately, the poor become business partners who can add value if they are directed properly and have equal opportunities to compete against sizeable firms.

Table 1.2 presents a comparison between traditional microfinance and Islamic microfinance based on economic empowerment.

Economic empowerment funds are established for the purpose of investing with the poor on a commercial basis. In this regard, the concept is similar to developmental *Waqf*. *Waqf* is an endowment that has great potential for social welfare. Traditionally, such charitable endowments are usually in the form of land and real estate. However, *Waqf* in the form of cash is also allowed. If established by cash endowment with the provision of supporting the poor, such *Waqf* is called cash *Waqf*.[13] Unlike traditional cash *Waqf*, which is invested in the bankable projects of an organized sector and the returns then used for the poor, developmental *Waqf* is invested in a portfolio of bankable and unbankable projects from the unorganized sectors of the poor.

When this approach to invest directly with the poor in viable opportunities is adopted, the impact on poverty alleviation multiplies because the returns from such investments are also spent on the poor. Economic empowerment fund resources are composed of developmental *Waqf* paid in – capital, donor countries, national financial institutions, international

---

[10] In the case of microfinance provided by the Islamic Development Bank through the Bank of Khartoum, the initial success of agricultural microfinance faded once the farmers were informed that the resource was zakat.

[11] Ahmed (2011), Cizakca (2004), and Kahf (2004) proposed the use of the cash *Waqf* concept for Islamic MFIs.

[12] Haneef et al. (2015).

[13] Kahf (2000, 2004).

Table 1.2 Islamic economic empowerment versus conventional microfinance.

Classic Microfinance	Microfinance Based on the Approach of Economic Empowerment
The fundamental need is for finance	There are several basic needs: access to project opportunities, access to partnerships, access to basic infrastructures, access to financing, and access to markets
The marginalized or poor individual is a credit borrower	The marginalized or poor individual is a business partner who has great potential for generating wealth
Gains from transactions with the poor are made even when the poor suffer	The practice followed is that of participatory finance: gains are made from transactions with the poor but solidarity with the latter remains Ethical finance is practiced; thus, ethical rules are followed
Individual micro-project microfinancing	Micro-projects, medium projects, integrated projects, small and medium-sized enterprises, large projects, micro/small/large financing
MFIs undertake the financing	MFIs are socioeconomic actors
MFIs operate with short-term clients	MFIs conduct business with their clients in the short, medium, and long terms depending on the projects' natures.
The clients manage their projects	MFI supports customers with the management of their projects until the customers become autonomous
MFIs manage the financing	MFIs manage the value chains in collaboration with a network of specialized partners
Microcredit	Financial engineering with different appropriate Islamic financing methods that ensure projects' profitability

Source Gundogdu (2018b)

financial institutions, corporate social responsibility programs, and *Zakat*. From the perspective of Islamic principles, however, *Zakat* should not be used as such because it is required to be a direct transfer of wealth. Hence, *Zakat* should directly be given from the rich to the poor.

In order to expand the impact on value chains, more needs to be done for the following.

- SDG #7: Affordable and clean energy
- SDG #8: Decent work and economic growth
- SDG #9: Industry, innovation, and infrastructure.

Once again, in order to assure the allocation of resources and work effort to viable and value-adding projects, the market markup rate should be used for project proposals related to these three SDGs. Infrastructure development and affordable energy projects can be undertaken with *Istisna* and/or *Ijara* agreements under public–private partnership (PPP) initiatives and SME involvement. If employment and economic growth are to be achieved, small and medium-sized enterprises (SMEs) require support in the form of financial resources. In this regard, two-step *Murabaha*, in addition to *Musharaka/Mudaraba*, is the most efficient tool for SME financing and resource mobilization. In order to increase the number of PPP projects, invested money can be collected, after repayment starts, by issuing investment *Sukuk* whereby investors give lump sums to financiers. The latter can then embark on new projects immediately instead of waiting for full repayment at the end of a 15- to 20-year tenor as practiced by MDBs. Thus, it is essential to involve private sector resources in order to bridge the investment gap. Such an approach may appear more expensive at first glance because PPP finance is more costly than public finance. Nevertheless, long-term cost–benefit analysis proves that cost efficiency in project production and maintenance after project completion makes PPP cheaper than public finance, regardless of the higher financing cost. Nevertheless, PPP should be opted only if there exists an element of value-for-money.

1.2   Grants for Hunger and Wealth Redistribution

In the case of grant resources (see Table 1.1), funds are not returned from beneficiaries to fund providers. The main grant resource in Islam is *Zakat*, which is an entitlement whereby the poor share the wealth of the rich. With regard to hunger and inequality, Islam prefers *Zakat*, a wealth distribution mechanism, to *Sadaqa*, which is almsgiving. *Zakat* is collected annually at a rate of 2.5 percent from the rich based on their net worth. Because it is collected annually from net worth, and not income, *Zakat* not only addresses the issues of hunger and inequality but also inhibits wealth accumulation among a very small number of people who would otherwise set exploitative prices as more factors of production accumulate under their control. Islam encourages accumulation of wealth but not in the hands of very few people. If all the factors of production are gathered in the hands of a few, such people would determine prices based on monopolistic and oligopolistic price setting, which is good for them but not for the poor. *Zakat* addresses the issues of hunger and inequality with direct and indirect effects: (1) the transfer of wealth to unfortunate people in the form of a direct effect on hunger and inequality, and (2) a decrease in prices by impeding the accumulation of the factors of production in the hands of a few in order to alleviate hunger and inequality.

Sadaqa, almsgiving, is not proposed as a means to address poverty; nor is it proposed as a means to address hunger and inequality in Islamic countries. *Sadaqa* is acceptable only in cases of emergency in order to correct the consequences of dire situations that emerge abruptly. If a situation that involves hunger and poverty is protracted, people should put their efforts into addressing such problems rather than encouraging the masses to become addicted to almsgiving – i.e., *Sadaqa*. These extreme examples of poverty, as outlined here, can be addressed with enabling environments that can be created from Islamic microfinance programs for which resources are mobilized with economic empowerment funds and developmental *Waqf*.

Because *Zakat* is an entitlement of the poor and represents their share in the wealth of the rich, the *Zakat* resources should not be kept or collected for developmental programs or invested for the poor. *Zakat* money should be given directly to the poor. On the other hand, establishing *Zakat* platforms is encouraged to mobilize more resources to support economic empowerment programs. The cost associated with establishing and managing such platforms can be covered from the *Zakat* collected. For example, people under pressure to feed their families use microfinance loans as emergency resources; thus, they cannot generate value addition with the loans that they receive. Hence, *Zakat* should complement economic empowerment funds. If microfinance beneficiaries are also victims of hunger, they should be able to use *Zakat* money to feed themselves while investing microfinance loans to develop their enterprises.

Zakat is the social safety net of Islam. It does not represent social transfer in the form of food stamps or a social security system; instead, it prefers the direct transfer of wealth from the rich to the poor. With such a feature, it alone can address the issues of hunger and inequality in communities. Unfortunately, though, *Zakat* collection rates are unsatis-factory. Indeed, the issue of low level of *Zakat* collection has been the subject of several academic studies.[14] Two reasons for such low *Zakat* collection levels may be people's lack of trust in *Zakat* collection agencies and the lack of efficient collection channels.

1.3   CONCESSIONAL RESOURCES FOR SOCIAL INFRASTRUCTURE DEVELOPMENT

As a general approach in Islam, an interest-free loan, *Qard Hasan*, is better than a grant. *Qard* as a concessional loan can be invested and the generated markup can be spent on development programs. Only the principal returns to the fund providers.

> Who is it that would loan Allah a goodly loan so He will multiply it for him and he will have a noble reward?
>
> Quran 57:11

In many verses in the Quran, believers are encouraged to give interest-free loans, *Qard Hasan*, in order to address protracted problems and break vicious circles. In contrast, *Sadaqa* is for emergencies and unlike *Zakat* it is voluntary. For this reason, the solution proposed by Islamic finance for social infrastructure revolves around concessional loans – i.e., *Qard Hasan*. Nevertheless, proposals to use *Qard Hasan* for microfinance, which should seek profitable value-adding activities, should not be considered.[15] The use of *Qard Hasan* can create zombie developmental programs that become reliant on concessional loans. Besides, it is improper to address infrastructure relating to basic necessities with commercially priced loans that give rise to price bubbles and exploitation of the poor. Moreover, *Zakat* is a direct transfer of money that addresses the issues of hunger and inequality and should not be used in developmental programs to address the following:

[14] For example, Kahf (1999) reported that the *Zakat* collection rate is only between 0.3–0.4 percent of gross domestic product (GDP) in Pakistan, Yemen, and Saudi Arabia. Further, Shirazi et al.'s (2009) calculation showed that the maximum *Zakat* collection rate ranges between 1.8–4.3 percent of GDP annually with institutional arrangements.

[15] Iqbal and Mirakhor (2007).

- SDG #3: Good health and well-being
- SDG #4: Quality education
- SDG #6: Clean water and sanitation
- SDG #11: Sustainable cities and communities.

These SDGs should be addressed with concessional resources: *Qard Hasan* but from a new perspective. The traditional understanding of *Qard Hasan* is to have the principal returned. However, the recipients of *Qard Hasan* should not have any markup repayment obligation, thereby breaking the vicious circle of poverty. In many instances, the poor do not have the means for regular payments. They do not even have the US$100 monthly installment toward the payment of the principal of *Qard Hasan* for home ownership. The same holds for other social investment programs related to the four SDGs listed above. Some of the flagship programs are given in Table 1.3.

All these programs in Table 1.3 are related to basic human needs: health, education, water, and shelter. Experience shows that even noninterest-bearing concessional loans do not enable the poor to make small monthly repayments to solve these problems. If the poor cannot solve these problems, they cannot integrate into global value chains and work to take care of themselves. First, we need to open the eyes of a blind person to enable him or her to work. The only solution is to mobilize resources with the concept of *Qard Hasan*, invest the collected funds in commercially priced transactions, and use the profits to help the programs' implementation. Unfortunately, the general tendency is to keep *Zakat* funds for such use. It is inappropriate to keep *Zakat* money for investments with the poor. *Zakat* should be directly distributed to the poor. Thus, we should change our understanding of *Qard Hasan* in order to use its resources for commercially priced SDG-related projects or investment *Sukuk*. Such an approach would support developmental projects and employment, while the returns on *Qard Hasan* can be used for supporting programs related to health, education, water, and shelter.

As stated earlier, the issues raised here concern human deprivation and have intangible aspects. Hence, from the *Maqasid* perspective, the related programs should not be financed with commercially priced loans. In addition to return on Economic Empowerment Funds, innovative resource mobilization tools with *Qard Hasan* should be employed to fund the programs. Returns on Economic Empowerment Funds' and *Qard Hasan*

Table 1.3 Contemporary development programs, by IsDB.

Program name	Description
Basic Education for the Poor	The program's main objective is to provide access to free, quality, basic education services for children in unserved, underserved, poor, and disadvantaged communities by the following means: increasing retention, improving learning achievements, increasing completion rates at primary level, and strengthening school management structures
Blindness Control	A partnership formed to address cataracts in less-developed countries (LDCs) and to develop human resources in the ophthalmic field
Coalition Program to Stop Obstetric Fistula	The program supports the use of skilled birth attendance to prevent obstetric fistula. Women with the condition directly benefit from treatment, rehabilitation, and reintegration into society
Drylands Initiative	To bring sustainable development to pastoral and agropastoral communities
Sustainable Villages Program	The program's primary objective is to reduce extreme poverty in the field with the help of low-cost, sustainable, and community-led interventions. The program's scope includes investment in sectors that directly relate to (1) agriculture and livestock, (2) primary education, (3) primary healthcare, (4) rural infrastructure, (5) business development, (6) the empowerment of women, and (7) the preservation of the environment with proper water and sanitation infrastructures
Vocational Literacy Program for Poverty Reduction	To improve the literacy competencies, job skills, and productivity of illiterate people and the poor through access to nonformal education, vocational training, and/or microfinance services

(continued)

Table 1.3 (continued)

Program name	Description
Affordable Housing Program	To use resources to subsidize monthly installment payments of the poor in order to support the ownership of homes with clean water and proper sanitation

Source Gundogdu (2018)

funds' commercially priced investments should be used for health, education, water, and shelter programs. The best resource mobilization tools to collect *Qard Hasan* are complementary currency in microfinance, crowdfunding, cash *Waqf*, and cash *Waqf Sukuk*.

Money collected with these instruments can be invested in economic empowerment funds, developmental *Waqf* funds, investment *Sukuk*, and two-step *Murabaha* for commercial returns. The profits can be used to help run programs for health, education, water, and proper shelter without generating additional burdens on the poor, who can then focus on self-sustenance.

1.4 THE NARRATIVE

This systematic inquiry into Islamic finance for development programs suggests that the perfunctory understanding of *Zakat* and *Qard Hasan* should change. *Zakat*, which addresses hunger and inequality, should be directly transferred from the net worth of the rich to the poor. It should not be withheld in the accounts of *Zakat* institutions under the pretext of investing the money for the benefit of the poor. *Qard Hasan*, on the other hand, should be withheld in the accounts for investing in mobilized resources for the benefit of the poor. The returns on *Qard Hasan* investment should be used to provide support in the form of education, health, water, and shelter for the poor. Even though it is voluntary, *Sadaqa* should not be part of development programs because it should only be used for emergency interventions in dire situations that occur occasionally. Protracted issues related to poverty and employment should be addressed by Islamic finance that seeks commercial returns and by focusing on value chains. While addressing value addition with Islamic microfinance through the economic empowerment concept, supportive infrastructure investment, such as in transport and energy, should also be identified to improve value chains. Such infrastructure development – project asset creation – can be undertaken with *Istisna* contracts, ideally in accordance with the PPP business model and SME provision as much as possible. Employment opportunities in downstream value chains should also be expanded through Islamic SME financing with two-step *Murabaha*. At a strategic level, commercially priced loans, grants, and concessional loans should be harnessed to relevant development programs. Further, the use of information and communications technology (ICT) platforms for resource mobilization, such as crowdfunding, will increase resource mobilization possibilities. However, the key for the success of resource mobilization is having the appropriate governance. Thus, resource mobilization platforms should be regulated and the rights of fund providers should be protected within a sound legal and risk management system. Fund providers should have assurances about the proper use of funds without any possibility of corruption or mismanagement.

SDGs are highly admirable as they list the intervention areas. What differentiates sustainable development from infrastructure development is the focus on sustainability. SDGs are connected to the development institutions' infrastructure development business.

SDG#1-No poverty is subject to the Agricultural Investment Sector of Multilateral Development Banks (MDBs). It can be tackled by providing an enabling environment to the rural population: microfinance and social infrastructure (education, health, water). Irrigation and drainage is a key component of the subject – and the whole of Ch. 9 is dedicated to the subject. When it comes to poverty, the concept of *Sadaqa*, *Waqf*, and *Zakat* are proposed as one-size-fits-all products. However, they have different roles and attributes. The experience and review of academic reflection suggest a confusion concerning Islamic charitable spending. The proposals and implemented programs include intervention that utterly contradicts with basic principles of *Infaq, Sadaqa, Waqf*, and *Zakat*. The reason these are named separately has to do with their differing roles, yet they are used interchangeably. The roles of different Islamic charitable spending should be defined to enable the development of to-the-point interventions in pursuit of sustainable development. Hence, Ch. 5 elaborates on different roles of Islamic social spending tools.

SDG#7-Affordable and clean energy, SDG#9-Industry, innovation, and infrastructure, and SDG#8-Decent work and economic growth fall under the economic infrastructure sector. As with the SDG#1-No poverty intervention, there is confusion with the provision of not only economic infrastructure but also social infrastructure (SDG#3-Good health and well-being, SDG#4-Quality education, SDG #6-Clean water and sanitation, and SDG#11-Sustainable cities and communities). Traditionally these infrastructures have been developed with:

1. Public procurement
2. Bilateral loans/grants
3. MDB sovereign loans/grants
4. Public–private partnership.

Public procurement and bilateral loans have embedded shortcomings. Public procurement is inflicted with irregularities. Bilateral loans do not fit the long-term aspect of infrastructure development. Parties involved in bilateral loans may not be able to sustain good relationships during the lifetime of the loan, which may extend over 30 years. Bilateral and some MDB loans exhibit some attributes that are not in the best interest of borrowing countries. These loans impose international competitive bidding procurement whereby firms from lending countries would win the bidding process. As a result the borrowing country would have to pay back the loan and at the same time pay to the winning firm that repatriates the money without enhancing the capacity of the local firms. Islamic finance rules and regulations applied with an *Istisna* contract is a good way to address the issue of MDB sovereign loans for infrastructure development. The details on fairness with Islamic finance contracts are provided in Ch. 2. Although Islamic finance differs from conventional finance with *Istisna* contracts, the issue of sustainability with infrastructure development, both in Islamic and conventional infrastructure development, pushes PPPs forward.

Presently public–private partnerships (PPPs) are proposed not only for economic infrastructure development but also for social infrastructure development. Chapter 3 identifies the sectors suitable for PPPs. PPPs appear to work better for economic infrastructure, yet can be problematic when used with large-scale infrastructures. Chapter 7 elaborates on the possibility of SME involvement in the provision of economic infrastructure as a technological trend to support the involvement of SMEs, particularly in affordable energy. Since large-scale infrastructures need to be financed using a large amount of funds, the involvement of SMEs in the provision of economic infrastructure necessitates alternative resource mobilization approaches. The issue from an Islamic finance perspective is discussed in Ch. 4. Chapter 6 provides a further insight into financial sector sustainability vis-à-vis the state of the Islamic finance industry in fulfilling sustainable development.

Affordability of services for final users is key while developing infrastructure. For social infrastructure, examining the matter from a consumer perspective would reveal the best intervention and resource mobilization tools for infrastructure development. Chapter 8 looks into the dilemma of financing education and health. Financing such services by themselves makes them less affordable. Chapter 9 makes an analogy to education and health and comes up with a sustainable solution for a water sector: Irrigation and drainage provision in pursuit of agricultural development. Actually, all these SDGs are somehow connected either directly or indirectly, and Ch. 10 provides a holistic approach in summarizing the most suitable business model for infrastructure development, resource mobilization, and remedies to tackle resource mobilization difficulties peculiar to Islamic finance. Unlike with conventional finance, the restriction of Islamic finance inflict efficiency problems for financial institutions while ring-fencing borrowers for fairness.

References

Ahmed, H. 2011. Waqf-based microfinance: Realizing the social role of Islamic finance. In *Essential readings in contemporary waqf issues*, ed. K. Monzer and M.M. Siti, 205239. Kuala Lumpur: CERT.

Ahmed, H., M. Mohieldin, J. Verbeek, and F. Aboulmagd. 2015. On the sustainable development goals and the role of Islamic finance. World Bank Policy Research Working Paper No. 7266. Available at SSRN: https://ssrn.com/abstract=2606839.

Cizakca, M. 2004. Cash waqf as alternative to NBFIs Bank. Paper presented at the International Seminar on Nonbank Financial Institutions: Islamic Alternatives, jointly organized by Islamic Research and Training Institute, Islamic Development Bank, and Islamic Banking and Finance Institute Malaysia, Kuala Lumpur, March 1–3.

Gundogdu, A.S. 2018. An inquiry into Islamic finance from the perspective of sustainable development goals. *European Journal of Sustainable Development* 7(4).

Gundogdu, A.S. 2019. Poverty, hunger and inequality in the context of zakat and waqf. *Darulfunun Ilahiyat* 30(1): 49–64.

Haneef, M.A., A.H. Pramanik, M.O. Mohammed, M.F.B. Amin, and A.D. Muhammad. 2015. Integration of waqf-Islamic microfinance model for poverty reduction: The case of Bangladesh. *International Journal of Islamic and Middle Eastern Finance and Management* 8(2): 246–270. https://doi. org/10.1108/IMEFM-03-2014-0029.

Iqbal, Z., and A. Mirakhor. 2007. Qard hasan microfinance (QHMF). http:// www.newhorizonislamicbanking.com/index.cfm?section=academicarticles& action=view&id=10461. Accessed April 2, 2009.

Kahf, M. 1999. Zakah: Performance in theory and practice. Paper presented at the International Conference on Islamic Economics Towards the 21st Century, Kuala Lumpur, August 1999.

Kahf, M. 2000. *al Waqf al Islami, Tatawwuruh, Idaratuh, Tanmiyatuh* (Islamic waqf, its growth, management and development). Damascus: Dar al Fikr.

Kahf, M. 2004. Shari'ah and historical aspects of zakat and awqaf. Background paper prepared for the Islamic Research and Training Institute, Islamic Development Bank.

Shirazi, N.S., M.F.B. Amin, and T. Anwar. 2009. Poverty elimination through potential zakat collection in the OIC-member countries: revisited. *The Pakistan Development Review* 48(4): 739–754.

Sinclair, H. 2012. *Confessions of a microfinance heretic: How microlending lost its way and betrayed the poor.* San Francisco, CA: Berrett Koehler Publishers.

Wilson, R. 2007. Making development assistance sustainable through Islamic microfinance. *IIUM Journal of Economics and Management* 15(2): 197–217.

Zarrouk, J. 2015. The role of Islamic finance in achieving sustainable development. *Development Finance Agenda* 1(3): 4–5.

CHAPTER 2

Islamic Versus Conventional Infrastructure Project Finance vis-à-vis Time-Overrun Issues

Islamic finance is able to provide the required instrumentality while also observing certain restrictions. There has been much comparison of Islamic finance with more conventional finance models. For those suspicious of the merits of Islamic finance, it should be noted that both Islamic and conventional finance supposedly carry out the task of bringing together fund providers and fund seekers to boost the economy. It is very often suggested that Islamic and conventional finance are similar, to the extent that most Islamic finance contracts can be changed to conventional finance contracts with only minor amendments.[1] Islamic finance appears to resemble conventional finance as a financial intermediator, and yet the Islamic finance business model – which is to say, the way in which financing is carried out – can curb potentially adverse side effects and may preclude the impoverishment of vulnerable people, given that its lending activities are framed by the Islamic belief system. Those who are critical tend to believe that both Islamic and conventional finance give rise to an imbalance in the economy and work against vulnerable people, and this is considered as a social failure of Islamic finance.[2] Although Islamic finance comes up with *Zakat* and *Waqf* to address social failures, the nature of

---

[1] Beck et al. (2010).

[2] Asutay (2007).

© The Author(s), under exclusive license to Springer Nature Switzerland AG 2021
A. T. Diallo and A. S. Gundogdu, *Sustainable Development and Infrastructure*, Palgrave Studies in Islamic Banking, Finance, and Economics, https://doi.org/10.1007/978-3-030-67094-8_2

Islamic finance itself is a way to protect vulnerable people and bring about fairness to finance. A multilateral development bank carrying out infrastructure development presents us with an excellent example of the merits of Islamic finance.

Unlike the reminder of the book, this chapter provides a micro comparison and investigation of the subject matter. Islamic economics and finance comprise a comprehensive discipline, and several aspects need to be borne in mind to avoid social failure. Islamic economic principles urge trade, investment, and availing financing to support them, yet they also acknowledge the fact that economic growth out of trade and investment is not sufficient to address the poverty issue. The Islamic proposition for poverty alleviation is to have *Waqf* for social infrastructure development such as health, education, and water, and *Zakat* for wealth redistribution. Moreover, Islamic finance principles indicate that some infrastructure development projects should not be carried out using banking services. Social infrastructure projects in the areas of health, education, and water should not be done through banks, but should instead be carried out with *Waqf* development. On the other hand, economic infrastructure projects for transport and energy should be subject to commercially evaluated financial transactions. In the same fashion, resources for economic infrastructure projects should be mobilized through commercially priced resources, while for social infrastructure projects resource mobilization should be obtained from concessional resources in the form of *Qard Hasan*. From a *Maqasid* point of view, social infrastructure projects should be transformed from infrastructure project finance to *Waqf* development in order to curb commodification of these basic human needs. The reflection suggests that economic infrastructure financing and the provision of social infrastructure in the form of *Waqf* development should continue to be subject of MDB business lines. The efficiency issue, hence, will still be key for scaling up MDBs' infrastructure engagement.

Multilateral development banks evaluate infrastructure projects based on four parameters: relevance, effectiveness, efficiency, and sustainability. Islamic Development Bank (IsDB) projects, similar to those of the Asian Development Bank (ADB) and the World Bank, may suffer from flaws in project formulation. The issue of sustainability is common across all MDBs, particularly in challenging countries, and requires bringing innovative solutions to MDB interventions. Unlike common impediments, the issue of efficiency (timely completion of projects) is more of a problem for Islamic finance. Strong *Shariah* restrictions on fee structuring in IsDB

Table 2.1   Infrastructure project evaluation parameters

Relevance	The assessment of the ex ante and ex post relevance of objectives in terms of consistency with country development priorities and the corporate priorities
Effectiveness	The assessment of the extent of achievement of the expected outputs/outcomes based on the project log-frame. It has two sub-parameters: • Progress toward output: can the project assets deliver the outputs such as daily needed electricity consumption? • Progress toward outcome: can the outputs deliver desired outcomes such as daily electricity production with project assets to alleviate poverty in the region?
Efficiency	The assessment of the extent to which the outputs and outcomes are efficiently delivered in terms of timeliness and cost
Sustainability	The assessment of the risks to sustainability of development outcomes. It includes evaluation of technical sustainability, institutional sustainability, financial sustainability, and environmental sustainability

Source The authors

financing agreements – as they impede upfront and commitment fees – appear as the root cause of excessive time overrun for project completion as compared to other MDBs. Although there are much more technical details, the parameters are listed in Table 2.1. The time-overrun issue is related to the efficiency parameter.

The *Shariah* restrictions in the IsDB financing agreement protects the borrower, yet such covenants giver rise to: (1) submission of unready and non-priority projects to IsDB and (2) the lack of urgency from beneficiary countries as there is no harsh upfront and commitment fee implications. On the other hand, such *Shariah*-compliant features also protect the lender because, unlike with other types, it is much easier to cancel Islamic infrastructure projects if needed since there are no associated upfront fee and commitment fee complications.

Because introducing upfront and commitment fees to *Shariah*-compliant financing agreements is not an option, measures such as QnP (quality and prioritization) were introduced to screen out unready and non-priority project proposals. However, there are key factors in the project cycle that affect the timely completion of projects – such as "Land Rights," "Project Management Unit Structure," "Capacity of Executing Agency," "Counterpart Funding," "Mode of Financing," "Conditions Precedent to Effectiveness" (particularly having Legal Opinion from borrowing country), etc.

2.1   Project Cycle of MDBs

In essence, project cycles, as well as the documents produced therein, are almost identical across all three MDBs: IsDB, World Bank, and Asian Development Bank. The project cycle stages are as follows:

1. Identification and engagement
2. Preparation/design
3. Appraisal
4. Negotiations and board approval
5. Implementation and support/implementation and monitoring
6. Completion and evaluation
7. Independent evaluation and monitoring.

First, a project is identified, and lenders engage with loan seekers based on the predetermined country engagement strategy. This engagement phase is followed by a period of technical assistance to loan seekers, mainly to prepare feasibility studies and the like. The next stage, appraisal, is the most critical of the project cycle, as a thorough appraisal with the selection of the right project components is key for the success of the project. It is only in this stage that the project cycles of the three MDBs differ. In the case of the ADB, draft legal agreement negotiations are delayed until after the appraisal; this can give rise to delays in project implementation, as making changes to the legal agreement *after* approving the financing terms can be cumbersome. Both the WB and the IsDB, however, prepare a draft agreement at this stage and embark on a loan-seeker review in the very early stages, to avoid back-and-forth negotiations in the approval stage; this is done because changing the main feature of the loan agreement very often necessitates changing the financing terms, which in turn involves cumbersome approval processes on the part of the MDBs' boards. Following the approval stage, the implementation stage – which requires extensive monitoring – can start. Once the project is completed, the MDBs produce project completion reports, to document the lessons learned and thereby improve future project management practices.[3] Table 2.2 provides the list of deliverables produced in each stage.

---

[3] In the case of the WB, the document is called the Implementation Status and Result Report (ISR).

Table 2.2 Deliverables in project cycle

Stages of project cycle	Islamic Development Bank (IsDB)	World Bank (WB)	Asian Development Bank (ADB)
Identification and Engagement	Member Country Strategy Paper (MCPS)	Country Partnership Framework (CPF)	Country Partnership Strategy (CPS)
	Project Concept Note (PCN) based on feasibility study prepared by loan seeker.	Project Concept Note (PCN) Project Information Document (PID) Integrated Safeguard Data Sheet	Concept Paper based on feasibility study prepared by loan seeker. Project Data Sheet
Preparation/Design	Technical Assistance (Special Program for Project Preparation-SPPP) Project Preparation Review Report-PPRR (Also used to be named as Project Concept Document-PCD) Procurement Arrangement	Technical Assessment by WB Feasibility study prepared by loan seeker. Environmental Assessment Report prepared by loan seeker. An Indigenous Peoples Plan Procurement Plan	Technical Assistance
Appraisal	Draft Project Appraisal Document (PAD) Draft Legal Agreement	Draft Project Appraisal Document (PAD) Draft Legal Agreement	Design and Monitoring Framework (DMF) Initial poverty and social analysis (IPSA)
Negotiations and Board Approval	Reports and Recommendations of the Management (RRM) Legal Agreement based on previously negotiated draft agreement	Memorandum of President Legal Agreement based on previously negotiated draft agreement	Reports and Recommendations of the President (RRP) Legal Agreement negotiated after approval

(continued)

Table 2.2 (continued)

Stages of project cycle	Islamic Development Bank (IsDB)	World Bank (WB)	Asian Development Bank (ADB)
Implementation and Support/Implementation and Monitoring	Project Implementation. Assessment Support Reports (PIASR)	Implementation Status and Result Report (ISR)	Midterm Review Report (MTR) Project Performance Report Change Request from beneficiary
Completion and Evaluation	Project Completion Report (PCR)	Implementation Completion and Results Report (ICR)	Project Completion Report (PCR)
Independent Evaluation and Monitoring	Project Performance Evaluation Report (PPER)	Project Performance Assessment Report	Project Performance Evaluation Report (PPER)

Source The authors

The cycle is completed with the generation of an independent operations evaluation department report that may highlight deficiencies in the MDBs' project management practices. Indeed, MDBs' experience with the project cycle represents significant added value for the countries involved. They identify loopholes, bring certainty to the process, and ensure the successful completion of very large, multiyear projects. It is not only the MDBs' project cycle discipline but also the soundness of procurement and disbursement standards that substantially contribute to proper project implementation. As with the project cycles themselves, across all three MDBs, procurement and disbursement guidelines tend to resemble each other, since their project finance experience has led them to take preemptive measures to avoid the pitfalls that would otherwise have led to project failure.

2.2   Comparison of Disbursement and Procurement Processes

The IsDB procurement guidelines (PGs) were approved in 2019, those of the WB were approved in 2011 and revised in 2014, and those of the ADB were approved in 2015. Comparisons of these PGs reveal that, save for minor differences, they are almost identical.[4] The ADB and IsDB PGs are slightly different and reflect the possibility of an electronic procurement system, along with integration with the existing electronic procurement systems of member countries. The ADB PGs moved some parts of the appendix to the main part of the guidelines; this makes the PGs easier to read. Besides, the ADB PGs introduce some thresholds with respect to timelines and quantities; in this respect, it differs from the flexibility seen in the WB PGs.

During project implementation, procurement actions precede the disbursement procedure. All three MDBs are nearly identical in terms of their main disbursement procedure frameworks. There are four disbursement procedures – namely, reimbursement, advance payment, direct payment, and commitment.[5] A reimbursement is a payment from the loan account to the borrower's account for payments that borrowers made from their own resources. Advance payment is a prior transfer of funds from the loan account for prospective expenditures.[6] In direct payment, MDBs, at the request of the borrowers, make direct fund transfers to the third-party beneficiary's account.[7] A direct payment procedure involves payment to suppliers against delivery documents, and it is a common disbursement practice used in Islamic finance. Under the commitment

---

[4] The IsDB PGs are available at: https://www.isdb.org/sites/default/files/media/doc uments/2019-06/IsDB_Official_Guidelines_Procurement_of_GoodsNWorks_ENG.pdf. Accessed September 18, 2019. The WB PGs are available at: http://pubdocs.worldbank. org/en/492221459454433323/Procurement-GuidelinesEnglishJuly12014.pdf. Accessed September 18, 2019.

The ADB PGs are available at: https://www.adb.org/sites/default/files/procurement-guidelines-april-2015.pdf. Accessed September 18, 2019.

[5] IsDB Disbursement Guidelines available at: http://www.tagtenders.com/UploadFiles/ Disbursement%20Manual.pdf. Accessed September 18, 2019.

World Bank Group Disbursement Guidelines available at: http://documents.worldb ank.org/curated/en/410851468161639013/pdf/385750ENGLISH01ement0Guide0 1PUBLIC1.pdf. Accessed September 18, 2019.

ADB Disbursement Guidelines available at: https://www.adb.org/sites/default/files/ adb-loan-disbursement-handbook-2017.pdf. Accessed September 18, 2019.

[6] Special Accounts for PMU expenditures are example of advance payment.

[7] As a separate account for project financial management, it might be noted that all three MDBs open loan accounts to allocate financing amounts. However, in the details therein, there are substantial differences. For example, in the case of the WB, a loan account is managed by the borrower, but for the ADB and the IsDB, a loan account is managed by the lender (i.e., the banks themselves).

procedure, MDBs irrevocably agree to reimburse a commercial bank for payments to the supplier against a letter of credit (L/C).[8]

In the case of the IsDB the advance payment option is used to make payment to a special account for the project management unit (PMU) expenses. However, a third party may also request advance payment against a bank guarantee and the amount is usually about 20 percent of the contract. In the case of advance payment, the markup is charged not from the date of withdrawal, but from when the money was transferred to the project account. In a *Murabaha* (installment sale) mode of financing, such markup practices are not permissible[9]; however, in the case of *Istisna* agreements, Islamic banks calculate the cost of the asset they created for the installment sale at the end of the production process. They may, however, use reference markups to calculate the cost of the asset that will be sold on installment to the borrower at the end of the production process.[10] This is fair, for in the case of reimbursement/retroactive disbursement, markup is calculated from the date of disbursement, rather than the invoice date. Although the IsDB allows reimbursement for procurements carried out by borrowers (given that transactions take place after the bank's approval date for the project), disbursement documents such as a supplier invoice or bill of lading are requested. Apart from such flexibility, the general principle of the IsDB is to affect disbursement to third-party suppliers, but not borrowers, in direct payment or irrevocable commitment to reimbursement (ICR) for letter of credit (L/C) commitment. The IsDB does not and cannot charge, due to *Shariah* restrictions, any fee for ICR, which is also an L/C confirmation, for L/C payments. This is one merit of Islamic finance, from the borrower's perspective – in particular, in the world's least-developed countries – as L/C confirmation for their banks would be difficult and very expensive.[11]

---

[8] The procedures are the same across all three MDBs, with basically the same content and only a few changes in terminology. For example, the ADB issues an irrevocable reimbursement undertaking, while the IsDB calls it an irrevocable commitment to reimburse (ICR).

[9] In this regard, such disbursements may lead to *Shariah*-compliance issues as IsDB now opts for installment sale over *Istisna*.

[10] See the IsDB disbursement guidelines, 4.56–4.57.

[11] This additional benefit of IsDB financing should be communicated to MC by project teams.

In essence, looking only superficially at similarities in the project cycle and PGs among the three MDBs will lead one to incorrect conclusions. The restrictions of Islamic finance readily emerge when one examines disbursements (e.g., there is no L/C confirmation fee charged to the borrower by IsDB due to *Shariah*-compliance restrictions), and they manifest themselves even more in the associated legal documents.

2.3   COMPARISON OF LEGAL AGREEMENTS, COLLATERAL, AND DEFAULT

It is clear that the project cycle and procurement procedures of all three MDBs, Islamic or otherwise, are similar. Such similarities should be expected, as the policies and business processes of all MDBs are grounded in decades of experience and best-practice benchmarking. However, it still does not suffice to say, despite the fact that they converge very much in terms of project finance, that Islamic finance and conventional finance are the same. As mentioned, differences emerge in terms of disbursement and become more prominent in the sphere of legal documents. For example, the agreements of the ADB and the WB stipulate commitment charges, even if there is no disbursement. In the case of the ADB, commitment charges start to accrue sixty days after the loan agreement is concluded, and any undisbursed amount is chargeable until the financial closing date.[12] In the case of the WB, both upfront fee and commitment fee are embedded in the legal agreement, in addition to interest charges.[13] Islamic finance principles allow for neither the upfront nor the commitment fee to be charged on the unused amount of an approved loan, and this feature favors the borrower. The use of several fee structures apart from interest charges can also lead to *Gharar*. The interest rate charged might appear very attractive and much cheaper than other alternatives, if one does not factor in fees. For example, the aim of a waste management project is to increase access to sewage collection

---

[12] ADB Loan Disbursement Handbook 2017. Financial closing date is the date on which loan account is closed. A 0.15 percent (p.a.) commitment fee is accrued on the full loan amount.

[13] The WB charges a 0.25 percent upfront fee, payable not later than sixty days after the effectiveness day. The commitment fee of 0.25 percent per annum is charged on the unwithdrawn loan balance.

services through the installation and rehabilitation of household connections. Should the project be delayed due to implementation difficulties, or unforeseen setbacks the burden is borne by the borrower, and this needs to be reflected in the upfront fee and commitment fee that households pay. On the other hand, if there were to be no such fees, lenders would be motivated to be extremely diligent in project appraisal – indeed, a lender would be much more motivated than the borrower to assess any potential implementation setbacks. In other words, lenders should add value rather than rely on fees to protect financial interests.[14] The collection of upfront fees and commitment fees would be unfair in cases of unforeseen delays or *force majeure*, and so because of *Shariah* restrictions the Islamic banks do not charge either of them. In this regard, the IsDB's markup for calculating the cost of asset production and amortization for an installment sale is *Gharar*-free. In view of such a borrower-friendly feature, to ensure adequate returns, Islamic banks should be more diligent in their project formulation, in order to avoid a lack of commitment from the borrower (as they cannot charge a commitment fee).[15]

In the case of the ADB and the WB, the loan agreements, as evaluated herewith, are silent on the issues of default cases and default interest rate. Such omissions are not acceptable from the Islamic finance perspective. The issue of default must be specified in order to inform the borrower about the consequences of repayment delays and hence preclude *Gharar*; relying on a commitment fee seems unfair. The IsDB's agreement clearly stipulates default cases. While Islamic banks cannot charge default interest, to preclude moral hazard, they are allowed to charge an amount that should be paid and place it in a *Waqf* account. That is to say, the bank

[14]To compare the legal documentation, the following agreements are used.

1. Loan agreement between the WB and the Empresa Municipal De Agua Potable Y Alcantarillado De Guayaquil, EP Emapag EP, for the Guayaquil Wastewater Management Project.
2. Loan agreement between the ADB and the Kingdom of Thailand for the Greater Mekong Subregion Highway Expansion Phase 2 Project.
3. *Istisna* agreement between the IsDB and the Government of the Republic of Kazakhstan for the construction of the Aktobe-Makat Road Project.

[15]This feature alone suggests that Islamic finance urges financial institutions to be more diligent in their lending practices.

cannot accrue default interest revenue. In this regard, the IsDB agreement clearly stipulates that 1 percent p.a. will be charged in the case of default, and that the borrower should deposit it into a separate *Waqf* fund account.

All three MDBs carry out very large project finance programs against a sovereign guarantee. However, the issues of upfront fees, commitment fees, amortization schedules, and default interest rates as set down in the agreements, given a sovereign guarantee as collateral, can lead to moral hazard.[16] Infrastructure project finance as practiced by the WB and the ADB is similar to the classic Islamic *Istisna* agreement, which predates Western-style conventional project finance. Governance and risk management safeguards converged conventional MDB project finance to Islamic project finance. Their resemblance in terms of the project cycle, procurement, and disbursement, however, completely disappears when one considers the legal documents they use to administer lending. The IsDB's legal agreement stipulates that the purpose of the loan is to generate assets, which are then sold to the borrower. The assets, as such, belong to the IsDB until the final installment sale. In this regard, the collateral feature differs, as the WB and ADB legal documents do not establish such asset ownership. Compared to an *Istisna* that is asset-backed, an installment sale contract of the IsDB is more similar to WB and ADB legal documents as an installment sale is an asset-based *Murabaha* sale.

However, installment sale contracts are not appropriate for Islamic infrastructure project finance. Islamic finance puts the burden of asset production responsibility on Islamic banks by using *Istisna* contracts. As Islamic banks are manufacturers of assets, in the case of a malfunction of assets, they have a responsibility toward those who are affected – unlike in the case presented in Case Box 2.1.

---

[16] The issue of moral hazard is relatively low in the case of MDBs that evaluate projects on a standalone basis to mitigate such moral hazard. Besides, MDBs are very peculiar in terms of the timely implementation of projects, given their internal follow-up mechanisms. The issue of moral hazard with respect to collateral would be much more prominent in the case of project finance lending by private banks.

Case Box 2.1 Holding Megabanks Accountable: An Examination of Wells Fargo

Ocasio-Cortez, Congress Women: "Should Wells Fargo be held responsible for the damages incurred by climate change due to the financing of fossil fuels and these projects?"

Sloan, CEO of Wells Fargo Bank: "I don't know how you'd calculate that, Congresswoman."

Ocasio-Cortez, Congress Women: "Say from spills, or when we have to reinvest in infrastructure building sea walls from the erosion of, um, from the erosion of infrastructure or cleanups, wildfires, etc."

Sloan, CEO of Wells Fargo Bank: "Related to that pipeline? I'm not aware that there's been any of what you've described that's occurred that's related to that pipeline."

Ocasio-Cortez, Congress Women: "How about, uh, the cleansup from the leaks of the Dakota Access pipeline?"

Sloan, CEO of Wells Fargo Bank: "I'm not aware of the leaks associated with the Dakota Access pipeline that you're describing."

Ocasio-Cortez, Congress Women: "So, hypothetically, if there was a leak from the Dakota Access pipeline, why shouldn't Wells Fargo pay for the cleanup of it since it paid for the construction of the pipeline itself?"

Sloan, CEO of Wells Fargo Bank: "Because we don't operate the pipeline; we provide financing to the company that's operating the pipeline."

Source: US Congress

The example in Case Box 2.1 indicates the perspective of conventional finance on infrastructure development. Banks do not accept any responsibility on malfunction of project assets. The Islamic perspective, however, clearly indicate that financiers have absolute responsibilities for project assets. *Istisna* contracts indicate as such. Avoiding this responsibility with an alternative underlying contact should not be the way. Islamic banks may replace *Istisna* contracts with two contracts: *Murabaha* and Service *Ijara*. Project finance involves the purchase of assets and services for the production of assets. There are features of *Istisna* contracts that make banks responsible for the asset they created. The alternative of using *Murabaha* and Service *Ijara* to procure assets and services is not proper as this means having two contracts to eschew responsibilities imposed by

Istisna. Using *Murabaha* for financing tangible goods is acceptable to a certain degree. However, financing services with Service *Ijara* contracts or *Murabaha* is not possible in Islamic finance. The issue is discussed in more detail in Ch. 8. Hence, *Istisna* is the only contract for infrastructure project finance. It imposes heavy responsibilities on financiers and brings about time overrun. These checks and balances are unfavorable for banks but good in general as they ensure sustainability. Since there is no way to amend them, and it is not advisable to do so due to sustainability concerns, Islamic banks need to be more diligent in their project management. That is, they should not be there to charge only markup but bring value addition for environmental and social safeguard. The issue of banks' responsibility will and should remain by using an *Istisna* contract, yet there is still the issue of efficiency that needs to be addressed.

2.4 Determinant of Time Overrun

When examining time overrun, if we assume the dependent variable to be Efficiency, then the independent variables would be Project Management Unit Structure, Counterpart Funding, Mode of Financing, Capacity of Executing Agency, and Land Right. These five variables would determine the likelihood of timely completion of projects. A description of these variables is provided below.

The Dependent Variable
Efficiency: If the project is finished within time and budget, it gets "1," "0" otherwise.
The Independent Variables
Land Right: If the land right issues are solved **before approval** or no land right issues exist, it gets "1," "0" otherwise. It is expected that in the case of there being no land right issues by the time of project approval, the probability of success in the form of "Efficiency" increases.
Counterpart Funding: If the counterpart funding is allocated/budgeted **before approval**, it gets "1," "0" otherwise. It is expected that if the counterparty funding is budgeted by the time of project approval, the probability of success in the form of "Efficiency" increases.
Mode of Financing: If the mode of financing is installment sale alone, it gets "1," "0" if the mode of financing is *Istisna*. It is

expected that an *Istisna* contract with an asset creation silent feature has a negative effect on the timely and within-budget completion of the project. An installment sale (*Murabaha*) contract is possible only in straightforward projects such as the procurement of fiber optic cables in an ICT first-mile project. Most of the infrastructure projects should be carried out with *Istisna* contracts.

Capacity of EA: If the EA has sufficient capacity to implement the project, it gets "1," "0" otherwise. An EA with a high capacity is expected to increase the likelihood of the success: timely and in budget project implementation. In this regard, a toolkit to evaluate the sufficiency of EA capacity is needed.

PMU: If there exist Type-1 PMU, it gets "1," "0" otherwise. There are different types of project management units. They can be mainly categorized based on financial liaison. PMU staff salaries paid by MDBs differ from PMUs under Executing Agency of the beneficiary country.

Although an econometric study can quantify the matter, such an exercise is impeded due to lack of a sufficiently large sample size. Nevertheless, the experience suggests that the efficiency parameter can achieved by ring-fencing based on the abovementioned variables. It is to be expected that in some cases where there exist strong EA, counterpart funds are available on time and there is no land right issue, the presence of PMU has not much contribution toward probability of success in the form of "Efficiency." It is also to be expected that in the case of land right issue and unavailability or counterparty funds, neither the presence of strong EA nor PMU can assure success. Finally, it is to be expected that some types of PMU presence is needed in case of *Istisna* contract to assure timely and within-budget completion of the projects. If all the determinants of success are aligned, the issue of time overrun with Islamic project finance can be addressed.

Addressing the efficiency parameter, in addition to sustainability, is important to ensure the relevance of the MDB business model for the provision of social infrastructure in the form of *Waqf* development. The transfer of project assets to *Waqf* would address the sustainability parameter. In the case of economic infrastructure, however, there is no such transfer possibility. Transferring the project assets to a government agency would result in the deterioration of the project assets, as they would be allowed to go to racks and ruin. However, public–private partnership can fill the bill to address such issues. MDBs role in economic infrastructure, transport, and energy should also transform from sovereign infrastructure finance into models involving private sector. Although PPPs have superior features in efficiency and sustainability parameters, they may lack relevance and effectiveness parameters in some sectors. Effectiveness has two sub-parameters: progress toward output and progress toward outcomes. Producing project assets with PPP may yield the desired output but it may also be counterproductive toward outcomes. For example, the provision of electricity (project output) can be achieved with a PPP gas-fired power-plant project, but this may not help with poverty alleviation (outcome). It may even impoverish households with unfair tariffing.

REFERENCES

Asutay, Mehmet. 2007. Conceptualization of the second best solution in overcoming the social failure of Islamic finance: Examining the overpowering of homoislamicus by homoeconomicus. *IIUM Journal in Economics and Management* 15(2): 167–195.

Beck, T., A. Demirgüç-Kunt, and O. Merrouche. 2010 Islamic vs. conventional banking: Business model, efficiency and stability. World Bank Policy Research Working Paper No. 5446. Washington, DC.

CHAPTER 3

Identifying Infrastructure Sectors for Islamic Public–Private Partnerships Projects

Islamic public–private partnership (PPPs) projects emerged as a viable solution to assist bridging the huge infrastructure investment gap related to sustainable development goals (SDGs). SDGs are ambitious, and the available development finance resources fall short of what is needed to deliver the SDGs.[1] It is estimated that from 2016 to 2030, about US\$5–6 trillion annual infrastructure investment is needed for SDGs and this amount is twice that of the present infrastructure investment.[2] The global infrastructure development-level ranking reveals that Organization of Islamic Cooperation (OIC) countries' median of 88 has fallen behind the world median of 81.[3] The infrastructure gap may be filled with blended finance, though with repercussions, and capital market securitization through private sector involvement.[4] Given the potential of asset-backed features, there is a natural fit between infrastructure PPPs

---

[1] World Bank (2015a: 1–2).

[2] Bhattacharyna et al. (2015: 9) and Woetzel et al. (2016: 17–31).

[3] Aijaz and Abayomi (2017: 11).

[4] OECD Definition of Blended Finance: "Blended finance is the strategic use of development finance for the mobilization of additional finance toward sustainable development in developing countries with additional finance referring to commercial finance." Available at http://www.oecd.org/dac/financing-sustainable-development/development-finance-topics/OECD-Blended-Finance-Principles.pdf. Accessed October 25, 2018.

© The Author(s), under exclusive license to Springer Nature Switzerland AG 2021
A. T. Diallo and A. S. Gundogdu, *Sustainable Development and Infrastructure*, Palgrave Studies in Islamic Banking, Finance, and Economics, https://doi.org/10.1007/978-3-030-67094-8_3

Table 3.1 Matching sukuk for resource mobilization

Proposed Islamic resource mobilization		SDGs	Programs
1. Commercially Priced Loans: Islamic Finance Modes (funds returned from beneficiaries of finance, principals plus market markups, to fund providers).	Economic Empowerment Funds Developmental *Waqf*	SDG #1: No poverty	Economic Empowerment Program: Islamic microfinance in value chain
	1. Investment *Sukuk* 2. Two-step *Murabaha / Musharaka*	SDG #7: Affordable and clean energy SDG #9: Industry, innovation, and Infrastructure SDG #8: Decent work and economic growth	1. Public–private partnership 2. Small and medium-sized enterprise line of financing

Source Gundogdu 2018b

and Islamic finance in the context of SDGs.[5] Table 3.1 indicates an Islamic finance framework and related SDGs to specific development finance programs and Islamic resource mobilization methods to scale up these programs. Private sector involvement is presented as an instrument to address:

- SDG #7: Affordable and clean energy
- SDG #9: Industry, innovation, and infrastructure
- SDG #8: Decent work and economic growth

A systematic securitization of Islamic PPPs with infrastructure investment *Sukuk* to mobilize private sector resources is a viable solution to avail more funds to infrastructure development programs.[6]

It is quite clear that SDGs and resource mobilization efforts to fill the infrastructure gap to achieve SDGs are also an opportunity to grow the Islamic finance industry. More importantly, given the alignment of SGDs with *Maqasid*, it is an excellent opportunity to expand Islamic finance while observing *Maqasid Al Shariah*. Should Islamic PPPs become more

---

[5] Aijaz and Abayomi (2017: 24).

[6] Gundogdu (2018b).

widespread, Islamic financial institutions would find leeway to invest in tangible assets produced by PPP projects. The securitization of Islamic PPPs with asset-backed *Sukuk* would attract pension funds, wealth funds, and *Takaful* companies and provide more liquidity management outlets for the treasury departments of Islamic banks. Nevertheless, private sector investment is based on risk–reward consideration and it is crucial to provide viable investment opportunities for which low return is balanced with low risk in a way that the private sector is convinced that this alternative is better than high-risk and high-return options. In this regard, there are elements related to the risk that need to be assured by Islamic PPPs for private sector involvement. As a general practice, financiers of PPPs factor these risks into the risk matrix attached to their credit documents and mitigate them. Besides, project-related holistic risk assessment has been the subject of many academic studies.[7]

On the other hand, there remains a substantial risk for countries regarding scaling up Islamic PPPs with blended finance and tapping into capital markets with infrastructure investment *Sukuk*. While attracting private investment to Islamic PPPs with risk mitigated by sovereign commitment, reckless scale-up would give rise to issues of debt sustainability and consequently deteriorate the livelihood of poor people, who are most affected by the side effects of public debt.[8] Since the adoption of the millennium development goals (MDGs) in 2000, the development finance landscape has changed substantially. Regardless of the GDP growth of emerging economies, inequality within many countries continues to rise, and the gap between the richest and the poorest is growing.[9] This alone indicates that regardless of GDP growth with multilateral development banks' (MDBs) intervention and capital inflows, the issue of poverty has not disappeared because, perhaps, some key success factors in poverty alleviation have been ignored. The formidable dilemma that, regardless of infrastructure investment, poverty does not disappear from this planet needs to be addressed.

One of the key issues in this respect is from which resources infrastructure projects should be financed. That is, who should pay for and shoulder the burden of these projects? When it comes to financing infrastructure

---

[7] Marcus and Chen (2004: 14).

[8] Kemal 2001: 267).

[9] World Bank (2015a: 5).

projects, resorting to available domestic resources is an option as many countries have reached a high tax-to-GDP ratio.[10] However, the alternative of utilizing domestic financial resources may not ensure the success of infrastructure projects because of the politico-economic constraints and the need to import capital expenditure (CAPEX) for projects, and also because it leaves the protracted issue of managing foreign exchange (FX) earning capacity unattended, particularly for the least-developed countries. Most importantly, a recent increase in the tax-to-GDP ratio in OIC countries is the result of higher transaction taxes (most notoriously value-added tax); this increases the burden on the poor, while it is the people above the poverty line who are most likely to benefit from infrastructure projects.[11]

In the end, SDGs might be seen as a convergence of conventional finance to Islamic finance since they put emphasis on the wider economic priorities rather than the interests of merely the corporations and financial institutions. This conversion should be welcomed by the Islamic finance industry as the truth is the ultimate outcome of human reflection. SDGs are definitely well aligned with *Maqasid Al Shariah*, and hence have gained attention from the Islamic finance community.[12] However, defining economic priorities and aligning them to Islamic finance should be a concern. Reflection alone might not be enough and recourse to faith-based guidance can define sustainable methods to address the short-comings of human reflection. Thus, the issue of putting SDGs in the context of the priorities of Islamic economics and finance for infrastructure PPPs still requires attention. We aim to address this in this chapter by shedding light on some of the overlooked aspects of infrastructure PPPs and offering guidance based on the priorities of Islamic economics and finance.

3.1   Islamic PPPs

Perhaps the best way to define Islamic PPPs is by examining the differences between Islamic PPPs and conventional PPPs. Unfortunately,

---

[10] As of 2015, the average tax-to-GDP ratio for developing countries is around 12%, which is only 3% lower than that of high-income countries (World Bank data).

[11] Salti and Chaaban (2010: 11) and Songco (2002: 45).

[12] Ahmed et al. 2015: 14–30.

there is no universally accepted conventional definition of a PPP.[13] The International Monetary Fund (IMF) and the Organization for Economic Cooperation and Development (OECD) each have their own definitions. The IMF defines a PPP as follows:

> "An arrangement where the private sector supplies assets and services that traditionally have been provided by the government. In addition to private execution and financing of public investment, PPPs have two other important characteristics: there is an emphasis on service provision, as well as investment, by the private sector; and significant risk is transferred from the government to the private sector."

The OECD gives the following definition:

> "An agreement between the government and one or more private partners (which may include operators and financiers) according to which the private partners deliver a service so the service delivery objectives of the government are aligned with the profit objective of the private partners and the effectiveness of the alignment depends on a sufficient transfer of risk to the private partners."[14]

Each PPP is different and unique, yet the main motivation is the quick delivery of public services and a means of risk sharing with a reduced financial burden on government.[15] This definition suggests that PPPs are only for the provision of public services and that there is no need to evaluate PPP project proposals for things such as hotels or slaughter houses; however, these do pop up from time to time.

Apparently, the provision of PPPs in sharing risks and rewards is aligned, at least in theory, to Islamic finance. However, modern PPP structures reveal little evidence concerning the transfer of risks to the private sector. There is substantial evidence to accuse PPPs of being a wealth transfer from the poor to corporations and financial institutions. There is no evidence of PPPs in as-is structures contributing toward poverty alleviation.[16] All this suggests that some aspects of infrastructure

---

[13] Ong and Leonard (2002: 2).

[14] World Bank (2015b).

[15] Osei-Kyei and Chen (2017: 113).

[16] World Bank (2015b: 8–9).

PPPs are missed. The same may hold for contemporary Islamic PPPs. In fact, in comparing financing cost against conventional alternatives, the difference between Islamic and conventional PPPs is not so much related to the structure but more to the financing contracts and commercial considerations of the project sponsors (equity investors). A joint report by the World Bank and the Islamic Development Bank, "Mobilizing Islamic finance for infrastructure public-private partnerships," explains how Islamic PPPs have been implemented across OIC countries. The key features of Islamic PPPs, which are included as case studies in the report, will be discussed hereafter.

PPPs are fundamentally infrastructure projects. Resources for projects can be obtained in two forms: corporate and project finance. In corporate finance, financiers take the risk of loan seekers and corporates, and they are paid even if the project is not performing properly. Hence, the lending decision is based on financial analysis of the balance sheet of the loan seeker. In the case of project finance, however, the debt repayment comes from the cash flow generated by project assets and there is only recourse on project assets generated by project sponsor via SPV.

Project finance with PPPs relieves corporates, namely private sector project sponsors (equity investors), from the risk of exposing all their assets in the case of the project failing. Since project sponsors are neither willing nor permitted to guarantee project loans in Islamic finance, and would incur due balance sheet liability should they do so, special purpose vehicles (SPVs) and government offtake guarantees are introduced to mobilize resources from financiers. These features allow project sponsors to mobilize debt from financiers.

Nevertheless, financiers expect the project sponsor to insert equity, in addition to a government offtake guarantee. Hence, standard PPP project resources are composed of equity from the private sector and debt from financial institutions. In *Musharaka* structures, financiers insert equity instead of debt, but such models would give rise to moral hazard and are likely to work against financiers. The debt-to-equity ratio would be 70:30 or even higher depending on the risk assessment by financial intuitions. Proportioning capital participation based on risk is advisable from an Islamic finance perspective. In case the project risk is perceived to be higher or there is not enough historical data to evaluate project risk, financiers ask for higher equity participation from project sponsors. For example, if there is only six months of data available for wind quality in the region, a financier could either back off from wind energy projects, request a wind guarantee from the government, or even request higher equity participation from the project sponsors to mitigate the risk. Taken together, the financiers' debt and project sponsors' equity insertion constitute the SPV capital. The presence of the SPV distinguishes PPPs from corporate finance and ordinary project finance since an SPV is a pivotal party that[17]:

1. signs a concession agreement with the government to provide public services,
2. signs a financing agreement with financiers as an *Istisna* contractor to deliver assets and as a lessee to make repayments (the most common Islamic PPP structure),
3. signs a contract with EPC contractors to construct the project (parallel *Istisna*),
4. is responsible for the operations and maintenance of project assets to provide public services as per concession agreement.[18]

Since the SPV is a separate legal entity, financiers are relieved from the risk associated with asset ownership. In addition, even if project sponsors become insolvent at any time during a PPP, projects would not be affected since the assets are registered in the name of SPV. All these features are strengthened should there be government offtake agreement guarantees. Because the government and project sponsors/SPV are independent legal entities, the repayment risk is mitigated in a *Shariah*-compliant manner. According to Islamic *Shariah*, a project sponsor cannot give a guarantee to a financier for SPV loan repayment obligations as they are connected parties. Independent third-party offtake guarantee by a government also makes PPPs excellent sources of *Sukuk* securitization. Unlike PPPs, it is quite difficult to securitize many infrastructure projects as *Shariah*-compliant fixed income *Sukuk*. SPV, not *Sukuk* holders, is responsible for risk associated with environmental and social safeguards as the manufacturer of assets should there be hazard due to imperfections in the project asset created.

---

[17] Ahmad et al. (2018: 3).

[18] According to *Ijara* agreements, maintenance, repair, and insurance of project assets are the responsibility of the lessor, that is, the financier. As a general practice, Islamic banks delegate these responsibilities, as well as ownership tax responsibilities, to the lessee, SPV, via a "Servicing, Maintenance, and Insurance Agreement."

Apart from the abovementioned peculiarities, Islamic and conventional PPPs are very similar structures and, as documented, Islamic PPP experiences are similar to conventional ones.[19] For instance, the presence of a project sponsor substantially contributes toward the sustainability of the project assets. First, PPP procurement decision is made by the private sector in a way to assure the best price for long service years to maximize the benefit out of procurement. In this regard, they are not less stringent than MDB procurement. PPP procurement is commensurate with MDB procurement. However, the decision to carry out a project should still be based on the presence of value-for-money. Value-for-money is the difference between the total life cycle cost of a public procurement project and the same for alternative PPP procurement in the provision of the same level of service quality. Besides, the affordability should be factored in. The issue of affordability is more acute in public goods. Health, education, and water services should be affordable for the public. The issue of affordability itself sheds a light on the problems of using PPPs in social infrastructure development.

The similarity is quite normal since the presence of bona fide transaction and risk management practices in project finance converges conventional finance to Islamic finance in PPPs. Accordingly, Islamic and conventional banks can even parallel finance the same PPPs.[20] However, this does not mean that there is no difference between Islamic and conventional finance in terms of PPPs. The presence of an Islamic finance agreement alone would ensure fairness to all parties. In Islamic project finance, the party producing the project asset has responsibility for not only environmental and social safeguards but also any legal obligations. Islamic finance contracts ring-fence and protect loan seekers and correct the imbalance found in conventional finance agreements. As a general principle, there are no upfront or commitment fees or default interest penalties incurred by Islamic banks in Islamic project finance contracts

---

[19] Abdul-Aziz and Kassim (2011: 151).

[20] The major obstacle for Islamic–conventional parallel financing is the pari passu clause. Unlike conventional banks, since Islamic banks own project assets according to most Islamic finance contracts, they would have debt seniority because of this ownership if the project fails. Conventional banks cannot have recourse to project assets. In practice, Islamic banks waive their seniority rights to ensure pari passu in parallel financing.

– that is, *Murabaha*, *Ijara*, *Istisna* – though, in practice, some Islamic banks do not comply with such strict rules.[21]

From a risk point of view, *Murabaha* is the least risky and *Istisna* is the riskiest for financiers; *Ijara* is in the middle. It is also worth mentioning *Musharaka* and *Mudaraba* options for PPPs. An Islamic bank may opt for equity investment in SPV via a *Musharaka* contract together with project sponsors. However, such an arrangement would decrease the merit of PPPs. Although Islamic finance contracts are categorized as risk sharing (*Musharaka* and *Murabaha*) and markup-based (*Murabaha*, *Ijara*, and *Istisna*), such categorization might not be perfect.[22] Because they involve profit–loss sharing, the contracts may appear more Islamic, yet *Musharaka* and *Mudaraba* are contracts by which Islamic banks mobilize resources for loans.[23] Such resource mobilization contracts should not be used for financing. The only exception for the advisability of *Musharaka* and *Mudaraba* for financing is microfinance projects.[24] Apart from microfinance, commercial loans are better to be financed with debt contracts (*Istisna*, *Ijara*, *Murabaha*) to avoid moral hazard and encourage healthy development of related securities for Islamic capital markets, which is key for the expansion of Islamic finance. From a *Shariah* viewpoint, PPPs should not be financed with bogus commodity *Murabaha* – aka organized *Tawarruq* contracts – since, according to the Islamic Fiqh Academy, such contracts are clearly not *Shariah* compliant.[25]

If there is no civil work component of PPPs, *Murabaha* and *Ijara* agreements can be used to fulfill the needs of SPV – for example, a financier can procure turbines for power PPPs or port cranes for transport PPPs. Although *Murabaha* and *Ijara* agreements appear similar, there is a substantial difference between them. *Murabaha* makes PPPs asset-based while *Ijara* contracts make PPPs asset-backed.[26] In many jurisdictions,

---

[21] Beck et al. (2010: 3–4).

[22] Ariffin et al. (2009: 153–163).

[23] Islamic banks can tap into conventional funds using the *Mudaraba* structure to make more funds available for Islamic PPPs. The Islamic Development Bank employed *Mudaraba* contracts to make use of the OPEC Fund and Saudi Fund for Development (World Bank 2015a).

[24] Gundogdu (2018a: 383).

[25] Gundogdu (2016: 251).

[26] There are asset-backed *Murabaha* practices, but only for trade finance. In the case of project finance, asset-backed structures can be established with *Ijara* contracts.

the state would not give ownership directly to financiers because of the legal constraints.[27] Under such circumstances, financiers opt to make a *Murabaha* sale. In the case of a *Murabaha* sale, since the ownership of the asset is transferred, there is no possibility of a secondary market should the PPP be securitized with *Sukuk*. In the case of *Ijara*, a financier can securitize their lease proceeds from SPV, as they legally own the project assets and can transfer ownership of these assets with *Sukuk*. It is important to note that in most countries local rules do not allow a lien on government-owned public assets. Hence, additional arrangements can be made to separate the agreement so that simple ownership rests with the government and use rests with the financier. Accordingly, an alternative, more purposeful solution to increase asset-backed options can be to take advantage of certain legal rights, such as to use the usufruct right, by separating simple ownership to make it rest with the state.[28]

In the case of most PPPs, there are civil work components whereby assets need to be created. Hence, *Istisna* contracts are used to create assets. After the creation of an asset, subsequent *Murabaha* or *Ijara* agreements can be employed to make an arrangement with SPVs. The most common structure in Islamic PPPs is the *Istisna–Ijara* structure.[29] In order to mobilize resources, an *Istisna* agreement followed by an *Ijara* agreement structure would provide the most conducive environment to tap into tradable *Sukuk*. However, in order to ensure the health of the *Sukuk* market and protect investors, securitization should start only after asset creation. That is, *Istisna* should not be the subject of *Sukuk* securitization to avoid exposing investors to production risk that may destroy the trust in the market should the project be delayed, which happens frequently, or fails, which also happens.

---

[27] The case of PPP hospitals in Turkey. "Mobilizing Islamic finance for infrastructure public-private partnerships." Available at http://documents.worldbank.org/curated/en/898871513144724493/Mobilizing-Islamic-finance-for-infrastructure-public-private-partnerships. Accessed October 30, 2018.

[28] The case of PPP of Madinah International Airport. "Mobilizing Islamic finance for infrastructure public-private partnerships." Available at: http://documents.worldbank.org/curated/en/898871513144724493/Mobilizing-Islamic-finance-for-infrastructure-public-private-partnerships. Accessed October 30, 2018.

[29] Aijaz and Abayomi (2017: 25–39).

3.2 Defining Success Factors

The viability and merit of PPPs are generally accepted, and the question of success factors in PPPs has been the subject of many studies. For example, robust engineering design and procurement have been identified as critical success factors.[30] Perhaps an assessment from the Islamic finance aspect can provide a more valuable insight into the discussion. The asset-backed possibilities and emphasis on risk sharing by Islamic finance make infrastructure PPPs an excellent area for Islamic banks to focus on. However, in order to reap the benefits of PPPs for the Islamic finance industry, proper preparation of bankable projects are as vital as identifying the most relevant resource mobilization methods, aligned to *Maqasid Al Shariah*, to finance Islamic PPPs. It is also important to note that transaction tax is not welcomed in Islam. Muhammad (PBUH) in his opening of Madina Market stated: "This is your market, let its space not be diminished and let no tax be taken in it."[31] Indeed, the hostility of Islamic economics and finance toward tax, and particularly transaction taxes, contradicts the blended finance approach as proposed by the development committee in the "From Billions to Trillions" report.

Islamic PPP projects should be better commercially priced rather than blending concessional loans from public resources with commercially priced private sector resources to incentivize corporations and banks. Commercially priced loans would ensure that project appraisal is based on realistic financial projection (such as internal rate of return) and impede the transfer of public resources to project sponsor/developers and banks. Incentivizing the private sector, as proposed by the blended finance approach, contradicts the general tendency to avoid subsidies to the public. Subsidies, such as fuel, deteriorate the livelihood of the poor due to the transfer of resources from the poor to middle- and upper-middle-income classes.[32] There is also no evidence that food subsidies alleviate poverty – rather, they keep the poor in a state of poverty. The Islamic proposition for poverty alleviation and hunger is more related to wealth transfer, *Zakat*, and economic empowerment to provide an enabling business environment for the poor.[33] The role of economic

---

[30] Osei-Kyei and Chan (2017: 113).

[31] Kister (1965: 274).

[32] Granado et al. (2012: 2234–2248).

[33] Gundogdu (2018a: 389–390).

infrastructure development finance is indirect. Indeed, if ring-fencing measures are not taken, infrastructure projects may exacerbate poverty and hunger parameters for the poor.

There are enough reasons to question the merit of incentivizing the private sector with blended finance in the context of poverty alleviation from a historical perspective. Regardless of decades of huge infrastructure development by MDBs and governments in developing countries, poverty persists and it is time to question the effectiveness of development finance for poverty alleviation and identify the bottleneck in infrastructure development projects. The issue may be related to focusing merely on infrastructure development while ignoring value chain and using incorrect resource mobilization approaches. The infrastructure projects related to basic human needs (social infrastructure) that are covered under:

- SDG #3: Good health and well-being
- SDG #4: Quality education
- SDG #6: Clean water and sanitation
- SDG #11: Sustainable cities and communities

should not be financed with PPP. The problems with using PPP for social infrastructure is discussed extensively in the literature.[34] Commodification of basic human needs is against *Maqasid Al Shariah* – as is using transaction tax collection to avail concessional public resources for incentivizing the private sector with blended finance to undertake PPPs in these sectors. To date, there is no evidence showing that blended finance has a positive impact on poverty alleviation.[35] Hence, the use of blended financing is not suitable for PPPs. However, blended finance should be used to address the aforementioned SDGs related to basic human needs or social infrastructure to avail more concessional loans (*Qard Hasan*) via the following platforms:

- Complementary currency
- Crowdfunding
- Cash *Waqf* /Cash *Waqf Sukuk*.

---

[34] Abdul-Aziz and Kassim (2011: 155).
[35] OECD (2016: 10).

To avoid a wealth transfer effect at the expense of the poor, from a *Maqasid* point of view, PPPs should be financed with commercially priced loans without blended finance, and infrastructure projects related to public goods and social infrastructure should not be subject to PPPs.

Infrastructure projects delivered with Islamic PPPs can be deemed successful if there is no recourse regarding sovereign guarantees or tax revenues, if they do not inflict a direct or indirect burden on the poor, and if there has been a fair distribution of risks and rewards. These factors need to be assured before scaling up Islamic PPPs and tapping into capital markets. The general risk factors and mitigation methods associated with PPPs are mature in practice as they are available in the annex of any PPP credit document and vastly evaluated in the literature. Instead, the focus here is to propose a framework to identify success factors for PPPs in fulfilling certain Islamic finance criteria. The PPPs fulfilling these criteria should be the subject of scale-up while unsuitable PPPs need to be avoided by Islamic financial institutions. The methodology of evaluating Islamic finance products, as will be explained in Chapters 4 and 8, suggests that any Islamic finance products contradicting *Maqasid Al Shariah* give rise to project-related/systematic risk or spur *Shariah*-compliance issues in legal documents.[36] Being *Shariah* compliant with risk-sharing features and asset-backed schemes does not guarantee alignment with *Maqasid Al Shariah* either. In addition to the alignment with *Maqasid Al Shariah* and *Shariah* compliance, PPP projects should also allow the development of Islamic capital markets with asset-backed tradable *Sukuk* to attract resources to infrastructure projects and scale up infrastructure investment without public resources.

Supporting trade is a pillar of Islam, as Muhammad (PBUH) stated: "nine out of ten portions of sustenance are from trade."[37] As a result, the selection of appropriate sectors in which to develop economic infrastructure related to value chain – transport (railroads, roads, airports, and seaports), and, to lesser extent, the energy versus social infrastructure such as health, education, and water – is key to success in Islamic PPPs. The projects that support capacity building of local value chains and connect these to the global value chain would be successful as they can increase the FX earning capacity and loan repayment capacity of the country.

---

[36] Gundogdu (2019a: 17).

[37] Ǧaribu'al Hadis cited in Kayed and Hasan (2013).

Hence, the most successful PPPs should primarily be economic infrastructure related, particularly transport sector, as long as they are within the aid-for-trade and trade facilitation strategy of the country, they are financially feasible (as evidenced by financial calculations on repayment without recourse to government guarantees), and there is a fair price formation in the offtake market.

As a general principle, asset-backed PPP structures, in which financiers have access to assets created during the life of the repayment, are superior to asset-based PPP structures from an Islamic finance viewpoint. Asset-based structures are *Shariah* compliant, yet, unlike asset-backed PPPs, *Sukuk* would not permit secondary market trading. Hence, one of the most important benefits of PPPs is to create a *Sukuk* pool for Islamic banks' liquidity management need, which is missed with asset-based PPPs. More important than securitization, the issue of fair risk sharing should be addressed. Risk, and also reward, should be shared fairly among the parties involved (financier, government, and sponsor) according to the principles of Islamic finance.[38] Hence, PPP structures in which governments bear all the risk are not acceptable from a *Maqasid* point of view. It is argued that profit should not be assured, and therefore a fixed return on investment should not be guaranteed in Islamic finance.[39] As an alternative to provide a fair solution, the usufruct right of financiers can give the opportunity to rent the project assets to the government and, in the case of default, the asset owner (financier) should be able to have control over the asset to make it generate income in the market.[40]

Greenfield *Sukuk* should be avoided since it may create negative carry for issuers as the *Sukuk* proceeds would be disbursed in a lump sum and delays or failure in project completion would discredit Islamic capital markets. Hence, the availability of project completion bonds in the form of *Takaful* is of utmost importance. Given that the *Takaful* industry may not have the capacity to provide such products, Islamic financial institutions can continue to resort to risk mitigation arrangements to ensure proper completion of the projects by project sponsors. However, governments should not provide any guarantee for completion so as to avoid

---

[38] Maghrebi and Mirakhor (2015: 85–115).

[39] Cross et al. (2012: 4).

[40] The government is not able to confer simple ownership of assets due to legal restrictions. In addition, there can be no lien on state property, so participating in certain ownership rights is a viable solution for financiers.

moral hazard. It is not feasible to make PPPs totally free from any risk to make them attractive to Islamic banks. In the end, they should also take risks like any other economic actors. In order to consider a PPP as being successful, there should be no recourse to government guarantee; therefore, the availability of completion bonds in the form of *Takaful* would make a substantial contribution to the success of Islamic PPPs. Even without this, financiers and project sponsors should assume project completion risk as they are supposed to be specialized in the sector and this is their economic value-add. The project completion risk should, as stated above, not be assumed by the government as the cost would be reflected on the poor. The use of *Takaful* to mitigate project completion risk, political risk insurance, and sovereign offtake obligation risk should be encouraged. Under the presence of such comprehensive *Takaful*, even greenfield *Sukuk* for PPPs would be possible. It is important here to define the use of *Takaful*: it should be encouraged as long as it supports investment and trade and it should be discouraged if it leads to moral hazard.[41] The issue of mandatory and voluntary early repayment of lease proceeds should also be addressed and factored in to ensure the fixed income nature of infrastructure investment *Sukuk* to be offered in Islamic capital markets. Besides, the production of additional assets after projected asset creation under an *Istisna* agreement would alter the repayment schedule and the effect on fixed income *Sukuk* should be addressed and factored in.

Transactions should be free from *Maysir* (speculation or gambling) and PPP contracts should be clear without *Gharar* (uncertainty). In order to ensure the absence of *Maysir* and *Gharar*, the decision to finance PPP projects should be based on realistic financial projections (such as internal rate of return) factoring affordability of services to be provided, robust engineering design, environmental safeguards, and a value-for-money evaluation. Apart from this, PPPs are naturally free from *Maysir*, with investment in bona fide projects, and *Gharar*, with well-defined content regarding lump sum, turn-key, and EPC.[42] The details of success parameters are presented in Table 3.2.

---

[41] Gundogdu (2019a).

[42] EPC refers to engineering, procurement, and construction. In infrastructure projects, these aspects are managed by defined guidelines based on decades of project experience.

Table 3.2   Success parameter for Islamic PPPs

Maqasid Al Shariah	Shariah *compliance*	*Resource mobilization*
No commodification of basic human needs. Avoid social infrastructure: such as education, health, and housing sectors for Islamic PPPs. Focus on economic infrastructure such as transport sector PPPs to improve local value chain and connect it to the global value chain to enhance FX earnings capacity of the country. Assure fair price formation in the market for goods and services to be provided (no monopoly and no subsidy). No government guarantee to financiers for project completion risk related to EPC contractors or project sponsor. Ensure realistic financial projections, robust engineering design, and environmental safeguard to avoid moral hazard due to government offtake commitments and inflicting a burden on the local population.	No use of commodity *Murabaha*, aka organized *Tawarruq*, for financing projects. Independent third-party guarantees only. No related party (such as project sponsor) guarantee to ensure loan repayment. Robust maintenance and operational arrangement of PPP assets as a requirement of *Ijara* contract. No upfront fee and commitment fee in the financing agreements.	No blended finance and concessional loans, but commercially priced *Sukuk*. Asset-backed structures (such as *Istisna* in asset creation to be followed by *Ijara* or stand-alone *Ijara* PPPs) to allow *Sukuk* to be tradable in the secondary market to enable liquid management opportunities for Islamic banks. No greenfield *Sukuk* unless there is a comprehensive *Takaful* coverage for project completion risk and project delay risk. Infrastructure investment s*Sukuk* should be issued only after project completion to prevent project completion risk impacting on Islamic capital markets. The issue of additional asset creation, mandatory or voluntary early repayment of lease proceeds should be addressed to avoid repercussions on Islamic capital markets via infrastructure investment *Sukuk*.

Source Gundogdu 2019b

From a risk point of view, Islamic PPPs may exclude civil work elements of the project and focus on CAPEX. That is, *Ijara* structures are more likely to succeed as opposed to *Istisna* vis-à-vis asset production risk. However, the value-add of Islamic banks is higher with *Istisna*. The use of *Ijara* instead of *Istisna* would increase the probability of success, but it will be at the expense of the principles of Islamic finance to fully engage with real economic activities. Hence, Islamic banks should engage in asset production to ensure the feasibility of the project and the timely and proper implementation of asset creation as their contribution to the economy. Ideally, *Istisna* contracts may be followed by *Ijara* at the end of the production period. And these agreements should be free from upfront fees and commitment fees.[43]

Robust maintenance arrangements and capacity assurance of the entity that will eventually operate the assets created, such as toll roads, airports, and so on, need to be designed during the project appraisal stage. This is vital for the success of any Islamic PPP as the maintenance and proper operation of assets is primarily the obligation of financiers in *Ijara* agreements. Most importantly, the prices of goods and services to be provided with PPPs should be affordable and determined in a well-structured competitive market: fair price formation is an integral part of Islamic understanding.[44]

3.3   PPPs Toward Sustainable Outcome

By observing the Islamic finance propositions shown in Table 3.2, in addition to the standard risk mitigation measures with PPP finance, Islamic PPPs can be used to fill the infrastructure gap in the context of SDGs while at the time ensuring the elimination of repercussions on the poor. SDGs are related to not only enabling infrastructure but also alleviating poverty and hunger. We should be ready to question infrastructure development as a panacea for poverty alleviation and hunger since, regardless of decades of massive infrastructure investment by MDBs and local authorities, both poverty and hunger still persist in the world. While addressing certain SDGs related to economic development, Islamic PPPs should not undermine SDGs related to poverty and hunger. The framework proposed – based on *Maqasid Al Shariah*, *Shariah* compliance, and securitizing Islamic PPPs with *Sukuk* for resource mobilization – reveals that certain types of PPPs are more likely to succeed and be fruitful for all parties involved while not deteriorating the conditions of the poor. Hence, Islamic PPPs should focus more on economic infrastructure, particularly the transport sector, under aid-for-trade and a trade facilitation agenda to enhance the capacity of local value chains and connect

---

[43] Gundogdu (2018b: 4).

[44] Gundogdu (2019a: 56–57).

these to the global value chain. These types of projects should not be implemented on an ad hoc basis without strategic priorities related to the value chain. Development programming should begin by addressing supply-side constraints to enhance value creation in local markets and subsequently, or in parallel, invest in economic infrastructure in a way to enhance countries' FX earning capacity. Such an approach would increase foreign exchange earning capacities and assure repayment of FX dominated loans.

The success of Islamic PPP projects depends on a thorough project appraisal being carried out that will decrease the probability of recourse on sovereign guarantees, enable the delivery of a robust engineering design, and guarantee environmental safeguards to ensure the durability and sustainability of project assets as well as securitization opportunities of projects financed in Islamic capital markets. The alternative infrastructure development approaches with tax resources should be avoided. Although the financing cost of PPPs is higher, privately led asset creation and maintenance can bring procurement gains to compensate for the higher capital cost of the private sector.[45] This also relates to the value-for-money concept. Finally, off-budget funding with contingency liability is much better than using tax revenues for infrastructure development. Hence, the PPP concept is the right approach for the transport sector should the checks and balances of Islamic economics and finance be observed. Social infrastructure projects such as for health, education, and water should be excluded from PPPs. The provisions of social infrastructure services are discussed further in Chapters 8 and 9. The only remaining economic infrastructure sector is energy. Unlike with the transport sector, the tariffing of households does not qualify to the energy sector as a best fit for PPPs. For the energy sector, traditional methods of infrastructure development with public procurement, PPP, and mixed intervention cannot solve the energy access problem of the poor. This suggests that new approaches are needed specifically for the energy sector – and these are presented in Chapter 7.

---

[45] OECD (2018).

REFERENCES

Abdul-Aziz, A.R., and P.S. Jahn Kassim. 2011. Objectives, success and failure factors of housing public-private partnerships in Malaysia. *Habitat International* 35 (1): 150.

Ahmad, U., Y. Ibrahim, and M.S. Minai. 2018. Malaysian public–private partnerships: Risk management in build, lease, maintain and transfer projects. *Cogent Business & Management* 5 (1). Published online December 1, 2018 at: https://www.tandfonline.com/doi/full/10.1080/23311975.2018.1550147.

Ahmed, H., M. Mohieldin, J. Verbeek, and F. Aboulmagd. 2015. On the sustainable development goals and the role of Islamic finance. World Bank Policy Research Working Paper No. 7266. Available at SSRN: https://ssrn.com/abstract=2606839.

Aijaz, A., and A. Abayomi. 2017. *Mobilizing Islamic finance for infrastructure public-private partnerships* (English). Washington, DC: World Bank Group. http://documents.worldbank.org/curated/en/898871513144724493/Mobilizing-Islamic-finance-for-infrastructure-public-private-partnerships. Accessed October 11, 2018.

Ariffin, N.M., S. Archer, and R.A.A. Karim. 2009. Risks in Islamic banks: Evidence from empirical research. *Journal of Banking Regulation* 10 (2): 153–163.

Beck, T., A. Demirgüç-Kunt, and O. Merrouche. 2010 Islamic vs. conventional banking: Business model, efficiency and stability. World Bank Policy Research Working Paper No. 5446. Washington, DC.

Bhattacharyna, A., J. Oppenheim, and N. Stern. 2015. Driving sustainable development through better infrastructure: Key elements of a transformation program. Global Working Paper. Washington, DC: Brookings Institution.

Cross, C.G., C.R. Nethercott, H. Rai, and M.A. Al-Sheikh. 2012. *Islamic project finance*. Latham & Watkins LLP. Practical Law Company. https://www.lw.com/thoughtLeadership/islamic-project-finance. Accessed October 11, 2018.

Granado, F.J.A., D. Coady, and R. Gillingham. 2012. The unequal benefits of fuel subsidies: A review of evidence for developing countries. *World development*, 40 (11): 2234–2248.

Gundogdu, A.S. 2016. Islamic electronic trading platform on organized exchange. *Borsa Istanbul Review* 16 (4): 249–255.

Gundogdu, A.S. 2018a. An inquiry into Islamic finance from the perspective of sustainable development goals. *European Journal of Sustainable Development* 7 (4): 381.

Gundogdu, A.S. 2018b. How different is Islamic finance? Abstract Book ISEFE 2018 Fall Symposium.

Gundogdu, A.S. 2019a. *A modern perspective of Islamic economics and finance*. Bingley, UK: Emeralds Publishing.

Gundogdu, A.S. 2019b. Determinants of success in Islamic public–private partnership projects (PPPs) in the context of SDGs. *Turkish Journal of Islamic Economics* 6 (2): 25–43.

Kayed, N.K., and M.K. Hassan. 2013. *Islamic entrepreneurship*. London, UK: Routledge.

Kemal, A.R. 2001. Debt accumulation and its implications for growth and poverty. *Pakistan Development Review* 40 (4): 263–281.

Kister, Meir Jacob. 1965. The parket of the Prophet. *Journal of the Economic and Social History of the Orient* 8: 272–276.

Maghrebi, N., and A. Mirakhor. 2015. Risk sharing and shared prosperity in Islamic finance. *Islamic Economic Studies* 23 (2): 85–115.

Marcus, J., and S.E. Chen. 2004. Identifying risk factors of boot procurement: A case study of stadium Australia. *Construction Economics and Building* 4(1).

OECD. 2016. *OECD DAC blended finance principles for unlocking commercial finance for the sustainable development goals*. Paris: OECD. http://www. oecd.org/dac/financing-sustainable-development/development-finance-top ics/OECD-Blended-Finance-Principles.pdf. Accessed February 6, 2020.

OECD. 2018. *Public–Private Partnerships: In pursuit of risk sharing and value for money*. Paris: OECD. http://www.oecd.org/gov/budgeting/public-privatepartnershipsinpursuitofrisksharingandvalueformoney.htm#B3. Accessed November 11, 2018.

Ong, H.C., and D. Lenard. 2002. Can private finance be applied in the provision of housing? Book of Proceedings FIG XXII International Congress.

Osei-Kyei, R., and A. Chan. 2017. Implementing public–private partnership (PPP) policy for public construction projects in Ghana: Critical success factors and policy implications. *International Journal of Construction Management* 17 (2): 113–123.

Salti, N., and J. Chaaban. 2010. On the poverty and equity implications of a rise in the value added tax. *Middle East Development Journal* 2 (1): 121–138.

Songco, J.A. 2002. Do rural infrastructure investments benefit the poor? Evaluating linkages: A global view, A focus on Vietnam. Policy Research Working Paper, World Bank, Washington DC.

Woetzel, J., N. Garemo, J. Mischke, M. Hjerpe, and R. Palter. 2016. *Bridging global infrastructure gaps*. McKinsey Global Institute, McKinsey & Company.

World Bank. 2015a. *From billions to trillions: Transforming development finance post-2015 financing for development: multilateral development finance* (in English). Washington, DC: World Bank Group. http://siteresources.wor ldbank.org/DEVCOMMINT/Documentation/23659446/DC2015-0002% 28E%29FinancingforDevelopment.pdf. Accessed October 28, 2018.

World Bank. 2015b. *World Bank Group support to Public-Private Partnerships; lessons from experience in client countries, FY02-12*. Washington, DC: World Bank Group. http://documents.worldbank.org/curated/en/405891 468334813110/pdf/93629-REVISED-Box394822B-PUBLIC.pdf. Accessed November 11, 2018.

CHAPTER 4

Sustainable Islamic SME Financing

The emergence of Islamic finance as an alternative to conventional finance in the modern age is perhaps one of the most remarkable events in the history of finance. While the foundations of conventional finance have been developed in the context of protecting capital owners, both lenders and borrowers agree on limits, rights, and obligations based on principles of the faith in Islamic finance. Islamic finance has interconnected, yet specific, intervention methods for SDGs based on the nature of the issues as presented in Table 4.1. Poverty and economic infrastructure (SDG #1-7-8-9) should be tackled with commercially priced loans, while the provision of social infrastructure (SDG #3-4-6-11) needs to be decentralized through community *Waqf*. Regardless of emphasis on *Zakat* for poverty, its role is auxiliary but still vital with linked indirect effects.[1]

4.1 THE ROLE OF SMES IN ECONOMIC INFRASTRUCTURE AND SDGS

The Islamic approach for poverty alleviation is more to do with economic infrastructure. SME financing is an economic activity, to support decent work and economic growth that necessitates commercially priced funding

---

[1] Gundogdu (2018b).

© The Author(s), under exclusive license to Springer Nature Switzerland AG 2021
A. T. Diallo and A. S. Gundogdu, *Sustainable Development and Infrastructure*, Palgrave Studies in Islamic Banking, Finance, and Economics, https://doi.org/10.1007/978-3-030-67094-8_4

Table 4.1 SMEs for SDGs

Proposed Islamic resource mobilization		SDGs	Programs
1. Commercially Priced Loans: Islamic Finance Modes (funds returned from beneficiaries of finance, principals plus market markups, to fund providers)	Economic empowerment funds Developmental Waqf	SDG #1: No poverty	Economic Empowerment Program: Islamic Microfinance in Value Chain
	Investment Sukuk Two-step Murabaha/Musharaka	SDG #7: Affordable and clean energy SDG #9: Industry, innovation, and infrastructure SDG #8: Decent work and economic growth	1. Public–Private Partnership 2. Small and medium-sized enterprise line of financing

Source Gundogdu (2018b)

to avoid zombie companies. Grant and concessional loans for this sector are not advisable for sustainability.[2] SMEs are of the utmost importance for employment and growth.[3] Besides, they are expected to have a bigger role in the provision of economic infrastructure. Presently, the public–private partnership (PPP) business model has proved to be superior to traditional public infrastructure development due to sustainability features. Private sector performance in management, operation, and maintenance of infrastructure assets can bring substantial benefits to compensate for higher financing costs associated with project finance.[4] Nevertheless, profit maximization motivation, which is acceptable in Islam, brings about repercussions in the case of centralized large-scale infrastructure that bestow unfair price formation capabilities to project sponsors. The best-case scenario is to provide social and economic infrastructure without large and centralized schemes. For social infrastructure (SDG 3-4-6-11): health, education, and water, Islamic proposition is *Waqf* to impede commodification of public goods. On the contrary, it

[2] Gundogdu (2018b).

[3] Abdulsaleh and Worthington (2013).

[4] Gundogdu (2019b).

is the private sector that dominates economic infrastructure (SDG 7-8-9): transport, ICT, energy. With the new technological trends, such as PV panels in the energy sector and prospective levitation technologies for transport, SMEs are expected to gain ground against PPP in the future. Hence, the roles of SMEs will expand from decent work and economic growth to incorporate the provision of economic infrastructure. Nevertheless, there is a need to reflect on protracted SMEs issues: (1) funding gap, (2) source of financing, and (3) SME characteristics and access to funds. These issues are extensively discussed in the literature, and in the following sections we shall examine these topics further.[5]

Funding Gap

The issue of a SME funding gap was first officially recognized in the United Kingdom by the Macmillan Committee, which was established by the government in 1931 to study the British financial system.[6] The funding gap is formally defined by two approaches:[7]

1. Positive approach: an equilibrium, in which the volume of lending is below that which would emerge in a competitive capital market with costless and complete contracting, no private information and rational expectation.
2. Normative approach: a market failure, the appropriate policy response to which is an increase in the volume of lending.

Put simply, a funding gap occurs if there exists a mismatch between the supply of capital and the demand due to enduring market failure.[8] The funding gap is the difference between funds available and funds that are required as working capital and CAPEX. The issue of information asymmetry, which is more acute between SMEs and outside stakeholders, makes the funding gap problem more severe for SMEs. Information asymmetry not only limits the access of SMEs to financial sources but also increases defaults. Hence, it leads to more expensive credit facilities as a

---

[5] Esho and Verhoef (2018) provided an integrated literature review.
[6] Predkiewicz (2012).
[7] Cressy (2002).
[8] Predkiewicz (2012).

default probability –which is higher with SMEs under information asymmetry – is factored into the financing costs.[9] Since SMEs do not have enough access to capital markets, they are more affected by funding gaps. The issue of a funding gap for SMEs is more acute in developing countries.[10] Accessing to formal financing resources from banks is particularly difficult in SMEs in Sub-Saharan Africa due to feeble financial infrastructure and unstable macroeconomic conditions.[11]

Source of Financing

Sources of finance available to SMEs are not different than that for large corporations, yet SMEs have more difficulty in gaining access to these sources.[12] The difficulty is more intense in developing countries.[13] Since SMEs are not listed in the stock exchange, they do not have access to the sources of organized markets.[14] As they are out of organized markets, they do not have an obligation to disclose information to the public. The lack of information disclosure exacerbates the information asymmetry between external stakeholders and SMEs.[15]

Financing source can be broadly categorized as being internal or external, debt or equity, formal and informal, long term or short term.[16] Some sources are more prevalent depending on regional location. For example, in Japan and Europe banks are the main source of SME financing – though the 2008 global recession curbed the European banks funding for SMEs.[17] In USA, banks are also the major source of funds.[18]

---

[9] Abdullah and Manan (2011).

[10] Collier (2009), Dong and Men (2014), Sacerdoti (2009), and Vasilescu (2010).

[11] Peria (2009) and Sacerdoti 2009).

[12] Beck (2007), Berger and Udell (1998), and Dong and Men (2014).

[13] Dong and Men (2014), Sacerdoti (2009), and Vasilescu (2010).

[14] Berger and Udell (1998), Dong and Men (2014), and Wagenvoort, 2003.

[15] Stiglitz & Weiss (1981).

[16] Abor (2007), Quartey (2003), Eniola and Entebang (2015), Hanedar et al. (2014), Khan (2015), Nguyen and Luu (2013), and Xiao (2011).

[17] Harrison and Baldock (2015), Lawless et al. (2015), Ono and Uesugi (2014), Vermoesen et al. (2013), and Wehinger (2012).

[18] Berger and Udell (1998) and Moritz et al. (2016).

The only exception for banks being the main source of funding is Africa, where SMEs rely mostly on informal sources.[19]

SME Characteristics and Access to Funding

Since most of the SMEs are not listed, their access to equity is restricted.[20] Regardless of efforts to have SMEs on the stock exchange, most of the SMEs are not able to list on stock exchanges.[21] The failure to achieve corporate governance parameters and the access to equity markets being confined to bank loans has led to research into SME characteristics. SME characteristics, such as asset structure, firm age, owners' characteristics, geographic location, and legal form, are thought to have an effect on access to funding. These characteristics affect access to funding.

Legally incorporated SMEs, sending credibility and formality signals to financial institutions, are more able to access external formal sources.[22] Yet the financing gap is still there. The location of SMEs, whether they are rural or urban, does not affect access to funding significantly.[23] On the other hand, owning fixed assets substantially increases the access to formal debt from banks.[24] This suggests that SME financing is influenced by several aspects. Lack of proper financial statements/information closure and fixed asset for collateral are still key factors.

SME financing alone as implemented today may not yield effective results for the evolving importance of SMEs in sustainable development efforts. Regardless of SME subsidies and lines, the issues related to SMEs and their potential capacity to contribute to SDGs remain questionable. Kersten et al. (2017) found no evidence of SME financing in contributing to poverty alleviation and economic growth. Beck et al. (2005), found no constructive income inequality effects of SMEs, as well for poverty alleviation and economic growth. SME financing has existed for decades and

---

[19] Beck and Cull (2014) and Quartey (2003).

[20] Wagenvoort (2003).

[21] Harwood and Konidaris (2015), Revest and Sapio (2013), and Sestanovic (2015).

[22] Cassar (2004) and Abdulsaleh and Worthington (2013).

[23] Hanedar et al. (2014) and Nguyen and Luu (2013).

[24] Abdulsaleh and Worthington (2013).

major aspects of this, including Islamic, are well covered in the litera-ture.[25] However, with the dissatisfaction concerning SME financing and its key role in SDGs, a detailed elaboration is needed on to-dos and not-to-dos of SME financing from an Islamic finance perspective as Islamic finance methods can perform better for SMEs.[26]

The literature on Islamic proposals focuses on arrays of contracts without identifying underlying issues. The root cause of the problem appears to be financial products and proper product development prac-tices. The Islamic finance industry tends to provide all conventional services to SMEs. With expanding business volumes and demand from Muslim communities, the Islamic financial institutions have launched product development initiatives to grapple with the requests coming from markets and to keep up with conventional financial institutions. In the process, they very often take resource mobilization contracts of Islamic finance for lending.[27] The approach has given rise to the emergence of questionable Islamic finance products. The problem is more acute in the case of SME financing due to risk management concerns. The newly developed Islamic finance products usually end up being non-*Shariah* compliant. Present Islamic finance products, which conform to legal requirements but which do not serve social needs, can be deemed as "pseudo-Islamic" products.[28] A compact framework is needed for systematic scrutiny to avoid these pseudo-Islamic products.

4.2   Islamic Financial Products and Product Development for SMEs

Islamic finance product development should start from a *Maqasid Al Shariah* perspective and extend to *Shariah* compliance and risk manage-ment safeguards while factoring local rules and regulations as well as operational efficiency.[29] As indicated in Fig. 4.1, the four pillars should

---

[25] Lima et al. (2020) and Abdulsaleh and Worthington (2013).

[26] Ibrahim (2003).

[27] Abdulsaleh and Worthington (2013) provides the accounts of Islamic finance products for SMEs.

[28] Habib (2011).

[29] Gundogdu (2019a).

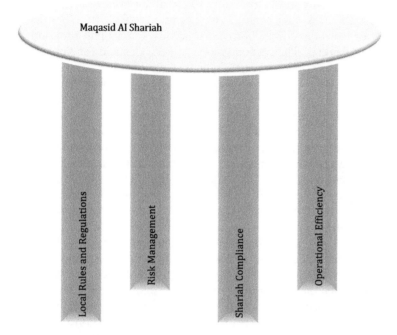

Fig. 4.1 Framework for Islamic finance product development (*Source* Gundogdu [2019a])

support the top of the table with the ultimate goal of progress toward *Maqasid Al Shariah*.

Islamic banks, in general, are deposit collecting banks and they are regulated by rules applicable to deposit banks. The lending practices of deposit banks are shaped for cash lending. The Islamic product development process unintentionally fits this reality. It is not surprising to observe the prevalence of organized *Tawarruq*, which is a cash lending, as a reaction to align Islamic finance business with local rules and regulations drafted for conventional deposit banks. Organized *Tawarruq* is labeled as "commodity *Murabaha*" but it has nothing to do with traditional *Murabaha*. Traditional *Murabaha* is similar to cash lending in debt creation. Nevertheless, there are certain limitations imposed on financiers with the contract. First, disbursement is direct to the accounts of a supplier in traditional *Murabaha* and tied to a transaction. Since deposit collecting pressurizes banks to distribute fixed returns to depositors, Islamic banks take measures for operational efficiency. They disburse funds of loans directly to borrowers' accounts in a lump sum and start charging markup. The pretext is loan seekers' demand for not revealing the presence of a loan to their suppliers.

It is also very common to observe disallowed upfront fees, commitment fee, and late payment charge clauses in the SME loan agreements. Although traditional *Murabaha* is a debt-creating instrument similar to cash lending, it impedes the side effect of cash lending with fee restrictions. The idea is to support economic activity in a sustainable manner. In the case of cash lending, debt is outstanding starting from the lump sum disbursement, while in traditional *Murabaha* only utilized funds amount for purchase is outstanding. Thus upfront and commitment fees exacerbate the burden on SMEs: viable business opportunities are not always available upfront and committed to SMEs. The feature of debt creation in conventional lending achieves superior operational efficiency for banks, to the detriment of borrowers. Observing restrictions of traditional *Murabaha* would make deposit collecting banks less efficient, but it would make the economy and financial system more sustainable in the long run. The stress of markup charged for idle loans manipulates businesses, particularly SMEs, to venture into risky transactions. SMEs have strength in flexibility to adopt micro realities of supply and demand in an economy.[30] However, they have a weak capacity of financial management and they very often use cash received from loans as a resource to pursue the agenda of business owners, such as real estate investment for big gains. As a result, SME loans that were intended to support sustainable economic activities end up being used for speculative investments. The flaws in financial products offered to SMEs and related adverse motivation of parties due to such products are not conducive to the proper utilization of SME loans. This appears to be a reason for weak SME financing contribution toward economic growth, poverty alleviation, and abating income inequality.

Financial management weaknesses and unreliable financial records of SMEs urge banks to adopt stringent risk management measures such as imposing late payment charges and taking collateral in the form of

---

[30] Paul (2020).

real estate mortgage and guarantees from business owners. The dynamics lead to moral hazard and adverse selection in SME financing.[31] Under KPI pressure, bank staff tend to favor the highest markup-potential client as long as the collateral quality is acceptable. Even if a lower markup-potential transaction is sound and has a solid contribution to the economy, the pressure to hit certain KPIs influences the decisions and actions of bankers. Relying on late payment charges with a quality mortgage is another cause of adverse selection. As long as there is a collateral cushion, bankers do not mind delays in repayment, which is an incremental profit. For sustainable SME financing in pursuit of SDGs, the issue of collateral and late payment charges should be factored in when directing SME financing business. Islamic finance has stringent rules on guarantees and collateral as well as on late payment charges. Late payment charges are acceptable but they should be transferred to separate *Waqf* accounts in order to deter moral hazard with both lenders and borrowers. In Islamic financing, collateral taking should be aligned with transactions. Collateral taking for risk management is perfectly acceptable if the process is aligned with the transaction.[32] For example, repayment risk in export financing should be mitigated with receivable insurance/*Takaful*. In the case of CAPEX financing, the *Ijara* contract constitutes an asset ownership right to recover in case of default.

More importantly, Islamic banks have the potential to engage more in asset-backed *Murabaha*. Prevailing *Murabaha* contracts are asset-based: debt is created out of genuine trade transactions, yet Islamic banks transfer ownership to borrowers immediately. In the case of asset-backed *Murabaha*, lenders make goods available for the borrower and release them in portion based on demand. It is a kind of inventory financing. Asset-based and asset-backed *Murabaha* have different realities. Asset-based *Murabaha* requires risk management methods similar to conventional finance. On the other hand, for asset-backed *Murabaha* risk management methods relate to asset management risk for goods/commodities financed.[33] Both asset-based and asset-backed *Murabaha* contracts can be used for working capital finance, which constitutes 90 percent of SME finance demand. Remaining CAPEX

[31] Berger and Udell (2002).

[32] Gundogdu (2019a).

[33] Gundogdu (2016a).

financing needs can be rendered with *Ijara* contracts. There is no cash lending in Islamic finance, except for the *Salam* contract for agricultural input financing.[34] As stated, cash lending to SMEs can encourage SME owners to indulge in booming stock or real estate markets. Observing Islamic principles on risk management concerning guarantees, collateral taking, and late payment would bring about sustainable SME financing and direct SMEs to their valuable roles in the economy. Proper use of Islamic finance contracts based on financial peculiarities of transactions – such as risk management, moral hazard, adverse selection, etc., – would save the economy from the peril of systematic risk created in the financial sector. Moreover, the proper use of Islamic finance would allow financial markets to work for sustainable development.

Unfortunately, the order of proper product development – which is first *Maqasid*, and then *Shariah* compliance, risk management, operational efficiency and lastly rules and regulations – is not practiced in real life. In the practice of Islamic product development, the process starts by first checking for rules and regulations to fit the products into a legal environment designed for conventional deposit banks. The process should start from *Maqasid* and end with rules and regulations. As long as a newly developed product fulfills all the aspects, it deserves to get rules and regulations to be changed if necessary. In the end, rules and regulations are there to assure the long-term sustainability of the system. Presently, KPI motivation of bankers and SME owners together with realities of the three pillars – i.e., rules and regulations, operational efficiency, and risk management – push the *shariah* compliance pillar to the last in the row of the product development process. The result is a mass scale organized *Tawarruq* with a low impact, similar to conventional financing, poverty alleviation, income inequality, and inclusive growth.

The issue has become even more absurd in relation to financing services. An Islamic finance contract for merchandise trade requires acquiring the ownership, somewhere in the process, of the tangible assets financed. An equivalent does not hold for trade in services. For instance, a bank cannot claim to acquire a high school teaching service for a kid from a private school and sell it to the father. In essence, it violates the principle of "Sell not what's not with you" principle of Islamic finance.

---

[34] Gundogdu (2010).

The Islamic proposition for such services is the prohibition of commodification of public goods. Islam advises the provision of public goods such as health, education, and water with *Waqf*. Financing trade in services can cause a major risk, as SMEs under liquidity pressures have capabilities to use fictitious services invoices, which is much easier than tangible asset-related invoices, to access liquidity. Such incidences would give rise to systematic risk. The issue of Islamic financial product development and financing services shall be exhaustively discussed in Chapter 8.

Although financing trade in services is not possible with *Murabaha* or *Ijara* due to the principle of "Sell not what's not with you," it is possible to finance consultancy services for projects with *Istisna*. *Shariah* acceptability appears as such consultancy work is the key to the success of project finance and involvement of Islamic banks is encouraged from the *Maqasid* perspective. However, project finance is more of a need for big corporations and SMEs in developed countries. An SME definition based on the number of employees and/or turnover indicates SMEs in developing countries may also need project finance.[35] Traditionally, project finance is a good fit for securitization with *Sukuk*. In the case of SMEs, a resource for *Istisna* project finance can be mobilized with *Mudaraba* and *Musharaka* but securitization with *Sukuk*, unlike for PPP projects, would lead to further complications and is not advisable in the SME sector for financial sustainability.

4.3 RESOURCE MOBILIZATION

Islamic finance is not short of contracts to fulfill the necessities of SMEs. As long as there is an alignment of a transaction with *Maqasid Al Shariah*, there is a *Shariah* compliant solution within the assortment of Islamic finance contracts, being asset-based or asset-backed, with *Murabaha*, *Ijara*, *Salam* and *Istisna*. The key is identifying appropriate financing contracts based on the specifics of the deal within the wider context of *Maqasid Al Shariah*. For instance, asset-backed *Murabaha* is a good fit for commodity and inventory financing but not CAPEX financing for SMEs; it should be *Ijara* for CAPEX. In the same fashion, Islamic

---

[35] The European Commission defines SMEs as those enterprises employing fewer than 250 persons that have a turnover of fewer than 50 million euros and/or a balance sheet total of fewer than 43 million euros (Commission Recommendation 2003/361/EC). SME defined in a developed country can be deemed as a big corporation in LDMCs.

banks can finance the construction of hospitals with *Istisna* contracts but health services should be provided under *Waqf* – not financed. *Salam* can be used as agricultural SME financing but not as a hedging mechanism in organized exchanges. More importantly, resource mobilization contracts should be delineated from the abovementioned lending contracts. *Mudaraba* and *Musharaka* are the resource mobilization main contracts of Islamic finance and it is advised that they should not be used to provide funds to SMEs. SME financing should also be based on realities to protect fund providers, which is not possible if Islamic resource mobilization contracts are used to fund SMEs.

Islamic finance works based on the profit–loss sharing principle but it is in the area of resource mobilization.[36] Despite being recommended in the literature, utilizing profit–loss sharing contracts such as *Mudaraba* or *Musharaka* to directly finance SMEs would be a disaster for the system.[37] Funds should be mobilized with *Mudaraba* and *Musharaka* contracts and resource mobilization should directly be connected to loan contracts of *Mudaraba, Ijara, Istisna, Salam*. Likewise, *Sukuk* should not be utilized in a way to replace SME loans similar to the conventional finance novelty of the SME mini-bond market.[38] Regrettably, corporate *Sukuk* is a method used by banks to convert loans to investments in their balance sheet. In doing so they eschew allocation of reserves for loans, improving their margins as well as capital adequacy ratio. This is not only a window dressing but also a means of regulation circumvention to gain an unfair benefit. Islamic banks issue corporate *Sukuk*, usually securitized with real estate, and then they purchase them. In some instances, these are marketed to depositors in case of dire liquidity situations. Such circumventive methods help to boost the KPIs of bankers, but lead to systematic risk in the long run for the economy.

Sukuk has the potential to lead to an unpleasant bundling issue in the SME sector. In the name of product development, gnomes would consider bundling the risk of different SMEs under *Sukuk* and sell them in the capital market as a novel product. One of the principles of Islamic finance is the prohibition of *Gharar*. It happens in the case of bundling obligation pertaining to different transactions. Adulteration in any market

---

[36] Gundogdu (2019a).

[37] By Oseni et al. (2013).

[38] Refers to Italy's emerging SME mini-bond market as cited in Altman et al. (2020).

is forbidden in Islam. Bundling different obligations with varying risk features for sale in capital markets is also adulteration and disallowed. Lending transactions should be directly linked to resource mobilization. Otherwise, bundling, similar to a pooling of deposits, would lead not only to systematic risk with negligence but also to negative carry feeding counterproductive motivations for banks.

It is common to have news headlines for Islamic banks indicating *Murabaha* syndication with Libor pricing. Although the name implies *Murabaha*, these are not *Murabaha* but "commodity *Murabaha*", aka organized *Tawarruq*. These types of syndicated loans are earmarked for trade and SME financing: in case of default, creditors have debt seniority. In reality, there is no direct connection of such syndicate loans to SME or working capital loans. There is no way to connect SME loan transactions: *Murabaha*, *Ijara*, *Istisna*, and *Salam*, to neither commodity *Murabaha* syndication nor *Sukuk*, as practiced in the market. Securitizing banks' assets with *Sukuk* and commodity *Murabaha* is a formidable problem. In deposit banking, both depositors and government have a stake in the bank. Thus, in some countries, there are restrictions on the securitization of banks' balance sheet assets – for instance, a lien on lease receivable is not allowed. In the case of a bank default, if the assets of the bank are securitized with such products, holders of such interests have debt seniority at the expense of other stakeholders. The government stake with a deposit guarantee would make the issue more complicated as the government has debt seniority over all others. Depositors, with limited guarantee cover for their deposits from governments, would be vulnerable as bankers, securitized paper holders, and government are much more educated about their rights and obligations.

With these complications, the deposit banking business model is not a good fit for Islamic finance at all. An ideal model would be based on the emerging crowdfunding concept.[39] A transition can be achieved through investment accounts to give alternative investment opportunities to depositors. Depositors can earmark some part of their funds for transactions in specific SME working capital and CAPEX financing. In such a system, since mobilized resources are not pooled but linked to a specific transaction, risk and return are fairly appropriated based on profit–loss sharing mechanism. The bank's responsibility is to offer risk

[39] Maizaitulaidawati and Razali (2019).

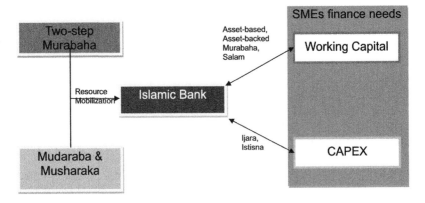

Fig. 4.2   SME lending and resource mobilization (*Source* The authors)

management and legal expertise while participating in lending with a small portion. Banks can categorize each transaction based on the risk profile and quality of the collateral. The higher the risk, the higher the expected return should be.

In general, SME financing should be carried out with *Murabaha* contracts for working capital and *Ijara* contracts for CAPEX financing as indicated in Fig. 4.2. *Salam* and *Istisna* contracts might present a minor share as tailor-made transactions. An ideal case for SME financing would entail fixed return lending contracts directly linked to profit–loss sharing resource mobilization contracts in tandem. The realities would necessitate exceptions. Although lending would be done better with fixed return contracts, in the case of microfinance profit–loss sharing contracts are advised based on *Maqasid* concern.[40] In the case of SME financing fixed return resource mobilization, two-step *Murabaha* should also be practiced alongside the profit–loss sharing resource mobilization contracts. For instance, in cases where local banks need FX loans to finance international trade transactions of SMEs, it can be extremely difficult to convince foreign lenders to assume the credit risk of local SMEs under profit–loss contracts. From a *Maqasid* point of view to support international trade, two-step *Murabaha* – by which international lenders take the risk of local banks and local banks link the borrowing to specific SME transactions

---

[40] Gundogdu (2018b).

– is advisable.[41] In the case of resource mobilization from the domestic market, resources can also be mobilized with profit–loss sharing contracts. The priority should be on *Musharaka* to enforce Islamic banks to put their stake in the transaction in order to inhibit adverse selection. The banks can act as lead arrangers in the proposed system similar to loan syndication. *Salam* and *Istisna* transactions can be subject of *Musharaka* resource mobilization. *Murabaha* and *Ijara* transactions can be funded with either *Musharaka* or two-step *Murabaha*. Unlike syndications, operational efficiency can be achieved with the proficiency of contemporary ICT that can link lending products directly to resource mobilization.

There is a compelling need to devise an Islamic framework for sustainable SME financing practices to make both lending and resource mobilization sustainable. SME financing within a well-considered framework could fulfill its wider emerging roles: (1) igniting employment and growth to achieve SDGs, (2) provision of economic infrastructure. From an Islamic finance perspective, the focus of the SME financing should be asset-backed *Murabaha* and asset-backed *Murabaha* for working capital; and *Ijara* for CAPEX financing, as in the case presented in Chapter 7. Islamic banks should mitigate risks based on the transaction in the form of receivable insurance/*Takaful*, or lien on machinery or goods financed. Systematic real estate mortgages, as collateral to mitigate risk, should be avoided to impede adverse selection. With real estate mortgages, the lender would choose higher markup paying loan seekers even if the business proposal was weak. It would decrease the fund allocation for value-adding economic activities and favor speculation. Islamic *Shariah* does not allow cash lending, such as overdraft windows, upfront fees, commitment fees, and late payment charges. In this regard, genuine Islamic loan contracts enable SMEs to focus only on their core business without getting distracted by financial management burden or negative carry. In order to avoid moral hazard, however, Islamic banks can charge late payment fees but they should transfer proceeds to separate *Waqf* accounts.

Unfortunately, there is no way to develop proper Islamic finance products for either SMEs or SDGs under the deposit banking business model. The pooling of resources and realities of this business model work against the priorities of Islamic finance. A better proposition would be directly

---

[41] Gundogdu (2009).

linking resource mobilization contracts, such as two-step *Murabaha*, *Mudaraba* and *Musharaka*, to specific loan contracts, such as *Murabaha* and *Ijara*. The contemporary capabilities of ICT enable such discourse to transform the landscape of Islamic finance in pursuit of achieving a sustainable financial economic system. However, more reflection is needed on risk management, regulation, and supervision for Islamic finance to streamline the industry in order to meet the requirements for sustainable development.

REFERENCES

Abdullah, M.A., and S.K.A. Manan. 2011. Small and medium enterprises and their financing patterns: Evidence from Malaysia. *Journal of Economic Cooperation and Development* 32(2): 1–18.

Abdulsaleh, A.M., and A.C. Worthington. 2013. Small and medium-sized enterprises financing: A review of literature. *International Journal of Business and Management* 8(14): 36–54.

Abor, J. 2007. Debt policy and performance of SMEs: Evidence from Ghanaian and South African firms. *The Journal of Risk Finance* 8(4): 364–379. https://doi.org/10.1108/15265940710777315.

Altman, E.I., M. Esentato, and G. Sabato. 2020. Assessing the credit worthiness of Italian SMEs and mini-bond issuers. *Global Finance Journal* 43(February). https://doi.org/10.1016/j.gfj.2018.09.003.

Beck. T.H.L. 2007. Financing constraints of SMEs in developing countries: evidence, determinants and solutions. In Financing innovation-oriented businesses to promote entrepreneurship. Unknown Publisher.

Beck, T., and R. Cull. 2014. SME finance in Africa. *Journal of African Economies* 23 (5): 583–613.

Beck, T., A. Demirgüç-Kunt, and R. Levine. 2005. SMEs, growth, and poverty: Cross-country evidence. *Journal of Economic Growth* 10: 199–229. https://doi.org/10.1007/s10887-005-3533-5.

Berger, A.N., and G.F. Udell. 1998. The economics of small business finance: The roles of private equity and debt markets in the financial growth cycle. *Journal of Banking & Finance* 22: 613–673.

Berger, A.N., and G.F. Udell. 2002. Small business credit availability and relationship lending: The importance of bank organisational structure. *The Economic Journal* 112(477): 32–32.

Cassar, G. 2004. The Financing of Business Start-Ups. *Journal of Business Venturing* 19(2): 261–283.

Collier, P. 2009. Rethinking finance for Africa's small firms. *Private Sector & Development, Proparco's Magazine* 1: 3–4.

Cressy, R. 2002. Funding gaps: A symposium. *The Economic Journal* 11(2): 1–27.

Dong Y., and C. Men. 2014. SME financing in emerging markets: Firm characteristics, banking structure and institutions. *Emerging Markets Finance and Trade* 50(1): 120–149. https://doi.org/10.2753/REE1540-496X500107.

Eniola, A., and H. Entebang. 2015. Small and medium business management-financial sources and difficulties. *International Letters of Social and Humanistic Sciences* 58: 49–57.

Esho, Ebes, and Grietjie Verhoef. 2018. The funding gap and the financing of small and medium businesses: An integrated literature review and an agenda. MPRA Paper No. 90153.

Gundogdu, A.S. 2009. Two-Step Murabaha as an alternative resource mobilization tool for Islamic banks in the context of international trade. *International Journal of Monetary Economics and Finance* 2(3/4): 286–301.

Gundogdu, A.S. 2010. Islamic structured trade finance: a case of cotton production in West Africa. *International Journal of Islamic and Middle Eastern Finance and Management* 3(1): 20–35. https://doi.org/10.1108/175383 91011033843.

Gundogdu, A.S. 2016. Risk management in Islamic trade finance. *Bogazici Journal* 30(2): 64–82. http://doi.org/10.21773/boun.30.2.4.

Gundogdu, A.S. 2018b. An inquiry into Islamic finance from the perspective of sustainable development goals. *European Journal of Sustainable Development* 7(4).

Gundogdu, A.S. 2019a. *A modern perspective of Islamic economics and finance.* Bingley, UK: Emeralds.

Gundogdu, A.S. 2019. Determinants of success in Islamic public–private partnership projects (PPPs) in the context of SDGs. *Turkish Journal of Islamic Economics* 6(2): 25–43.

Habib, A. 2011. *Product development in Islamic banks.* Edinburgh: Edinburgh University Press.

Hanedar, E.Y., Y. Altunbas, and F Bazzana. 2014. Why do SMEs use informal credit? A comparison between countries. *Journal of Financial Management, Markets, and Institutions* 2(1): 65–86.

Harrison, R.T., and R. Baldock. 2015. Financing SME growth in the UK: Meeting the challenges the global financial crisis. *Venture Capital* 17(1–2): 1–6.

Harwood, A., and T. Konidaris (2015). SME exchanges in emerging market economies: A stocktaking of development practices. World Bank Publications. https://elibrary.worldbank.org/doi/abs/10.1596/1813-9450-7160.

Ibrahim, B.A. (2003). Poverty alleviation via Islamic banking finance to micro-enterprises in Sudan: Some lessons for poor countries. Institute for

World Economics and International Management (IWIM), Sudan Economy Research Group, Discussion Paper, University of Bremen.

Kersten, R., J. Harms, K. Liket, and K. Maas. 2017. Small firms, large impact? A systematic review of the SME Finance Literature. *World Development* 97(September): 330–348.

Khan, S. 2015. Impact of sources of finance on the growth of SMEs: Evidence from Pakistan. *Decision* 42(1): 3–10.

Lawless, M., B. O'Connell, and C. O'Toole. 2015. Financial structure and diversification of European firms. *Applied Economics* 47(23): 2379–2398.

Lima, P.F.D., M. Crema, and C. Verbano. 2020. Risk management in SMEs: A systematic literature review and future directions. *European Management Journal* 38(1): 78–94. https://doi.org/10.1016/j.emj.2019.06.005.

Maizaitulaidawati, M., and Haron Razali. 2019. Financial sustainability of SMEs through Islamic crowdfunding. In *Handbook of research on theory and practice of global Islamic finance*, ed. Abdul Rafay. Philadelphia, PA, USA: IGI Global.

Moritz, A., J.H. Block, and A. Heinz. 2016. Financing patterns of European SMEs: An empirical taxonomy. *Venture Capital* 18 (2): 115–148.

Nguyen, N., and N. Luu. 2013. Determinants of financing pattern and access to formal-informal credit: The case of small and medium sized enterprises in Vietnam. *Journal of Management Research* 5 (2): 240–258.

Ono, A., and I. Uesugi. 2014. SME financing in Japan during the global financial crisi: Evience from firm surveys. *International Review of Entrepreneurship* 12 (4): 191–218.

Oseni, U.A., M.K. Hassan, and D. Matri. 2013. An Islamic finance model for the small and medium-sized enterprises in France. JKAU: *Islamic Economics* 26/2:151–179.

Paul, J. 2020. SCOPE framework for SMEs: A new theoretical lens for success and internationalization. *European Management Journal* 38 (2): 219–230. https://doi.org/10.1016/j.emj.2020.02.001.

Peria, M.S.M. 2009. Bank financing to SMEs: What are Africa's specificities? Private Sector & Development. *Proparco's Magazine* 1: 5–7.

Predkiewicz, K. 2012. Is it possible to measure a funding gap? Research Papers of the Wroclaw University of Economics, No. 271.

Quartey, P. 2003. Financing small and medium enterprises (SMEs) in Ghana. *Journal of African Business* 4 (1): 37–55.

Revest, V., and A. Sapio. 2013. Does the alternative investment market nurture growth? A comparison between listed and private companies. *Industrial and Corporate Change* 22 (4): 953–979.

Sacerdoti, E. 2009. Credit to the private sector in Sub-Saharan Africa: Developments and issues. *Private Sector & Development, Proparco's Magazine* 1: 8–12.

Sestanovic, A. 2015. SME stock exchanges: Should they have a greater role? Zagreb, Croatia: EFFECTUS – College of Finance and Law.

Stiglitz, J.E., and A. Weiss. 1981. Credit rationing in markets with imperfect information. *American Economic Review* 71 (3): 393–410.

Vasilescu, L.G. 2010. Financing gap for SMEs and the mezzanine capital. *Ekonomska Istrazivanja* 23 (3): 57–67.

Vermoesen, V., M. Deloof, and E. Laveren. 2013. Long-term debt maturity and financing constraints of SMEs during the global financial crisis. *Small Business Economics* 41: 433–448.

Wagenvoort, R. 2003. Are finance constraints hindering the growth of SMEs in Europe? EIB Papers, ISSN 0257-7755, European Investment Bank (EIB), Luxembourg, 8(2): 23–50.

Wehinger, G. 2012. Bank deleveraging, the move from bank to market-based financing, and SME financing. *OECD Journal: Financial Market Trends* 1: 65–79.

Xiao, L. 2011. Financing high-tech SMEs in China: A three-stage model of business development. *Entrepreneurship & Regional Development* 23(3–4): 217–234.

CHAPTER 5

Economic Empowerment, *Zakat*, *Waqf*, and Social Infrastructure

As a religion, Islam encourages entrepreneurship and wealth creation while obliging believers to allocate some part of their wealth for good causes, as is clearly indicated in the Quran.[1] Indeed, many verses in the Quran explicitly express the unacceptability of continuing to accumulate wealth without allocating some amount to those in need of support.[2] Hence, the issue of spending in the interest of good causes is an important topic in Islamic economics and finance. This topic has been discussed throughout Islamic history, as poverty is viewed as a matter to be handled similarly to struggles against disbelief (*Kufr*) in Islam. Muhammad (PBUH) said: "O Allah! I seek refuge from disbelief (*Kufr*) and poverty."[3] Hence, the realities of the contemporary world require a

---

[1] You can never have extended virtue and righteousness unless you spend part of what you dearly love for the cause of God. God knows very well whatever you spend for His cause (3:92).

[2] And let not those who [greedily] withhold what Allah has given them of His bounty ever think that it is better for them. Rather, it is worse for them. Their necks will be encircled by what they withheld on the Day of Resurrection. And to Allah belongs the heritage of the heavens and the earth. And Allah, with what you do, is [fully] Acquainted (3:180).

[3] Sunan an-Nasa'i 5485.

© The Author(s), under exclusive license to Springer Nature Switzerland AG 2021
A. T. Diallo and A. S. Gundogdu, *Sustainable Development and Infrastructure*, Palgrave Studies in Islamic Banking, Finance, and Economics, https://doi.org/10.1007/978-3-030-67094-8_5

systematic elaboration of how best to structure spending for the cause of Allah (*Fisabilillah*).

5.1 Categorizing Islamic Charitable Spending

There is often a confusion concerning several pertinent terms of Islamic charitable spending, namely, *Infaq*, *Sadaqa*, *Zakat*, and *Waqf*.[4] These terms are intended to represent different types of spending and should not be combined or used interchangeably. The Islamic view suggests beginning with your community: start with your family (*Infaq*) and then expand your giving to relatives and the neighborhood in which you live. The word *Infaq* relates to *Nafaqa*. It is obligatory for every Muslim to work for and spend money on family members who are not eligible to receive *Zakat*. In particular, it is essential for parents to assure that their children have the relevant education and basic assets necessary to fulfill their obligations in adulthood toward their children and parents. Thus, they should be well-versed in the contemporary skills required to create value, and subsequently allocate some part of their wealth to those closest to them in need of support. Hence, allocation of resources for *Zakat* and *Waqf* should come only after obligations toward family members have been met. The exception to this principle is *Sadaqa*, which is a voluntary act performed by the giver in cases of urgent need and, unlike *Zakat*, is not obligatory.[5] Members of a community should address emergency issues with *Sadaqa*.

On the other hand, if the problem is not sporadic but persistent, the issue should be addressed with tools other than *Sadaqa*. The intractable issues of poverty, hunger, and inequality should be addressed by enabling a business environment capable of economically empowering people (Islamic microfinance) with the support of *Zakat* and *Waqf*. Chapter 1 systematized the role of Islamic social transfer in the context of sustainable development goals (SDGs) related to economic empowerment (Islamic microfinance), *Zakat*, and *Waqf*.[6] Unfortunately, *Zakat* is assumed to be a major mechanism to address the issue of poverty, yet guidance of Muhammad (PBUH) suggests economic empowerment by means other

---

[4] Siddiqui (2008).

[5] Heck (2018).

[6] Gundogdu (2018b: 381–390).

than *Zakat*. Indeed, there is substantial confusion regarding the different facets of *Zakat* itself. The distinction between hunger and poverty is key to understanding the role of *Zakat* in this context. Although there are different definitions of poverty and hunger, perhaps the best conventional categorization lies in the context of local purchasing power: "National Poverty Line" and "National Hunger Line."[7] The Islamic understanding of poverty is slightly different than conventional one. According to Islam a person with a proper shelter with utilities and needed appliances, including transport, is not poor. Purchasing power parities enter into the picture in defining *Zakat* obligation and eligibility.

The way in which *Zakat* and *Waqf* are presented as a panacea is not reasonable. Different tools should have different scopes of work to justify their presence. The principles of Islamic social transfer effectuate people-to-people platforms. The Islamic social safety net is formed by the intersection of *Infaq*, *Sadaqa*, *Zakat*, and *Waqf*. The tax-based, government-centric social security system is not typically embraced. For example, *Sadaqa* resources might be mobilized by crowdfunding. In principle, the piling up of resources by governments or institutions, religious or not, is not considered laudable. Resources should be collected and summarily distributed from account to account, not withheld to invest for return, so as to avoid misappropriation and corruption by those running charitable institutions. Only in this regard is a government's supervisory role welcomed and needed. The role of institutions, religious community leaders, and governments as distributors of charity for the sake of political agendas is not acceptable in Islam.[8] It is clear that there exist moral hazard, adverse selection, and incentive concerns in the delivery of Islamic social transfer services.

---

[7] A comprehensive elaboration is provided in the World Bank document on the definition of poverty (siteresources.worldbank.org 2018). World Bank (2018), "The definition of poverty." Available at: http://siteresources.worldbank.org/INTPOVERTY/Resources/335642-1124115102975/1555199-1124115187705/ch2.pdf (accessed December 12, 2018).

[8] O you who have believed, do not invalidate your charities with reminders or injury as does one who spends his wealth [only] to be seen by the people and does not believe in Allah and the Last Day. His example is like that of a [large] smooth stone upon which is dust and is hit by a downpour that leaves it bare. They are unable [to keep] anything of what they have earned. And Allah does not guide the disbelieving people (2:264).

5.2   The Role and Specifications of Zakat

Several aspects of *Zakat* are very often confused, and in practice the use of *Zakat* funds often defeats the intended purpose of *Zakat*. In Islam, *Zakat* is not meant as a tool for direct poverty alleviation of individuals. Rather, *Zakat* is a means of addressing the societal issues of hunger in transition, and wealth inequality that may result from market imperfections. The effects of *Zakat* and *Waqf* on poverty alleviation are indirect, and their goal is to support systemic poverty alleviation efforts. Historical accounts support this proposition because – despite reports of continued surpluses in *Zakat* collection (beyond the amount of *Zakat* that could be distributed) – the issue of poverty has been prevalent in Muslim societies.[9] Sporadic periods of plentitude notwithstanding, eradication of visible poverty could not be sustained in the long-run. The belief in Islam is that poverty should be directly targeted by entrepreneurship and trade, and doing so requires the economic empowerment of vulnerable people. *Zakat* and *Waqf* mechanisms are needed to grapple with hunger, poverty, and inequality; yet, when it comes to poverty, the focus should be on economic empowerment. Creating dependency on charity is not encouraged in Islam, as indicated in the hadith in Case Box 5.1.

Case Box 5.1 Muhammad (PBUH)'s Exemplary Case for Economic Empowerment

A man of the Ansar community came to the Prophet (PBUH) and begged from him. (#1) He (the Prophet) asked: Have you nothing in your house? He (the man) replied: Yes, a piece of cloth, which we wear, or which we spread (on the ground), and a wooden bowl from which we drink water. (#2) He (the Prophet) said: Bring them to me. He (the man) then brought these articles to him and he (the Prophet) took them in his hands and asked to the assembly of people: Who will buy these? A man said: I shall buy them for one dirham. He (the Prophet) asked twice or thrice: Who will offer more than one dirham? Another man said: I shall buy them for two dirhams. (#3) He (the Prophet) gave these to him and took the two dirhams and, giving them to the man of the Ansar, he said: Buy food with one of them and take it to your family, and buy

---

[9] Hafidhuddin and Beik (2010).

an axe and bring it to me. (#4) He then brought it to him. The Prophet (peace be upon him) fixed a small branch of wood (as a handle) on it with his own hands (#5) and said: Go, cut and gather firewood and sell it, and do not let me see you for a fortnight. (#6) The man went away, cut and gathered firewood and sold it. When he had earned ten dirhams, he came to him and bought a garment with some of them and food with the others. (#7) The Prophet (PBUH) then said: This is better for you than begging which should come as a spot on your face on the Day of Judgment.

Source: Al-Baihaqi, Abu Bakr Ahmad Ibn Husain, Kitab Shuʾab al-Iman, Bab al-Hathth ʿalaʾ Tark al-Ghill was al-Hasad/ Mishkat, Kitab al-Adab, Hadith No 505 as cited by Obaidullah (2016b)

This example of Muhammad (PBUH) suggests that the Islamic approach to poverty alleviation is entrepreneurship and trade. Indeed, what is illustrated in the hadith is very similar to contemporary Islamic microfinance practices with economic empowerment approaches.[10]

Ideally, the economic system should be designed to enable people to take care of themselves while creating a surplus. This requires measures which can ring-fence vulnerable people against exploitation occurring in the form of *Riba*, or high input prices followed by low offtake prices. A phrase common among Indonesian rural populations summarizes this phenomenon: "*tuku larang, adol murah*" (too high a price when you buy, too low a price when you sell).[11] Vulnerable people need protection from exploiters and economies of scale in their business transactions – that is, economic empowerment. Hence, Islam forbids *Riba* and assures fair price formation in markets by disallowing monopolies and the taking advantage of financially strained people by offering them prices below the market worth. The economic empowerment approach of Islamic microfinance aims at balancing economies of scale for vulnerable people by aggregating demand and supply in order to obtain the best prices for them. This approach also introduces a profit–loss sharing financing mechanism, thus ring-fencing them against loan sharks. The Islamic approach indicates that not *Zakat* but entrepreneurship and trade are ultimately the key to poverty alleviation and prosperity. However, while *Zakat* does have

[10] Gundogdu (2018b: 381–390).

[11] Muhtada (2008).

a role to play in support for poverty alleviation, there remains a certain confusion concerning the principle.[12]

The traditional understanding of *Nisab* to determine which people are liable to pay *Zakat* (*Muzakki*) may not be relevant in the contemporary world. However, the essence of *Nisab* is still valid: one must have some assets after fulfilling *Infaq* obligations and making voluntary *Sadaqa* payments. In the same fashion, *Zakat* should be allocated based on purchasing power parity in a community. Hence, *Zakat* should be distributed to *Mustahiqeen* – those who are below the hunger line and wish to engage in economic activities.[13] Continuing to allocate *Zakat* to those who do not want to help themselves might in fact be seen as a kind of oppression (*Zulm*). This is because such a practice would put generations of offspring into a poverty trap. In this regard, *Zakat* should be used to address hunger to accompany Islamic microfinance.[14] However, microfinance institutions should operate based on market dynamics without *Zakat* or *Waqf* equity contributions, so as to assure value addition and profitmaking and avoid creating zombie microfinance intuitions. In cases where Islamic microfinance beneficiaries are also afflicted with hunger, *Zakat* support directly to individuals is advised only as a transition mechanism. The use of *Zakat*, *Sadaqa*, and *Waqf* as buffers against non-performing loans (NPLs), guarantee funds, or equity in Islamic microfinance is not acceptable, since *Zakat* is meant to be a people-to-people direct wealth redistribution mechanism.[15] However, the mainstream proposal for a profit–loss sharing mechanism between microfinance institutions (MFIs) and microfinance beneficiaries (MFBs) is accurate, as fixed return contracts in microfinance may allow MFIs

---

[12] Qaradhawi (1995). The confusion relates to the following major aspects of *Zakat*:
Who should give *Zakat* (Muzakki)?
Who should be beneficiaries of *Zakat* (Mustahiq)?
Who should distribute *Zakat*?
Where should *Zakat* be distributed?
Cash vs. in-cash-kinds of *Zakat* allocation.
Calculation of *Zakat* based on market value net worth vs. income generated from assets.
Can we accumulate *Zakat* funds and use return from investments as proceeds for distribution?

[13] Mustahqeen are clearly identified in Quran at verse 9:60.

[14] Gundogdu (2018b: 381–390).

[15] Hassan (2010) and Obaidullah and Abdullateef (2011).

to put all the burden on MFBs without providing conducive business opportunities – that is, economic empowerment.[16]

Once the issue of hunger is addressed in a community, *Zakat* should continue its role as a wealth redistribution mechanism to correct market imperfections. However, it is important to note that *Zakat* is a measure of wealth, not GDP. Comparing *Zakat* collection as a percentage of GDP as indicated by some scholars suggests that *Zakat* is assumed to be a kind of tax based on annual income streams such as GDP, not wealth stock redistribution.[17] *Zakat* funds cannot be used to create return on investment so as to use their proceeds for charitable purposes. The wealth accumulation in *Zakat* funds hints at a major issue, as *Zakat* funds should be distributed and not withheld for any reason. Issues already exist concerning *Zakat* distribution mechanisms. The contemporary *Zakat* collection mechanisms used by institutions might not be proper, as many concerned Muslims have doubts about the integrity of those running these institutions.

Although many scholars observed cynicism as a major impediment to performance of *Zakat* collection by institutions, perhaps Muslims with generations of experience have justification for their skepticism.[18] Indeed, the doubts of Muslims are justified since *Zakat* funds keep increasing; yet these institutions have accommodated the needy only with the returns on their investments.[19] This practice is against the spirit of *Zakat*: wealth redistribution. We are not ready to suspect any Muslim preferring to give his/her *Zakat* directly to real people, known to them, but not to institutions. Due to political economy constraints, it is not a straightforward process to audit the integrity of institutions in investments so as to prevent misappropriation via complicated financial mechanisms. With his full authority, Prophet Muhammad (PBUH) audited *Zakat* employees. Today, no one has such authority. Hence, people-to-people *Zakat* platforms under government supervision are necessary to gain the trust of devoted Muslims. No one, including religious clergy and government officials, should enjoy the power to distribute money collected from people for charitable purposes to society.

[16] Gundogdu (2018b: 381–390).

[17] Kahf (1989: 1–23) and Ahmed (2004).

[18] Obaidullah (2016a: 349–364).

[19] Obaidullah (2016b).

The spirit of *Zakat* also impedes the payment of *Zakat* to any institution, but directs it to people alone. People-to-people platforms without any patronage and with transparent government supervision would increase formal *Zakat* collection. The key is to have highly credible platforms, not institutions, because, given the political economy, it is a big challenge for *Zakat* institutions to be seen as trustworthy. The cost of people-to-people *Zakat* platforms can be covered with some part of the *Zakat* collected.[20] It is clear in Islamic tradition that *Zakat* is meant to be distributed where collected. *Asabiyah* in the form of geographical origin is not acceptable. For example, a person living abroad is not allowed to send *Zakat* to his neighbors in this home country while he has a needy neighbor nearby. However, it is acceptable for a person to give *Zakat* to his needy relatives living in another area, and surplus *Zakat* in one area can be distributed in another area.[21]

Zakat can be collected in the form of cash or cash-in-kind. However, it should not be in the form of food stamps, and recipients should be able to liquidate the cash-in-kind for cash, as per the principles of *Tamlik*. The principle of *Tamlik* necessitates the transfer of ownership to a *Zakat* beneficiary (*Mustahiq*) with all the rights of ownership.[22] In the contemporary world, there exists another concern regarding one type of cash-in-kind distribution: company shares. Unfortunately, given that there is no proper dividend distribution practice in many Muslim countries, the distribution of company shares is problematic. The practice is also problematic as it would negatively affect the sustainability of companies. Those who establish the companies should, and need to, maintain control over decision-making by retaining voting power in the company. Company share distribution methods were used in this way in Iran. In due course, the Iranian company owners purchased back, at lower than market prices, the shares from *Mustahiqeen* (*Zakat* beneficiaries). Although there was some improvement in poverty, the issue of inequality persisted in Iran.[23] It is perhaps because of the lack of understanding of the issues pertaining *Zakat*. An alternative is proposed that companies should pay *Zakat* based

[20] Quran at verse 9:60.

[21] Decree No. 3 on Transfer of *Zakat* Money to Other Areas, delivered by the First Symposium of *Zakat* Contemporary Issues, Cairo (1988).

[22] Anwar (1995).

[23] Salehi (2017).

on their balance sheets and income statements. Some scholars conclude that the orthodox position of having earnings as a *Zakat* base is consistent and makes economic sense.[24] However, extensive literature on *Zakat* bases, either orthodox or innovative, is not in line with the spirit of *Zakat*.[25]

1. Such practices only dilute fair price formation in the market as *Zakat* payments would be factored as costs similar to taxes. It is clear that Islam does not favor tax-based, particularly transaction tax, systems.[26] Nevertheless, tax credits for *Zakat* are a good way to phase out tax funded social transfer systems. The resulting direct wealth transfer systems would thereby abate the burden on the states.[27] *Zakat* should be collected based on market value net-worth, but not income generated from assets.

2. *Zakat* is an obligation of real persons, not legal entities. During judgment day, individuals, not legal entities, will be accountable for having met *Zakat* obligations. Hence, *Zakat* should be collected based on the net worth of individuals.

Zakat collection based on company shares is more plausible, but the repercussions should be addressed. In this regard, people can transfer some of their company shares to a temporary corporate *Waqf* that can use the cash receipt from the company shares dividends for social infrastructure development. However, there should be a fair dividend distribution mechanism in place to assure the *Tamlik* right to the *Waqf* while addressing the sustainability concerns for the company. Company shareholders can postpone their *Zakat* obligation for a certain period of

---

[24] Obaidullah (2016a).

[25] For example, OIC Fiqh Academy Decree No. 2 on *Zakat* on Building and Non-arable Land (2nd session) ruled out levying 2.5 percent of revenues of assets. However, such an approach would defeat the spirit of *Zakat*: Wealth distribution. At the end, 2.5 percent would be factored in the rent and deteriorate the situation of people who do not have assets/wealth but have to pay higher rents with little hope for accumulating some sort of assets/wealth. The wealth and assets would stay and accumulate at the hands of very few with such an approach to *Zakat* base.

[26] Gundogdu (2019a).

[27] The *Zakat* Management Act of Indonesia No: 38/199 is a good example of tax-deduction.

time, and, at the end of the temporary corporate *Waqf*, they can opt to pay their *Zakat* obligation based on the market value of the shares or extend the duration of the temporary corporate *Waqf*. Such a solution would allow growth and sustainability of profitable companies in the service economy while allowing social transfer obligations to be met through the *Waqf* mechanism. Under such an approach, shareholders cannot keep deferring their *Zakat* obligation forever, as *Tamlik* principles would give substantial voting power to *Waqf* beneficiaries.[28] In a similar fashion, people can also defer some part of their *Zakat* payment obligation to a future time with temporary cash *Waqf*. Such a practice would serve as a cushion should they have financial sustainability concerns for the future.

5.3   The Role and Specifications of *Waqf*

Unlike *Zakat*, which is a direct wealth transfer and resource mobilization method to address imbalances in a community, traditional *Waqf* is a business model that serves as an alternative to public or private ownership. The *Waqf* model works very well within social infrastructure asset management, such as health centers, educational institutions, and water and sanitation infrastructure management. The role of *Waqf* should be understood vis-à-vis restriction on the use of *Zakat* funds. The use of *Zakat* funds for social and economic infrastructure such as hospitals, schools, libraries, bridges, and highways (unlike proposed by Anwar), is not accepted.[29] Decree No. 1 on Investment of *Zakat* funds by the Third Symposium of *Zakat* Contemporary Issues, Kuwait (1991) allows the use of *Zakat* for social infrastructure development. However, again, such practices contradict the principle of *Zakat* being an obligatory people-to-people wealth redistribution mechanism. The issue of social infrastructure development is supposed to be addressed with *Waqf*, a voluntary act, and this is how the *Waqf* concept emerged as a separate charity tool in Islam, distinct from *Zakat*. Indeed, the Islamic *Waqf* model as a legal entity is believed to be inspiration for secular trusts, endowments, and

---

[28] Hashim (2010).
[29] Al Qaradawi (1994).

foundations.[30] However, there are key differences between a trust and a *Waqf*.[31]

Both public and private ownership in social infrastructure have repercussions that give rise to sustainability and fairness issues. *Waqf*, with its fundamental principles of perpetuity, inalienability, and irrevocability, assures proper management of assets, and relies upon community engagement to meet basic human needs. In cases of private ownership, commodification of basic human necessities gives rise to inequalities in society. In the case of public ownership, the issues of corruption and maintenance emerge. *Waqf* is a viable business model to engage communities that are the beneficiaries of the services provided by these assets (*Mawquf alaihi*). Hence, the issues of commodification and maintenance are less likely to inflict inequities on people. Unfortunately, throughout history, the use of *Waqf* was not fully related to social infrastructure development. Very often people used the *Waqf* mechanism to avoid taxes, or the confiscation of inheritance by the state.[32] The use of *Waqf* to circumvent such adversities is a rational behavior.

1. Islamic economic principles eschew tax collection-based systems.[33]
2. Inheritance rights are well-protected in Islamic jurisprudence, to the extent that one cannot allocate all his inheritable assets to a *Waqf*.[34]

Taxes imposed by the state and acting as a hindrance to rightful inheritance give rise to the second-best option for the people: the family *Waqf*. The best option (having a tax-free economic system and allowing for wealth transfer to posterity via inheritance) has not been realized. Islam encourages wealth accumulation, as doing so supports the freedom of individuals to have a free say in society. In a case where mass numbers of people have no wealth attached to them, they might keep quiet even

---

[30] Cizakca (2000).

[31] For example, in a trust, the property ownership vests with the trustee; in the case of *Waqf* ownership vests with Allah. A Waqif (*Waqf* endower) does not have power to revoke *Waqf*, while in the case of trust settlor can revoke trust.

[32] Timur Kuran (2001) provided detailed numbers in the case of Ottoman Awqaf in this context.

[33] This refers to prohibition of tax collection by Muhammad (PBUH) at the establishment of Medina Market as cited in Kister (1965).

[34] Obaidullah (2013).

under heavy oppression. Hence, wealth attached to individuals is a kind of safeguard against the rise of oppression. However, uncontrolled wealth accumulated in the hands of a very few is not acceptable in Islam. Everyone should have some assets, and wealth should not be accumulated at the expense of *Infaq*, *Sadaqa*, or *Waqf*. Furthermore, wealth should be redistributed among the people by means of *Zakat*, so that more individuals possess a certain amount of capital and can have a free say in matters concerning society.

The connection between *Zakat* and *Waqf* should be discerned: wealth allocated for *Waqf* is not part of the *Zakat* base. This was another reason for the development of the family *Waqf*. Tax circumvention and protection against confiscation might appear as reasonable causes to create a family *Waqf*, but *Zakat* avoidance is not acceptable at all. The "charity begins at home" principle is not related to *Waqf*, but rather to *Infaq* and inheritance. The guiding purpose of *Infaq* and inheritance in Islam is to prepare posterity for the future. They should obtain the best possible education to prepare themselves to adapt to upcoming technologies. By making use of a certain amount of inherited wealth, and generating enough of their own wealth to sustain their families, they will be well-positioned to contribute to society via *Sadaqa*, *Waqf* and *Zakat*. While it is not acceptable to avoid *Zakat* by means of family *Waqf*, as it was funded by cash-in-kind *Zakat* payments from company shares (corporate *Waqf*), *Zakat* payments can be postponed by means of a temporary cash *Waqf* model. Temporary cash *Waqf* may not observe all three principles of traditional *Waqf*: perpetuity, inalienability, and irrevocability. Nevertheless, these principles are not based on the Quran and might be revisited as long as the philosophy of *Waqf* (to provide social infrastructure to vulnerable people) is observed. Perhaps, the perpetuity, inalienability, and irrevocability principles of traditional *Waqf* were brought forth due to concerns about those who established a family *Waqf* with circumventive intentions. The principles dictate that *Waqf* assets (*Mawquf*) cannot be sold. However, this principle is circumvented by *Hukr* contracts, which in practice also allow for inheritance of *Hukr*. Additionally, cases of *Ibdal* (changing *Waqf* assets [*Mawquf*] with cash), and *Istibdal* (changing *Waqf* assets [*Mawquf*] with new assets) have been often recorded in the history of *Waqf*.[35] These types of practices had already rescinded the

---

[35] Heyneman (2004).

perpetuity, inalienability, and irrevocability principles of traditional *Waqf*. Indeed, temporary cash *Waqf* is perfectly acceptable, since it was justified as having similar economic benefits for social infrastructure development, and offered assurance to *Muzakki* with financial sustainability concerns. In this regard, temporary cash *Waqf* is similar to the corporate *Waqf* approach. The approach, however, is different from social responsibility programs.

Unlike social responsibility programs and unacceptable *Zakat* practice based on income statements (which are calculated like taxes by company management and create inefficiency), the company shares benefits from dividends, and cash *Waqf* benefits from returns on investments. While the company focuses on profit maximization, and a cash *Waqf* focuses on maximizing return on investment, the dividend payments from profit-maximized companies and return on investments from a cash *Waqf* can both be used on social infrastructure development.[36] A mechanism to ensure that more resources for social infrastructure development are derived from corporate *Waqf* and cash *Waqf* is needed.[37] The company shareholders and individuals may opt to postpone some part of their *Zakat* obligation by means of corporate *Waqf* and temporary cash *Waqf*. Such postponement should be fine, as it addresses the concerns of both *Mustahiq* (one eligible to receive *Zakat*) and *Muzakki* (one liable to give *Zakat*). *Muzakki* may have some wealth for now, but perhaps he is not sure of the future, as economic conditions five years from now may lead to a life under the poverty line. Hence, upon termination of temporary cash *Waqf*, he may have access to the funds. If conditions improve or stay as is, s/he may continue to allocate the wealth to temporary cash *Waqf*. The money collected in temporary cash *Waqf* can be invested as *Qard Hasan*, in which the return on investment is spent for social infrastructure development (such as affordable housing, temporary health programs, etc.), while the principle is returned to the original owner.[38] This is a different understanding of *Qard Hasan*, and it is necessary, as it has been observed in many instances that vulnerable people are not even

---

[36] The cash *Waqf* seeking high-risk investment for profit maximization categorized as investment bank by some scholars. While cash *Waqf* categorized for *Waqf* administered based on zero-downside risk with moderate return approach.

[37] Mohammed Obaidullah (2013) provided permissibility of such *Waqf* in the context of legal comparison across countries.

[38] Gundogdu (2018b: 381–390).

able to pay interest free loans for education, health, water, sanitation, and affordable housing projects. Hence, using the return on investment from a temporary cash *Waqf* is a viable solution to address social infrastructure development requirements.[39] Moreover, another definition of *Waqf* is "withholding an asset while releasing its usufruct."[40]

Accordingly, there is a need to adapt the traditional *Waqf* business model into the realities of the contemporary word. In this regard, finite *Waqf* as opposed to permanent *Waqf* can fit the bill. Traditionally, *Waqf* is a business model intended to deliver social goods, such as education, health services and water supply, which are better off not being commodified. Given the evolving needs of society, the temporary cash *Waqf* model can be a viable resource mobilization tool for social infrastructure development.

In an Islamic economic system, rich and able people should focus on profit maximization with their companies and on increasing the economic surplus. They should then allocate some part of their wealth after *Infaq* and *Sadaqa* to temporary cash *Waqf*, corporate *Waqf*, and *Zakat* in order to make more people rich and able. The concern might be that these individuals may attempt total avoidance of *Zakat* with temporary cash *Waqf* and corporate *Waqf*. However, the very nature of the decrease in purchasing power of money in temporary cash *Waqf* over a long period of time and the controlling power of company shares would tend to balance toward preference for *Zakat*. Hence, both temporary cash *Waqf*, corporate *Waqf*, and *Zakat* are expected to work hand in hand for the benefit of the social safety net. On another note, like keeping accumulated *Zakat* in funds without making distributions, having returns on investment of cash *Waqf* and corporate *Waqf* into the corpus of *Waqf* is not acceptable. Nevertheless, if needed, the return of temporary cash *Waqf* and corporate *Waqf* can be used for commercial return, for *Waqf* development, and to provide physical assets for schools, hospitals, water, and sanitation social infrastructure.

It is of the utmost importance to note the fact that Islam does not accept masses of people staying idle and depending on social transfer of capital from governments or wealthy people, as this is against human

---

[39] Gundogdu (2018b: 381–390). Indeed, the men who practice charity and the women who practice charity and [they who] have loaned Allah a goodly loan – it will be multiplied for them, and they will have a noble reward (57:18).

[40] Obaidullah (2013).

dignity. Everyone should work toward attaining a certain amount of wealth, as economic empowerment contributes to individuals' willingness to participate in free speech in society. Ultimately, people dependent on government support or wealth transfer from the rich would be very obedient, even in the face of extreme oppression and malevolence in their society. Hence, the concept of economic empowerment within Islamic microfinance should be the central element of poverty alleviation in Islamic economies and financial systems. Economic empowerment programs should not depend on *Waqf* and *Zakat*, but programs should be designed based on economic viability to ensure value addition. *Zakat* has direct societal effects on hunger and inequality. *Waqf* is a business model intended to operate social infrastructure, but temporary cash *Waqf* and corporate *Waqf* models can both be used for resource. Both *Zakat* and *Waqf* have unique, indirect, and valuable roles to play in poverty alleviation. However, for sustainable and long-term results, the focus of poverty alleviation efforts should be on economic empowerment.

In brief, *Zakat* is for SDG#2-5-10 (which tackle hunger and inequality) and *Waqf* is for SDG#3-4-6-11 (which tackle social infrastructure). SDG#1 (No poverty) should be handled with economic empowerment interventions. A *Waqf* model can be used as a business model for managing social infrastructure and resources can be mobilized with cash *Waqf* type instruments. However, the issue of *Waqf* asset development is there. Hence, the multilateral development banking (MDB) business model for not only social infrastructure development but also economic infrastructure development is still relevant and much needed. The MDB business model should transform into *Waqf* asset production for social infrastructure. As for economic infrastructure, it should shape for PPP and SME development as will be discussed in Chapters 3 and 7. Parameters of Islamic finance provide an equitable solution in infrastructure financing while leading to a time-overrun bottleneck. Although Islamic finance is much more equitable in infrastructure project development, the issue of efficiency still exists. Time overruns inflict resource mobilization efforts. Hence, the issue of time overruns needs to be resolved for scaling-up Islamic infrastructure asset development.

REFERENCES

Ahmed, Habib. 2004. *Role of zakat and awqaf in poverty alleviation*. Jeddah: Islamic Research and Training Institute, Islamic Development Bank Group.

Al-Qaradawi, Yusuf. 1994. *Fiqh al-Zakat*. Cairo: Maktabah Wahbah.

Anwar, Muhammad. 1995. Financing socio-economic development with zakat funds. *Journal of Islamic Economics* 4: 15–32.

Cizakca, Murat. 2000. *History of Philanthropic Foundations*. Istanbul: Bogazici University Press.

Gundogdu, A.S. 2018b. An inquiry into Islamic finance from the perspective of sustainable development goals. *European Journal of Sustainable Development* 7(4): 381.

Hafidhuddin, Didin, and Syauqi Beik. 2010. Zakat development: Indonesia's experience. *Jurnal Ekonomi Islam al Infaq* 1: 40–52.

Hashim, M.A. 2010. The Corporate Waqf: A Malaysian experience in building sustainable business capacity. Paper delivered at Dubai International Conference on Endowments, February 16–17, Dubai, United Arab Emirates. https://www.unescwa.org/events/dubai-international-conference-endowm ents-innovative-sources-finance-small-and-medium-sized. Accessed January 13, 2019.

Hassan, M.K. 2010. An integrated poverty alleviation model combining zakat, awqaf and micro-finance. Seventh International Conference: The Tawhidi Epistemology: Zakat and Waqf Economy, January 6–7, Bangi, Malaysia. http://www.ukm.my/hadhari/publication/proceedings-of-seventh-internati onal-conference-the-tawhidi-epistemology-zakat-and-waqf-economy. Accessed January 13, 2019.

Heck, Paul. 2018. *Taxation in encyclopaedia of the Qurʾān*. Washington, DC: Georgetown University Press.

Heyneman, Stephen. 2004. *Islam and social policy*. Nashville: Vanderbilt University Press.

Kahf, Monzer. 1989. Zakat: Unresolved issues in the contemporary fiqh. *IIUM Journal of Economics and Management* 2: 1–23.

Kister, Meir Jacob. 1965. The parket of the Prophet. *Journal of the Economic and Social History of the Orient* 8: 272–276.

Kuran, T. 2001. The provision of public goods under Islamic law: Origins, impact, and limitations of the *waqf* system. *Law & Society Review* 35(4): 841–898.

Muhtada, Dani. 2008. The role of zakat organization in empowering the peasantry: A case study of the Rumah Zakat Yogyakarta Indonesia. In *Islamic finance for micro and medium enterprises*, ed. Mohammed Obaidullah and Salma Abdullateef. IRTI, Islamic Development Bank: Jeddah.

Obaidullah, Mohammed. 2013. *Awqaf development and management*. Jeddah: Islamic Research and Training Institute, Islamic Development Bank.

Obaidullah, Mohammed. 2016a. Revisiting estimation methods of business zakat and related tax incentives. *Journal of Islamic Accounting and Business Research* 7: 349–364.

Obaidullah, Mohammed. 2016b. *Zakat management for poverty alleviation.* Jeddah: Islamic Research and Training Institute.

Obaidullah, Mohammed, and Salma Abdullateef. 2011. *Islamic finance for micro and medium enterprises.* Jeddah: IRTI, Islamic Development Bank.

Qaradhawi, Yusuf. 1995. *Fiqh Al-Zakah.* Trans. Monzer Kahf. Jeddah: Center for Research in Islamic Economics, King Abdulaziz University.

Salehi, Djavad. 2017. Poverty and income inequality in the Islamic Republic of Iran. *Revue Internationale Des Etudes Du Développement* 1: 113–136.

Siddiqui, Abdur Rashid. 2008. *Qur'anic Key Words.* Markfield: The Islamic Foundation.

CHAPTER 6

Islamic Finance Strife: Risk Management, Regulation, and Supervision

Islamic finance, unfortunately, has a strong potential to divert from the intended course, which might be defined as healthy surrounding for *Nafs*, if practices are based on simplistic drives such as profit maximization or compliance with demand from the market. Referencing the philosophy of Islam would be an omen to keeping Islamic finance on track. Protection of the human self (*Nafs*) and wealth (*Mal*) has been identified as two of five pillars of *Maqasid Al Shariah* as preached by Ghazali centuries ago.[1] Although such protection is in line with Quran verses which are very clear on right of ownership, the benefit of wealth in other verses comes with checks and balances. As Al-Rumi stated, *Nafs* is like a ship and worldly wealth is like the sea. The ships needs the sea to roam on the surface, yet, if sea water enters, the ship sinks into sea. The idea is empowering people in achieving sound hearth which is the more accurate definition of *Maqasid Al Shariah*, aka purpose of divine rules.[2]

In this regard, Islam is not against financing but there is also no leeway for a forever expanding financial system which will, in the end, take the

---

[1] *Al Maqasid Al Shariah*: human development and well-being to be realized by ensuring the enrichment of *Nafs* (human self), *Mal* (wealth), *Nasl* (posterity), *Aql* (intellect) and *Din* (faith).

[2] Gundogdu (2019).

© The Author(s), under exclusive license to Springer Nature Switzerland AG 2021
A. T. Diallo and A. S. Gundogdu, *Sustainable Development and Infrastructure*, Palgrave Studies in Islamic Banking, Finance, and Economics, https://doi.org/10.1007/978-3-030-67094-8_6

whole economy hostage – registering profits for itself and billing its failures to citizens through central banking arrangement as the lender of last resort and state tax imposition capabilities. Islamic banks could be deemed to be in the same course as conventional banks as they seem to be part of the above mentioned scheme. Some of their practices would literally convert them into conventional banks. Regardless of these, Islamic banks present a strong opposition to the entry of conventional banks or non-Muslim banks to the Islamic finance sector. The main argument is doubtful sources of funds as equity, arguing one needs to have *Halal* (permissible) funds to establish a business. If this is a valid stand, the same should apply to deposit and customer's investment fund from doubtful sources as stipulated in *Shariah* Advisory Committee (SAC) of Bank Nagara in Case Box 6.1.

Case Box 6.1 Resolution on Deposit or Customer's Investment Fund from Doubtful Sources
Resolution

The SAC, in its 58th meeting dated 27 April 2006, has resolved that Islamic financial institutions are allowed to accept application to open deposit account or investment account from a customer without conducting investigation to ascertain whether the sources of the customer's fund are permissible (*halal*), forbidden (*haram*), or a mixture of the two. Notwithstanding this, the SAC has no objection for Islamic financial institutions to establish an internal screening process to ascertain whether the sources of the fund received are *Shariah* compliant.

Source: Bank Nagara

In reality, Islamic banks do not take the position to refuse any funds from doubtful sources or funds brought by non-Muslims for depositing. As another note, in practice Islamic banks do not participate in syndication of conventional banks, yet they accept the participation of conventional banks to the Islamic syndication as an underlying contract for lending practice is Islamic. In the explanation of the SAC resolution, there is reference to business relationships, as permissible, between Muslims and

Table 6.1 Islamic finance strife

Issue	Solution
Accruing late payment charges as profit	Savings Deposit Insurance Fund/*Waqf* Fund
Factoring/Islamic discounting	Receivable financing with receivable *Takaful* as risk mitigated without recourse to seller
Commodity *Murabaha*	Letter of Credit based alternatives
Sukuk, controversial ones	*Intifa Sukuk*
Hedging: Islamic SWAPS/forwards	Natural hedging/*Takaful*

Source The authors

non-Muslims during *Rasulullah SAW*.[3] Allowing conventional banks to enter Islamic finance might benefit the Islamic finance sector as long as they comply with Islamic *Shariah* in their practice. *Shariah* compliance has already been highlighted as an issue that needs to be addressed by the existing players in the sector. In Table 6.1, several problematic practices of Islamic financial institutions and *Shariah* compliant alternatives are provided.

6.1 Late Payment Charges

There are several conventional finance products that are very close to Islamic finance; leasing and post-finance for international trade would count as good examples. Beck et al. (2010) indeed highlighted this issue as they state that many Islamic finance contracts can be converted to Islamic finance contracts with little change. This would be expected for transactions of conventional banks connected to the real economy. Islamic banks would diverge from conventional banks in being unnecessarily sophisticated and disconnected, from bona fide transaction, to products offered by conventional banks. In essence, in the case of leasing and post-finance, the main distinction would be interest charges on funds that are overdue. Conventional financial institutions would have overdue clauses in loan agreements that would generate additional profit in the case of late payment by their clients. Islamic financial institutions are not permitted to have any charges for late payment because the repayment

---

[3] Detail for the resolution is available at: http://www.bnm.gov.my/microsites/financ ial/pdf/resolutions/11_part05.pdf. Accessed April 16, 2014.

date and amount are fixed at the time of disbursement. And, according to the Quran, in the case of inability to repay by obligor, a devout Muslim needs to act as follows:

> And if the debtor is in straitened circumstances, then (let there be) post-ponement to (the time of) ease; and that ye remit the debt as almsgiving would be better for you if ye did but know.
>
> Quran 2:280

Unfortunately, devout Muslims can be subject to deception as very often unwillingness to repay would be presented as straitened circumstances. As a result, Islamic financial institutions have traditionally imposed late payment charges to deter such possibilities and protect their interests. These late payment charges are transferred to a *Waqf* fund for charity purposes. In practice, the control of *Waqf* fund is with the bank and the use of the fund creates a gray area. For example, if an Islamic Bank uses the fund for food distribution to the poor and displays its logo, this can also be called marketing. Some Islamic banks have already received a *Fatwa* from their *Shariah* boards for accruing late payment charges as "profit deprivation." This practice, which is not permitted by Islamic *Fiqh* Academy, would convert Islamic banks to conventional ones regard-less of their very legitimate Islamic finance products such as *Murabaha* or *Ijara*. The implication is immense, as customers of Islamic banks have been promised to be provided with Islamic products, yet the reality might be other way around.

Shariah minds are instrumental in the process. The products are stamped by scholars, who are paid by the producer of the product, as *Shariah* compliant. In any country, there would be a food codex and the government would regulate and supervise the market to ensure that what the customer gets is what has been labeled by the producer. In the case of cheating, the government can ban the producer. This is the case even for *Sujuk* but not *Sukuk*. The Dana gas *Sukuk* case is iconic as is presented in Case Box 6.2.

Case Box 6.2 Shariah Minds for Dana Gas *Sukuk*

Dana Gas, a *Sharjah*-based company listed on the Abu Dhabi stock exchange has caused an upheaval in the US$100 billion *Sukuk* market.

The company announced that its *Mudarabah Sukuk*, issued in 2007, restructured in 2013 and which matures in October 2017 has been declared non-*Shariah* compliant by its *Shariah* committee and therefore unlawful for repayment as per terms. Dana Gas was therefore proposing the exchange of that *Sukuk* with another that had half the previous dividends and without a conversion feature. In effect, the *Sukuk* holders would be short changed. Adding insult to injury, the company blamed *Shariah* evolution as the reason for its inability to play by agreed rules. According to a news report, the company had issued a statement that "Due to the evolution and continual development of Islamic Financial instruments and their interpretation, the company has recently received legal advice that the *Sukuk* in its present form is not *Shariah* compliant and is therefore unlawful under UAE law. As a result, a restructuring of the current *Sukuk* is necessary to ensure that it conforms to the relevant laws for the benefit of all shareholders". In essence, Dana Gas was blaming changes in *Shariah* interpretation for its woes. The fact that a basic requirement of the *Shariah* is to uphold the terms of a contract agreed to, appears to have been lost. Furthermore, even where *Shariah* interpretation changes, the fact that applying a change retrospectively to an agreed contract, goes against natural justice appears to also have been missed. This is not the first time *Shariah* interpretation has jolted *Sukuk* markets. In 2009, Investment Dar, a Kuwaiti company had tried to rescind its obligations to a bank using *Shariah* arguments. In this case however, Investment Dar's *Shariah* committee had barred the company from using *Shariah* principles to argue its case.

For a *Sukuk* market that in many ways is still in its infancy, these are unnecessary problems. More than anything, it points to the need for improved *Shariah* governance. Many would agree that the Dana Gas issue could not have happened in the Malaysian *Sukuk* market which has a tight and well-functioning *Shariah* governance framework. In Malaysia, a national body puts out resolutions, justified and clearly articulated in written form which become the guideposts for *Shariah* committees at the firm/bank level. Under the country's IFSA (Islamic Financial Services Act), individual *Shariah* committee members are held personally liable to ensure compliance with the national resolutions. This assures synchronicity in interpretation and execution of *Shariah* rules. Such a governance framework however is sorely lacking elsewhere.

This has huge implications not just for future growth of sukuk but of Islamic finance in general. *Shariah* scholars are not the only ones required to interpret and make judgement calls. Many spheres of business, accounting, law, engineering, and others require its practitioners to make judgements but they are guided by well codified rules/regulations. Accountants for example have clear accounting standards like GAAP and IFRS that are accepted internationally. Similarly, lawyers and judges are guided by statutes. The professions are also guided by professional bodies that require accreditation and ensure that their members behave in ways intended to serve society as they are supposed to. The *Shariah* fraternity, however, appears to have neither of these. There are no internationally accepted *Shariah* standards nor are there institutions that can chastise or hold scholars accountable for their decision. As long as such standardization and governance mechanism are missing, Islamic finance is likely to witness Dana Gas type issues from time to time.

Source: Bacha (2020)

In a citizen oriented country, public authority should have *Shariah* monitoring and take necessary action to avoid gray areas. For example, in case of late payment, one solution would be transferring late payment fees to a "Savings Deposit Insurance Fund" which might be used in case of market disruption to assist Islamic banks in pursuit of financial market stability. However, the deposit banking business model is not a good fit for Islamic finance. Hence, crowdfunding types of arrangement should inflict lenders with losses due to delays. The late payment charges can better be accumulated in a central *Waqf* account to be used as concessional resources in the service of sustainable development programs.

Today, public authorities are inclined to regulate Islamic financial institutions like conventional banks. This is reflected in the diversion from the essence of Islamic finance: to be part of bona fide transaction. From risk management, regulation and supervision points of view, neither public authorities nor bankers are willing to indulge in bona fide transaction as it implies different rules of the game. The question is: Should Islamic finance have its own rules or try to fit the rules of the conventional system? The inclination to fit Islamic finance into the conventional system gives rise to strife on products offered, particularly for treasury operations and working capital needs.

6.2   WORKING CAPITAL FINANCE

One of the main areas of confusion regarding *Shariah* compatibility is the misconception about fulfilling certain criteria to fit the transaction to the frame: the existence of buying and selling in tripartite arrangements is very often confused as being enough to enable *Shariah* compliance. Bill discounting practices are very often confused as being alternative means in Islamic finance because the bill is generated as the end product of bona fide transaction. Today several Islamic financial institutions practice factoring under the name of *Bai Al-Dayn* (Islamic factoring) or Islamic discounting. Nevertheless, in the case of bill discounting, whether checks or drafts, what is traded by financial institutions are not underlying assets but debt obligations. There is *forstyrrende* (disturbing) pressure from the industry on *Shariah* bodies for a green light to *Bai Al-Dayn*. The subject was discussed in the 16th Convention of Islamic *Fiqh* Academy at Makkah on January 5–10, 2002, and the following was forbidden:

1. Sale of debts to debtors with a deferred payment plan exceeding debt amount as this can be considered as *Riba Al-Fadl* and *Riba An-Nasiah* (*Jadwalah Ad-Dayn*).
2. Sale of debts to a third party with a deferred payment plan whether the debt is paid with the same type of kind or not – as this can be considered as sale of debt with debt (*Bai' Al-Kali* which is clearly prohibited by Prophet Muhammad).

In its very essence, route of the prohibition goes back to very basic principle of Islam: "No sell-off before actually possessing it" or "Sell not what is not with you." Regardless of loud and clear prohibition, some Islamic financial institutions are still very keen to indulge in *Bai Al-Dayn*: *Bai Al-Dayn* is easy to transact and there is a mature market with regulations and supervisions. As true believers, Muslims may opt to dismiss market opportunities or not to operate under the rule of conventional system. However, the main concern in this debate revolves around financing expanding local and international trade. This economic realty urges to develop *Shariah* compliant products alternative to factoring/bill discounting with corresponding supervisory rules and regulations. Import financing under a letter of credit (L/C) and documentary collection has been long practiced by Islamic banks and can be deemed as mature business practice. Regardless of critics on *Murabaha* syndrome, in Islamic finance, there need not to be issue as long as standards set by AAOIFI's FAS-2: *Murabaha* and *Murabaha* to the purchase orderer observed. The main critiques of *Murabaha* are related to debt creation, markup feature, collateral, risk/agency issues.[4] Some of this critiques can be addressed by resorting to more asset-backed *Murabaha*, though asset-based *Murabaha* can also fit the bill for *Shariah* compliance. On the other hand, resorting to asset-backed *Murabaha* would necessitate change in risk management practices as Islamic financial institutions needs to manage: third-party risk of insurance, collateral manager, etc., as well as commodity risk of price, quality, and quantity. That is, Islamic financial institutions should have not only different regulations/supervision but also sui generis risk management guidelines.[5]

In import financing obligor and an Islamic financial institution can enter into a *Murabaha* sale whereby the Islamic financial institution buys goods from an exporter and sells these to the importer – its client and obligor. The challenge comes with export financing as the buyer of the goods to be financed is in another country where establishing legal obligation to repay is a hurdle. The same difficulty exists for supply/purchase financing and receivable financing in a local market should the seller not have contractual relationship with financiers. As a result, some Islamic financial institutions resort to discounting bill/draft received from buyer abroad with recourse to seller – their clients and seller. Alternatives to *Dayn* are proposed as follows[6]

1. *Wakala* agreement between seller/exporter and Islamic financial institutions by which the former acts as an agent of the latter to conclude export transaction.
2. Export proceed assignment to the latter.
3. *Takaful* arrangement for export receivable insurance.

Islamic products can be offered within the existing banking structure. Conventional banks are willing to offer Islamic finance products through loans to their clients who hold only current accounts and are not involved

---

[4] Gundogdu (2016b).
[5] Gundogdu (2016a).
[6] Gundogdu (2016b):

with interest transactions. One reason for such a customer profile is security; an affluent client with sizable capital might not keep his/her money in a private Islamic bank that has meager equity. Hence, intervention of the state present itself as an alternative in many countries as there are state enterprises operating interest-based banking. As a matter of citizens' rights, the same service would be asked by devout Muslims for enjoying the security of keeping money in a state-owned bank. Another alternative would be allowing Islamic windows by big banks or state-owned banks. Although these are second and third types of best options, an instrumentality of investment account can serve for directly linking lending with resource mobilization in the transition toward a crowdfunding business model.

Yet the main impediment remains in the form of regulatory arrangements. In order to operate working capital lending and resource mobilization, banks need to be allowed to hold the ownership of goods financed. Banking regulatory and supervisory agencies tend to be strict in implementation of banking laws that disallow banks to own goods financed from a risk management point of view. This discretion is reasonable and implemented to protect financial stability as owning would bring about risk inherent with goods which might not be managed by banks properly. Two-step *Murabaha*, which is standard Islamic trade finance line, could be a solution to overcome this problem since ownership is simultaneously transferred from fund provider to line bank and from line bank to its client. The diffusion of this product depends on regulatory arrangements to allow banks to assume ownership in case of simultaneous transfer to third parties. Such transitional arrangement might be needed in the course toward perfect Islamic finance habitat. If embedded in the exchange system, two-step *Murabaha* can also be a good omen for liquidity management for Islamic financial institutions.[7]

6.3   Treasury, Fund Management, and Investment Practices

Unless pooling in resource mobilization with deposit banking is abandoned, liquidity management has been and shall be one of the major

---

[7] Gundogdu (2016c).

problems of Islamic finance practice. The main issue is interbank place-ment; it is not permissible as there is no bona fide transaction to underlie financial transaction. Under such limitations, an Islamic financial insti-tution would be exposed to negative carry if it cannot find investment opportunities; limitations are imposed with *Shariah* rules. Accordingly, efforts exerted by regulators to find solution to his protracted problem. International Islamic Liquidity Management Corporation, an interna-tional body established by central banks and money authorities, is one of the attempts to solve this problem. Nevertheless, proposals provided throughout could not avoid heavy criticism due to the obsession for a commodity *Murabaha* element as is already practiced in the London Metal Exchange. In the end, what would be the difference between drinking alcohol in KL instead of in London from a *Shariah* perspec-tive? Commodity *Murabaha* is a *Tawarruq* transaction administered in an organized commodity exchange on precious metal contracts. It is defended by treasury practitioners as there exist buying and selling. Never-theless, there is no intention of delivery of precious metal traded as the purpose of this organized activity is exchange of money with "markup." The Islamic *Fiqh* Academy discussed this activity of Islamic financial institutions in its 17th session and disallowed this practice, as shown in Table 6.2.

As proposed a two-step *Murabaha* can be embedded to stock/commodity exchange for liquidity management alternative tool. This proposal can fill the bill for the following reasons.

1. Two-step *Murabaha* is a mature Islamic finance line by which banks can lend to each other as alternative to commodity *Murabaha*.
2. Since there are buyer, seller, and shipping documents, bona fide transaction is assured – which is missing with commodity *Murabaha*.
3. In the case of two-step *Murabaha* there are two sales with indepen-dent markup and tenor so line banks can raise funds through tenor difference between two sales.
4. The underlying trade finance transaction is administered by centuries-long developed protocols such as INCOTERMS, UCP, URC or Bill of Lading conventions.
5. The presence of line bank as obligor would facilitate cross-border money placement as international investors can allocate risk expo-sure limit to line banks.

Table 6.2 The resolution of the Islamic *Fiqh* Academy regarding *Tawarruq*

Praise be to Allah alone, and peace and blessings upon the Messenger of Allah, his household and his companions. To proceed: the Islamic *Fiqh* Academy of the Muslim World League in its seventeenth session held in Makkah, 19-23/10/1424 AH/13-17/12/2003, examined the topic of *Tawarruq* as it is being practiced by some banks at present

After listening to the research papers presented on the topic, and after discussions about it, it became apparent to the Academy that the *Tawarruq* which is being executed by some banks nowadays is that, typically, the bank will undertake to sell a commodity (other than gold or silver) from the international commodity markets, or some other market, to the seeker of *Tawarruq* (*Mustawriq*) for a deferred payment, with the bank committing itself – either by a stipulation in the contract or in accord with customary practice – to represent the buyer in selling it to another buyer for cash and delivering the payment to the *Mustawriq*

After consideration and study, the Academy has decided the following:

First:

Dealing with the form of *Tawarruq* described in the introduction is not allowed, for the following reasons:

(1) The commitment by the seller in the contract of *Tawarruq* by proxy to sell the commodity to another buyer or to line up a buyer makes it similar to the prohibited *Inah*, whether the commitment is explicitly stipulated or is merely customary practice

(2) This practice leads in many cases to violation of the *Shariah* requirement that a buyer must take possession of a commodity in order for any sale after that to be valid

(3) The reality of this transaction is based on the bank providing cash financing with an increase to the party called the *Mustawriq* through purchase and sales transactions it conducts, which are in most cases pure formalities. The aim of bank from this procedure is to get an increase on what it gave in the way of financing. This dealing is not the real *Tawarruq* known to the scholars, which the Academy previously ruled was lawful in its fifteenth session, if the transactions are real and if certain conditions that the Academy explained in its resolution are fulfilled. The differences between the two have been made clear in the research papers presented on the topic. Real *Tawarruq* consists of an actual purchase of a commodity for a deferred payment that brings it into the ownership of the buyer and which he takes actual possession of and becomes responsible for; after which he will sell it for cash to fulfill his need. He may be successful in achieving that goal or not. And the difference between the two prices, the spot price and the deferred price, does not enter into the ownership of the bank, which involves itself in the process in order to make acceptable the increase it obtains on the financing it provides to the person through what are in most cases only formal transactions. The features of real *Tawarruq* are not present in the previously explained procedure practiced by some banks

Second:

The Academy advises all banks to stay far away from forbidden dealings in obedience to the command of Allah, the Exalted. As the Academy appreciates the efforts of the Islamic banks to rescue the *Ummah* from the tribulation of *Riba*, it advises them to use real Islamic transactions, not purely formal transactions, which, in reality, are nothing but financing operations with an increase for the financer

(continued)

Table 6.2 (continued)

Allah is the One Who guides to the right path; may the peace and blessings of Allah be upon our Prophet, his household and companions

Source Islamic Fiqh Academy

The main body of the product is available to fit this into liquidity management through stock/commodity exchange which requires additionally connecting trade finance activities of Islamic financial institutions with their treasury activities. The major drawback of this product would be lack of a secondary market, as after simultaneous *Murabaha* sales, there is only debt obligations of parties which if traded would create non-*Shariah*-compliant factoring/discounting. The availability of a secondary market is vital for the day-to-day transactions of conventional banks, and some argue that the same holds for Islamic financial institutions. In the case of trade finance, tenors are short to 3–6 months and Islamic financial institutions can arrange their liquidity management practices as hold to maturity.[8] In the end, being ruled by different principles should be reflected on internal practices for Islamic banks; by following *Shariah* principles, Islamic financial institutions would have their sui generis liquidity management practices such as risk management, regulations, and supervisions.

Although it is at the center of several issues and criticism, *Sukuk* can allow secondary market trading which may abate the burden on Islamic financial institutions as another fixed income instrument. However, the *Sukuk* as an Islamic finance instrument has come under the spotlight (Usmani 2008). The major issues pertaining to *Sukuk* can be summarized as follows.

1. Very often *Sukuk* issued are securitized on non-permissible contracts of commodity *Murabaha* or Bai Al-Inah.
2. The role of SPV or trustee.
3. Prevalence of asset-based *Sukuk* which would not confer any access to underlying asset in case of default.

[8] Gundogdu (2018).

Due to these features, many *Sukuk* today are criticized as being a replica of securitized bonds of the conventional system. The main issue is the hesitation of an asset owner to transfer ownership of the asset which might be lost even after full repayment in case of conflict. The solutions to this concern by both issuer and fixed income seeker can be better searched in Muslim business practice. In this regard, *Intifa* (usufructuary) as practiced in land registry can be solution. *Sukuk* can be backed by a usufructuary right as it can be separated from simple ownership of the asset during the tenor of *Sukuk*. Usufructuary right should be transferable during the tenor of *Sukuk* to allow secondary market. The owner of usufructuary right can rent this asset to the owner or third party for a fixed income. The usufructuary right can be sold to another fixed income seeker in the secondary market during the validity period. Such implementation is based on day-to-day *Shariah*-compliant activities of Muslims, would not require existence of an SPV or trustee, and would give access to usage of an asset in the case of default. With a clear difference from conventional bonds, such *Sukuk* would require specific security exchange commission regulation and supervision. The benchmark again can be from the real economy; transport public–private partnership (PPP) projects could be particularly suitable for *Intifa Sukuk*. In the case of default of state, *Sukuk* holders would have access to tolling fees through availability mechanism in PPP. From a risk management point of view, *Sukuk* holders would have fallback to usufructuary right, hence, stronger risk management capabilities. This would change *Sukuk* from debt security into an investment tool for raising funds for big infrastructure projects – hence, diverting funds from a debt market to an investment market. *Sukuk* should be used mindfully for mobilizing resources for infrastructure projects. It should not be a debt creating tool but an investment means for those with access funds. SME loans should be transformed into *Sukuk* to circumvent the regulatory environment.

In case of *Sukuk* default, is it possible to develop hedging tools such as Islamic CDS? This question would give rise to another hard talk: Islamic hedging. There have been many efforts to mainstream Islamic SWAPS, forward contracts, etc., as the Islamic finance industry has developed the idea of having an Islamic version of any product offered by their conventional counterparts. Looking into details, there would be several contracts between parties with Arabic names and relatively complicated diagrams but in essence one party guarantee the other in exchange of markup. These contracts are again based on commodity *Murabaha* or two *Wad* contracts. The only exception might be some FX forward contract intended to mitigate risk of receivables from a *Murabaha* sale. The concept of markup is acceptable in the case of buying/selling of goods – but is it also acceptable for risk or debt? The Islamic finance industry can resort to *Salam*, in the case of only agricultural input financing. However, using *Salam* as treasury practice should not be the case for devout Muslims. Islamic financial institutions can develop their risk management guidelines, which would be more stringent than those of conventional banks, for natural hedging and investment decisions instead of imitating conventional hedging mechanisms to count on probability calculations – that is, *Gharar* and *Maysir*.

If hedging mechanisms are not used, credit analysis developed by the conventional system can be applied to Islamic finance to manage risk associated with investment decisions. This would result in the credit analysis guidelines developed by the conventional system being strengthened by principles of Islamic finance: being informed of underlying transaction – paying to supplier in most cases – can enable proper risk management for the sector. Also, development of the *Takaful* industry would give more room to hedging possibilities. The main impediment on this front is the size of the *Takaful* industry, the number of *Takaful* participants, and the sectorial/geographic diversity of participants. In the case of a currency collapse in one country or a price collapse in one commodity, participants from different countries/sectors should shoulder the fallen if needed and expect the same should it happen to them. That is, *Takaful* diversified participation is key for its use as risk management tool. Islamic hedging solutions would not be possible without successful development of the *Takaful* industry, not only for *Sukuk* but also for trade finance operations such as marine cargo insurance, professional indemnity insurance, export receivable insurance, and political risk insurance for project finance. The defining line for *Takaful* is very simple: *Takaful* should be used as long as it supports trade (SME working capital finance and CAPEX finance) and investment (*Sukuk* to mobilize resources for infrastructure projects), and it should be avoided if it leads to moral hazard.

Regardless of all problems in practice of Islamic finance, Islamic finance can still stand as an alternative to the conventional system. For example, most of the Islamic banks still do not offer overdraft or debt-bridging products which are a major cause of credit risk and bubble. Nevertheless, there is an urgent need to address the problems of late payment charges, trade finance, and treasury/investment practices to halt Islamic finance inclination toward the conventional system. This would require the development of sui generis risk management practices, regulations, and supervision. From an Islamic finance industry point of view, solutions to limitations would come from imitating real sector practices as has been practiced by Muslim business communities for centuries but not the conventional finance system. Saying that, finance infrastructure developed by the conventional system, such as SWIFT, UCP 500, or ISIN, should be appreciated because without such infrastructure it would not be feasible to operate *Shariah*-compliant products. Islamic finance is heavily transaction based, and it is contemporary technology, mostly developed by non-Muslims, which allows the implementation of these transactions. Hence, for the diffusion of Islamic finance and principles to happen, the Islamic finance industry should focus on the *Shariah* compliance of transactions, be open to outsiders (Muslim or non-Muslim) to join to the sector as long as they abide by *Shariah*, and ask for governments to impose regulations and supervision suitable to Islamic finance. In the end, depositors of an "as-is" business model, or participants of crowdfunding in a "to-be" business model, who entrust the management of their hard-earned money to Islamic finance either through Islamic banks or windows, should be assured by governments they get a *Halal* return, as promised.

With a gradual move from deposit banking to the use of investment accounts and finally to a full conversion to the crowdfunding platform, the Islamic finance industry can bring forth a sustainable financial system. Risk management, rules, and regulations can be adjusted to pave the way for new business models which can cater for SME financing and infrastructure projects. The engagement of Islamic finance in economic infrastructure is straight forward as its features are in perfect alignment for Islamic financial product development. The product development for social infrastructure is more convoluted. Unlike projects, CAPEX, and working capital transactions, all of which include tangible assets, social infrastructure is classed as public goods. Health and education services, for instance, are intangible assets, and the Islamic finance perspective vis-à-vis financing services is discussed in ch. 8. The root cause of the problem, however, lurks in the financial product development procedures.

REFERENCES

Bacha, O.I. 2020. Dana Gas Sukuk: The need for improved shariah governance. https://www.researchgate.net/publication/339165026_Dana_Gas_Sukuk_The_Need_for_improved_Shariah_Governance.

Beck, T., A. Demirgüç-Kunt, and O. Merrouche. 2010. Islamic vs. conventional banking: business model, efficiency and stability. World Bank Policy Research Working Paper No. 5446. Washington, DC.

Gundogdu, A.S. 2016a. Risk management in Islamic trade finance. *Bogazici Journal* 30(2): 64–82. https://doi.org/10.21773/boun.30.2.4.

Gundogdu, A.S. 2016b. Exploring novel Islamic finance methods in support of OIC exports. *Journal of Islamic Accounting and Business Research* 7(2).

Gundogdu, A.S. 2016c. Islamic electronic trading platform on organized exchange. *Borsa Istanbul Review* 16(4): 249–255.

Gundogdu, A.S. 2018. The rise of Islamic finance: Two-step Murabaha. *Asia-Pacific Management Accounting Journal* 13(1): 107–130.

Gundogdu, A.S. 2019. *A modern perspective of Islamic economics and finance.* Bingley, UK: Emeralds Publishing.

Usmani, M.T. 2008. *Sukuk and their contemporary application.* South Africa: Mujlisul Ulama of South Africa.

CHAPTER 7

Islamic Approach Toward Energy Sector Infrastructure Development

Sustainable development goals (SDGs) are now also at the center of energy infrastructure sector. In order to achieve SDGs in filling the electricity infrastructure gap by 2030, it is estimated that, per annum for low and middle-income countries, 2.2 percent of GDP investment (4.5 percent of total infrastructure) and 0.6 percent of GDP maintenance spending (2.7 percent of total infrastructure) is needed. Most of the Islamic countries fall under this category. The numbers suggest that almost half of the infrastructure investment needs to be allocated for the energy sector: Infrastructure is interdependent and electricity is the key for other infrastructures such as transport, water supply, ICT, and provision of oil and gas. Use of tax revenues to fill the financing gap is not a feasible solution in poor countries as it has been tried for decades. Neither is it advisable from an Islamic economics point of view since it results in wealth transfer from communities to the few. This policy discourse also coincides with the general opposition in Islam concerning tax levied on people as a means of control.[1]

---

[1] Gundogdu (2019a).

© The Author(s), under exclusive license to Springer Nature Switzerland AG 2021
A. T. Diallo and A. S. Gundogdu, *Sustainable Development and Infrastructure*, Palgrave Studies in Islamic Banking, Finance, and Economics, https://doi.org/10.1007/978-3-030-67094-8_7

111

7.1   Setting the Parameters
to Evaluating New Business Models

Affordable and clean energy is an important part of SDGs and, as mentioned previously, the financing gap is huge to fill the bill for the much needed infrastructure investment.[2] Affordable and clean energy, SDG-7, is key not only for SDG-9 (Industrial Innovation and Infrastructure Development) and SDG-8 (Decent Work and Economic Growth) but also for health, education, etc. Energy is interconnected with 125 out of the total of 169 SDG targets.[3] Affordable energy is indispensable to support economic growth by connecting underdeveloped areas to the global value chain (GVC) and to developing upstream and downstream value chains. It is suggested that a better and earlier connection to GVC will yield improvements in economic performance.[4] Therefore, GVC is being presented as a viable solution for developing countries. Nevertheless, there is a structural impediment: a lack of both production capacity and transport infrastructure to enable some countries to get connected. Under the Aid-for-Trade agenda, introduced in WTO Hong Kong ministerial meeting, infrastructure investment in the energy sector and transport (ports, airports, roads) is key to enable the connection of vulnerable communities in developing countries to the GVC.[5]

On the other hand, development finance experience suggests that neither technological advancement and infrastructure investment nor global value chain approaches could abate the poverty issue. Connection to GVC increases a multinational firm's productivity.[6] Although the multinationals, as lead firms in the GVC, acquire higher profit margins, the supplier firms from developing countries entering the GVC experience a greater decline in margins.[7] A similar pattern is observed for the labor market: both the GDP of countries and the profits of companies are

---

[2] Ratio of needed investment to current investment is 3.04. IsDB GVC Report, p. 7.

[3] WB, ESMAP, SE4ALL (2017).

[4] Antras and de Gortari (2017).

[5] Vijil and Wagner (2012).

[6] Constantinescu et al. (2019).

[7] Choi et al. (2019).

increasing, yet the share of labor in income is falling.[8] Besides, multinationals avoid both corporate tax and transaction taxes, e.g., value-added tax, with opportunities created out of cross-border operations within the GVC, hence the tax burden keeps increasing on households.[9] Therefore, there is a strong case for community-centric alignment of the GVC – as does of the provision of economic infrastructure from an Islamic perspective.

Poverty exists and it will not abate – and is more likely to worsen – with repetitive turbulence in global financial markets. Although it has been argued that people get out of poverty with infrastructure development and GVC, the subject also needs Islamic reflection. The income approach to poverty, such as living below $3.2 per day for lower-middle-income countries or $5.2 per day for upper-middle-income courtiers as a definition of poverty, is not in line with Islamic understanding. Islamic perception of poverty is related to asset ownership and liabilities. From a conventional economics point of view, a person making a reasonable income is not poor even if this income is generated out of massive debt by soaking up negative net worth. In Islam, such a person can observe *Infaq* and *Sadaqa*, yet not be liable for *Zakat* – hence, deemed as not rich but poor should the negative net worth be factored in.[10] The income approach to poverty is also very problematic as under adverse market conditions those who have supposedly gotten out of poverty through debt would go back to poverty whenever the market mechanism stop precipitating an income stream generated out of overall loan growth. Hence, the conventional income approach to poverty is misleading and contradicts the Islamic view.

Unfortunately, there is no one-size-fits-all Islamic business model when it comes to infrastructure development. In addition to political economy concerning wealth transfer through infrastructure project development with conventional financing approaches and tariffing; sustainability and resilience are another issue across infrastructure developed. Many projects are poorly designed, operated, and maintained.[11] The connection of local communities to the global value chain cannot happen if assets remain in

---

[8] Refer to the World Bank Development Report 2020 (World Bank 2019, p. 86).

[9] IMF (2019).

[10] Iqbal and Lewis (2014).

[11] Hallegatte et al. (2019).

ruin or unmaintained and if the debt burden piles up with no prospect of a return on infrastructure investment in the case of weak sustainability and resilience features. Hence, the Islamic business model should also factor such sustainability and resilience issues to impede supply disruption and enable the proper operation and maintenance of project assets.

In the case of social infrastructure (health, education, and water) Islam recommends a *Waqf* business model to assure community ownership of project assets – such ownership overcomes sustainability concerns, while avoiding commodification of these public goods and wealth transfer from communities to the very few. Nevertheless, the issue of resilience remains for both economic infrastructure and social infrastructure, even under *Waqf*. Resilient infrastructures can be defined as assets such as power lines that can withstand external shocks, particularly natural hazards.[12] Resilience measures should be embedded into economic infrastructure, and in the case of energy this is critical since other infrastructure is highly affected by energy supply disruption.[13] According to Rentschler et al. (2019a), disrupted infrastructure services bring about USD 120 billion direct impact cost (reduced utilization rates and sales losses), and USD 65 billion coping costs (generator investment and generator operation costs) for firms in the low- and middle-income countries annually.[14] Disruption also has a direct impact, indirect impact, and coping cost for households. Disruption leads to diminished well-being of households, lower productivity of family firms, higher morbidity, and mortality.[15] Reliable access to electricity has a more favorable impact on human development parameters than electricity access alone.[16]

Besides, the provision of reliable electricity without disruption is key for the upstream value chain upgrade. For example, moving from natural fiber production to upstream yarn and fabric production requires a reliable undisrupted electricity supply. In the power sector, storms are the main cause of the disruption as flying debris hits lines and lightning

---

[12] Hallegatte et al. (2019).

[13] Wender et al. (2017).

[14] Disruption would also have an indirect impact on firms: higher barriers to market entry and lower investment.

[15] Rentschler et al. (2019a).

[16] Zhang (2019).

strikes conductors leading to short-circuits causing damage to assets.[17] Comparing non-natural shocks to natural shocks, the latter causes longer outages.[18] Factoring resilience into project design expands the need for more financing. If only exposed assets (based on disaster risk management data) are upgraded for resilience, a 3–6 percent incremental investment is needed. If all new assets are upgraded for resilience against winds, floods, and earthquakes, a 30 percent incremental investment is needed.[19] Nevertheless, such incremental investment is worthwhile as more resilient energy systems would decrease the costs inflicted due to disruption.[20] The same holds for maintenance. Not only would good maintenance decrease the risk of disruption but also the sunk cost for resilient infrastructure would decrease maintenance costs.[21]

Unlike social infrastructure, in the case of economic infrastructure (transport/first-mile ICT and energy sector), Islamic principles of fair price formation encourage private companies' involvement in the provision of these services. Yet, again, the issues of unfair wealth transfer and unfair competition should be dissolved. Transport and ICT infrastructure – particularly first-mile ICT infrastructure: international submarine cables or terrestrial cross-border links – can be provided with minimum unfair wealth transfer while addressing sustainability issues using an Islamic PPP business model which aims to ring-fence unfairness in conventional PPPs.[22] The very nature of such infrastructure requires large project companies. Since there exists usually one large asset, there would be large project companies involved until a need arose for novel methods and technologies that would allow SME participation in asset production and distribution. In addition, from an Islamic perspective, the model proposed would need to tap into alternative financing resources, not concessional loans or grants; commercially priced financing is advised for economic infrastructure finance. New models for the energy sector should enable

[17] Panteli and Mancarella (2015).

[18] Rentschler et al. (2019b).

[19] These figures indicates the monetary value of disaster risk management data.

[20] Schweikert et al. (2019).

[21] Rozenberg and Fay (2019).

[22] Gundogdu (2019b).

massive resource mobilization opportunities in order to fill the financing gap.[23]

As stated, from an Islamic economics and finance point of view, transport and ICT (particularly the first-mile) infrastructure can be addressed with a modified Islamic PPP business model. The question of affordable and clean energy problem remains. There emerges a need to address this issue with a new business model including an alternative financing mechanism to avoid financial strain on the government budget. Hence, alternative project finance mechanisms, such as crowdfunding, and energy provision schemes, such as off-grid renewable energy as a viable business model, appear as potential solutions. This track can be a resolution for affordable and clean energy for economic development without exacerbating wealth inequality with a tariff-based distribution mechanism. Such discourse can also inhibit exploitation of communities by large corporations and banks via public debt burden created out of large-scale production infrastructure and distribution networks. The new technological trend provides a sustainable, affordable, and resilient energy provision opportunity which can be replicated across regions with resource mobilization possibilities for scaling up. The new trends bring forth the possibility of electricity generation using solar and wind for energy, heating, and cooling over non-renewable and non-environmentally friendly alternatives.

Based on elaboration up until now, the newly emerging Islamic energy infrastructure business models can be evaluated based on the parameters presented in Table 7.1.

Section 7.2 discusses the traditional reform approaches to the energy sector and its propositions for a solution. Section 7.3 introduces the case of the newly emerging Islamic business model for affordable energy. Section 7.4 evaluates the case presented based on empowerment, sustainability, and scale-up criteria, and it concludes with remarks on traditional reform approaches vs. the emerging Islamic solution.

[23] Development Committee: From Billions to Trillions: Transforming Development Finance. Accessed February 6, 2020. Available at: https://siteresources.worldbank.org/DEVCOMMINT/Documentation/23659446/DC2015-0002(E)FinancingforDevelopment.pdf.

Table 7.1 Evaluation parameters for energy infrastructure business model

Empowerment	The extent to which the business model uses innovative solutions to address the issues with features not proposed in traditional energy sector solutions to get aligned with an Islamic perspective, defined as empowering communities and community SMEs
Sustainability: maintenance, affordability, and resilience	The extent to which the business model has embedded measures and techniques to ensure that the project assets will not deteriorate and go to rack and ruin after project completion and will continue to deliver envisioned outcomes Is institutional sustainability adequate to assure proper maintenance? The extent to which the business model can provide energy without disruption. Can this business model provide a resilient infrastructure? The extent to which energy provision is affordable to assure long-term profitability
Scale-up: replicability and resource mobilization	The extent to which the business model can be replicated across other countries/communities and accelerate resource mobilization to finance accelerated replications

Source The authors

7.2 TRADITIONAL REFORM PROPOSALS FOR THE ENERGY SECTOR

In the second half of the twentieth century, following their independence, developing countries adopted a public procurement option for asset production, transmission, and distribution of electricity as a discourse to provide access to energy to ignite economic growth. In the 1980s/1990s, wider principles of the Washington Consensus changed the paradigm for the energy sector. The paradigm change coincided with the disintegration of the Soviet Union and growing dissatisfaction with publicly owned utilities concerning inefficiencies, subsidies, and financial constraints.[24]

---

[24] Bacon and Besant-Jones (2001).

The Washington Consensus is a dogmatic belief, which indoctrinated the adaptation of so-called market-led development strategies for developing countries. The dogmatism assumes that such strategies would lead to economic growth, which would then benefit all with a so-called "trickle down" effect. The problem is, what looks perfectly convincing on paper may in reality bring about totally the opposite results. Case Box 7.1 the account of the Washington Consensus by the person who coined the term.

Case Box 7.1 Washington Consensus

John Williamson coined the term Washington Consensus. Ten reforms that constitutes the list, with reflection of Williamson on each, are as follow:

1. **Fiscal Discipline**: This was in the context of a region where almost all countries had run large deficits that led to balance of payments crises and high inflation that hit mainly the poor because the rich could park their money abroad.

2. **Reordering Public Expenditure Priorities**: This suggested switching expenditure in a progrowth and propoor way, from things like nonmerit subsidies to basic health and education and infrastructure. It did not call for all the burden of achieving fiscal discipline to be placed on expenditure cuts; on the contrary, the intention was to be strictly neutral about the desirable size of the public sector, an issue on which even a hopeless consensus-seeker like me did not imagine that the battle had been resolved with the end of history that was being promulgated at the time.

3. **Tax Reform**: The aim was a tax system that would combine a broad tax base with moderate marginal tax rates.

4. **Liberalizing Interest Rates**: In retrospect I wish I had formulated this in a broader way as financial liberalization, stressed that views differed on how fast it should be achieved, and – especially – recognized the importance of accompanying financial liberalization with prudential supervision.

5. **A Competitive Exchange Rate**: I fear I indulged in wishful thinking in asserting that there was a consensus in favor of ensuring that the exchange rate would be competitive, which pretty much implies an intermediate regime; in fact Washington was already

---

beginning to edge toward the two-corner doctrine which holds that a country must either fix firmly or else it must float "cleanly."

6. **Trade Liberalization**: I acknowledged that there was a difference of view about how fast trade should be liberalized, but everyone agreed that was the appropriate direction in which to move.

7. **Liberalization of Inward Foreign Direct Investment**: I specifically did not include comprehensive capital account liberalization, because I did not believe that did or should command a consensus in Washington.

8. **Privatization**: As noted already, this was the one area in which what originated as a neoliberal idea had won broad acceptance. We have since been made very conscious that it matters a lot how privatization is done: it can be a highly corrupt process that transfers assets to a privileged elite for a fraction of their true value, but the evidence is that it brings benefits (especially in terms of improved service coverage) when done properly, and the privatized enterprise either sells into a competitive market or is properly regulated.

9. **Deregulation**: This focused specifically on easing barriers to entry and exit, not on abolishing regulations designed for safety or environmental reasons, or to govern prices in a non-competitive industry.

10. **Property Rights**: This was primarily about providing the informal sector with the ability to gain property rights at acceptable cost.

Source: Williamson (2004)

Energy sector reforms in the 1990s focused on four packages: private sector participation in production and distribution, vertical and horizontal unbundling, competition particularly in the wholesale market, and creation of autonomous regulatory authority.[25] The security of an undisrupted, efficient, and reliable supply of electricity was the intended outcome of the reform packages of the 1990s. The reforms were supposed to create competition and increase investment for an undisrupted supply increase. Security of supply would have been achieved with increased investment while competition in the private sector would have supported social inclusion, yet environmental sustainability was not a factor. The reform propositions were derived from conventional economic theory, which has imperfect assumptions. However, the reform packages of the

[25] Foster et al. (2017).

1990s proved not to be applicable in practice, at least universally.[26] Developing countries partially implemented the 1990s model. Their endeavors were mainly confined to the creation of regulatory authority and Independent Power Projects (IPPs) by the private sector in the electricity production side, hence most countries ended up with a hybrid model.[27]

As a result, communities were stuck between government patronage and empowered corporations. Although the reforms of the 1990s highlighted the importance of fairness – particularly the importance of tendering against direct contracting of IPPs to avoid irregularities, as well as the issue of unfair risk mitigation guarantees by governments to IPPs for demand risk (take-or-pay clauses), termination risk, exchange rate risk, and fuel price risk to protect public interest – the issue of empowerment remained unresolved. The reform agenda sought private sector involvement in production and distribution, while the transmission segment, deemed as a natural monopoly, was left for public ownership. Most viable and profitable segments were cherry-picked for the private sector, while government investment in transmission lines to create an enabling environment for the private sector should have continued. This would have given rise to another aspect of empowerment as an investment in transmission lines could have been done, under the agenda, by multilateral development banks providing loans to countries, while production and distribution by the corporation could have been financed by big banks in commercial terms. Nevertheless, even big banks opt for a public–private partnership (PPP) model to mitigate off-take risk with a government off-take guarantee. Some countries even extend risk mitigation measures to provide project completion risk for financiers in their PPP regulatory framework. The 1990s reform agenda opened up a business opportunity for corporations and banks while burden and risk ended up with the public sector in the form of investment in transmission lines, land acquisition, MDB loans, and government guarantees. Neither tariffing of communities nor full-scale empowering of corporations and banks have abated. Nevertheless, private sector efficiency, particularly in the distribution segment, have not ended up being higher than the public sector,

---

[26] Besant-Jones (2006).

[27] Gratwick et al. (2008).

hence many countries have reverted the distribution segment from the private sector to the public sector.[28]

As a result, an alternative solution cannot be the 1990s agenda, or the hybrid system where the 1990s agenda ended up, and archaic full government involvement because all of these approaches empower a few corporations or banks, being government cronies, at the expense of people. Besides, these past approaches have not been able to yield a result for the emerging agenda: affordable and clean energy access for all (SDG-7) and clean energy (Paris Climate Change Accord). Universal and clean electrification cannot be achieved by allowing the private sector and banks to pursue commercial incentives especially for rural areas. Today, the new technological trend and decrease in investment cost make solar energy for off-grid electrification a viable solution. Such discourse to empower people, unlike traditional government involvement or the 1990s reform agenda, is in perfect alignment with *Maqasid Al Shariah*.

7.3 CASE OF "UNLOCKING ENERGY ACCESS FINANCE THROUGH CROWDFUNDING"[29]

The emerging solution comprises a distributed renewables for energy access (DREA) system and a crowdfunding platform to finance local SMEs for the installation of the DREA system. DREA is an alternative to the traditional approach of a large power system composed of large production facilities and extended large-scale networks for distribution. The traditional approach is not able to fulfill the energy access need, particularly for remote areas, as 840 million people still have no access to electricity.[30] DREA systems are stand-alone, off-grid as well as mini-grid systems, which generate and distribute energy out of a centralized electricity grid. These systems are capable of providing not only lighting but also electricity for cooking, heating, cooling, and household appliances. Market trends support DREA systems as recently sunk cost have

---

[28] pp. 14–15 of the report entitled "Rethinking Power Sector Reform in the Developing World", 2019, World Bank.

[29] Product developed Within Islamic Development Bank by Bandar Alhoweish.

[30] Tracking SDG 7, 2019. Accessed February 6, 2020. Available at: http://docume nts.worldbank.org/curated/en/517781558037625254/Main-Report (see International Energy Agency; International Renewable Energy Agency; United Nations Statistics Division; World Bank; World Health Organization 2019).

significantly reduced. With such a trend, replacing kerosene, estimated to cost USD 15 per month for a household, with a DREA system such as solar home system (SHS), estimated to cost USD 12 per month under 24 months leasing, appears as a cost-saving which has huge growth potential.[31] In the emerging model, local SMEs, which are in dire need of working capital to scale-up, will have a pivotal role in the setting up of solar house systems (SHS). Traditionally, SMEs have been under pressure with regard to working capital: inherent governance issues and the lack of financial statements hinder their access to formal loans from banks and to supplier financing (see ch. 6). SME access to finance is more acute for developing countries.[32] Appendix A shows the financing intervention in cooperation with a crowdfunding company (CC).

1. A multilateral development bank (MDB) signs a "Master *Murabaha*" agreement with the solar partner (SP), which is a local SME. This *Murabaha* agreement will provide a format for a "promissory note" which will be used as proof of debt obligation in the implementation phase. MDB also opens an e-wallet account with an accredited payment institution.
2. MDB signs an "agency" agreement with the crowdfunding company (CC) in which MDB appoints CC (for a pre-determined fee) to administer and manage the financing facility.
3. CC checks for conditions precedent to disbursement vis-à-vis the agreement prior to disbursement request from the SP.
4. CC makes direct disbursement to the supplier (manufacturer of SHS) upon receipt of funds from MDB.
5. After the supplier delivers the SHS to SP, the form of offer and form of acceptance crystalizes the sale price to be paid by SP.
6. SP signs lease agreements with the end beneficiaries and installs the SHS.
7. SP collects lease receipts from the end beneficiaries and transfers repayments of the sale price, in installments, to CC.
8. CC distributes the funds received from installment sales to participants in accordance with the pre-determined structure.

---

[31] Calculated by the product development team.

[32] Dong and Men (2014).

The Debt Seniority Feature to Attract More Resources

In order to mobilize additional funds from the private sector, development banks come up with debt seniority mechanisms. The most common practice is an A Loan/B Loan mechanism for blended financing.[33] This is a tranche approach by which a lead financier gets the first-loss hit up to a certain percentage to attract more resources for sectors new to financial markets and where there is no track record to assure investor confidence in the deal.

In this pursuit, the MDB initially proposed to have the first-loss tranche, as a pilot project, to encourage crowd who has low-risk appetite and limited resources allocable for risky SME financing ventures in developing and least developed countries. In the case of default by solar partners (SMEs), MDB absorbs losses up to a certain percentage. In this way, the crowd would be exposed to credit risk only after mass scale credit default by Solar Partners. However, after the *Shariah* review, the mechanism was abandoned and a tenor-based debt seniority mechanism was introduced. Tenor-based debt seniority provides comparable, to the first-loss tranche, assurance to the crowd by having the priority of repayments to the crowd ahead of MDB. MDB gets repaid its portion in a bullet payment after one year after full repayment to crowd in prior installments. Hence, there is no repayment to the MDB until full repayment has been made to the crowd investors. By maintaining the benefits of the traditional first-loss tranche, MDB have the opportunity to mobilize more resources from the crowd in a *Shariah* compliant manner out of debt seniority created in tenor.

7.4   EVALUATION OF THE EMERGING SOLUTION

Empowerment

The crowdfunding for resource mobilization is an alternative to traditional financing. Given that the deposit banking business model empowers bank owners and core financial systems, people-to-people methods would empower communities as people have direct access to investment even when they have little capital. This discourse would also alleviate the burden on governments as the deposit banking business model comes

---

[33] OECD (2016).

with guarantees to depositors in case of system failure. Crowdfunding mechanisms match Islamic finance principles in resource mobilization: profit-loss sharing. Although local SMEs have a strong involvement in installation, the supply of assets favors lead firms in the global value chain. Nevertheless, noting that the provision of renewable energy with solar would replace fossil fuel consumption, the introduction of SHS would not deteriorate foreign exchange positions, and it is environmentally friendly. As an improvement, it is advisable to have SHS assets produced in regions close to SHS installation areas as much as economies of scale allow. Such interventions would enhance the empowerment of local communities against multinational lead firms in the GVC. There is no need for long-distance distribution cables – besides, electricity production assets are not centralized. Both production and distribution are decentralized, which boosts overall resilience noting that proper maintenance measures are there. The scheme empowers small investors, communities, and community SMEs. There is no room for big corporations except for lead SHS suppliers in the GVC.

Sustainability: Maintenance, Affordability, and Resilience

As per *Ijara*, SP should be responsible for regular maintenance of the SHS and the cost should be factored into the lease payments. Regular maintenance increases the lifetime of assets, decreases the probability of disruption, and increases resilience. This alone shows us another merit of Islamic finance as the owner of the asset is also responsible for maintenance in the *Ijara* contract, and such features bring about an overall economic benefit to society. It is important to note that adequate anchoring, proper engineering design, and bracing would help both maintenance and resilience. In the engineering design stage, there should be a focus on maintenance and resilience requirements to ensure sustainability. However, local SMEs may not consider resilience as their priority. Hence, the scheme should impose resilience engineering design components in the system. Besides, in order to avoid asset loss due to hazards, a micro-*Takaful* component can be added to the financing package. Such discourse would also enhance credit risk and support resource mobilization efforts for scale-up. In addition to maintenance, the scheme has the potential to create redundancy in a meshed network, and this would also decrease disruption risk. In a similar fashion, SHS is not less affordable than traditional fuels as per the estimated costs.[34]

Scale-Up: Replicability and Resource Mobilization

Many countries are rich in solar renewable energy, and the proposed SHS system has a strong replicability potential. Alternative renewable energy production solutions, such as wind, can even further enhance the replicability of the scheme.[35]

Scale-up requires strong credit fundamentals and there are improvement opportunities with the scheme. First of all, there is a delivery risk which needs to be mitigated. Unlike that which is proposed in the transaction flow in Step 5, the form of offer and acceptance should be exchanged at the disbursement stage not at the delivery stage to avoid delivery risk. In case of adverse market conditions such as a drop in the price of asset financed, during shipment, a buyer may shun from accepting the sale price based on changing market prices with other pretexts.

Evaluating the structure, MDB mobilizes resources from crowd investors in a *Musharakah* and appoints CC as *Mudarib*. Under *Musharakah* resource mobilization both losses and returns should be distributed on a pro-rata bases. As the first-loss tranche approach constitutes *Shariah* concern, so do tenor arrangements. In the end, both methods create debt seniority which is not aligned to principles of the profit-loss sharing principle of *Musharakah*. The cause of credit risk is the lack of collateral in case SP fails to fulfill its commitments. Hence, the concern of the crowd can be addressed by risk mitigation mechanism: collateral taking. The most valuable and resalable parts of the SHS can be collateralized for investors. However, in the proposed scheme, under the *Ijara* agreement, SP has legal access to the physical asset while investors take the credit risk of SP with an asset-based *Murabaha*. The financing structures can be changes to back-to-back *iIara* by which investors, crowd, and MDB can have access to physical assets that can be used to mitigate the credit risk. Nevertheless, since the SP is obligor and

---

[34] For household kerosene spending of USD 15 per month versus USD 12 per month leasing payment under 18–24 months lease plan.

[35] Identified on pp. 71–118 of Renewables 2019 Global Status Report. Accessed February 6, 2020. Available at: https://www.ren21.net/gsr-2019/.

has a vested interest in the physical asset, establishing a lien on SHS would not be feasible on the ground. There might be two alternative solutions:

1. Have a collateral manager on the ground to limit the access of SP to collateralized asset.
2. Restrict the role of SP to asset and service (maintenance) provider and have a microfinance institution, approved by the local authorities to be obligor.

These two alternatives may be used based on the realities on the ground and the legal structure in each country. In any case, the ideal situation is to have ownership of the SHS rather than having a pledge in place.

Traditional approaches of government ownership, the 1990s agenda, and the hybrid model as the end product of the 1990s reforms are missing community empowerment criterion. These approaches empower big corporations, banks, and government cronies, and they are not able to deliver emerging agenda: SDG-7 and Paris Climate Accord for clean and affordable electricity for all. The case presented, "Unlocking Energy Access Finance through Crowdfunding," empowers communities, and has strong potential to deliver results for the emerging agenda. The new development in battery storage, plummeting cost of photovoltaic units, and a digitalized power grid already provide viability for decentralized, affordable, and clean energy opportunities.

Conventional economics and finance theories have proposals based on assumptions to frame a perfect set up. In many cases, their proposals do not work. Unlike conventional theories, Islamic principles are not based on assumptions. As stated, the Islamic view proposes neither theories nor assumptions to operationalize such theories in a hypothetically perfect market. The Islamic economics and finance approach acknowledges the existence of imperfection with people and markets and proposes perfect to-dos and not-to-dos for imperfect people and markets. In this regard, the case of "Unlocking Energy Access Finance through Crowdfunding" shows strong potential to fill the bill upon further fine-tuning based on Islamic to-dos and not-to-dos.

However, the success of this emerging solution requires massive SME financing to provide resources for solar partners (SPs) in a sustainable manner. Funds for SMEs are either insufficient or provided in a way to undermine financial sustainability. The Islamic finance approach for SME financing, presented in ch. 4, can address the matter in identifying the root causes and proposing solutions.

REFERENCES

Antras, Pol, and Alonso de Gortari. 2017. On the geography of global value chains. NBER Working Paper 23456 (May). Cambridge, MA: National Bureau of Economic Research.

Bacon, Robert W., and John Besant-Jones. 2001. Global electric power reform, privatization, and liberalization of the electric power industry in developing countries. *Annual Review of Energy and the Environment* 26 (1): 331–359.

Besant-Jones, John E. 2006. Reforming power markets in developing countries: What have we learned? Energy and Mining Sector Board Discussion Paper No. 19. Washington, DC: World Bank.

Choi, Jieun, Emiko Fukase, and Albert Zeufack. 2019. Global value chain (GVC) participation, competition, and markup: Firm-level evidence from Ethiopia. Background paper, World Bank, Washington, DC.

Constantinescu, Cristina, Aaditya Mattoo, and Michele Ruta. 2019. Does vertical specialization increase productivity? *World Economy*. Published electronically April 10. https://doi.org/10.1111/twec.12801.

Dong, Y., and C. Men. 2014. SME financing in emerging markets: Firm characteristics, banking structure and institutions. *Emerging Markets Finance and Trade* 50 (1): 120–149. https://doi.org/10.2753/REE1540-496X500107.

Foster, V., S. Witte, S.G. Banerjee, and A. Moreno. 2017. Charting the diffusion of power sector reforms across the developing world. Policy Research Working Paper 8235, World Bank, Washington, DC.

Gratwick, Katharine N., and Anton Eberhard. 2008. Demise of the standard model of power sector reform and the emergence of hybrid power markets. *Energy Policy* 36 (10): 3948–3960.

Gundogdu, A.S. 2019a. *A modern perspective of Islamic economics and finance.* Bingley, UK: Emeralds Publishing.

Gundogdu, A.S. 2019b. Determinants of success in Islamic public–private partnership projects (PPPs) in the context of SDGs. *Turkish Journal of Islamic Economics* 6(2): 25–43.

Hallegatte, Stephane, Jun Rentschler, and Julie Rozenberg. 2019. *Lifelines: The resilient infrastructure opportunity. Sustainable infrastructure.* Washington, DC: World Bank.

IMF (International Monetary Fund). 2019. Corporate taxation in the global economy. Policy Paper 19/007 (March 10), IMF, Washington, DC.

International Energy Agency; International Renewable Energy Agency; United Nations Statistics Division; World Bank; World Health Organization. 2019.

Tracking SDG 7: The Energy Progress Report 2019: Main Report (English). Washington, DC: World Bank Group.

Iqbal, Z., and M.K. Lewis. 2014. Zakat and the economy. In *Handbook on Islam and economic life*, ed. M. Kabir Hassan and Mervyn K. Lewis, ch. 23, pp. 453–475. Cheltenham, UK and Northampton, MA, USA: Edward Elgar Publishing.

Mariana Vijil, and Laurent Wagner. 2012. Does aid for trade enhance export performance? Investigating the infrastructure channel. *World Economy* 35(7): 838–868.

OECD. 2016. *OECD DAC blended finance principles for unlocking commercial finance for the sustainable development goals*. Paris: OECD. http://www. oecd.org/dac/financing-sustainable-development/development-finance-top ics/OECD-Blended-Finance-Principles.pdf. Accessed February 6, 2020.

Panteli, M., and P. Mancarella. 2015. Influence of extreme weather and climate change on the resilience of power systems: Impacts and possible mitigation strategies. *Electric Power Systems Research* 127 (October): 259–270.

Rentschler, J., M. Kornejew, S. Hallegatte, M. Obolensky, and J. Braese. 2019a. Underutilized potential: The business costs of unreliable infrastructure in developing countries. Background paper for this report, World Bank, Washington, DC.

Rentschler, J., M. Obolensky, and M. Kornejew. 2019b. Candle in the wind? Energy system resilience to natural shocks. Background paper for this report, World Bank, Washington, DC.

Rozenberg, J., and M. Fay. 2019. *Beyond the gap: How countries can afford the infrastructure they need while protecting the planet*. Washington, DC: World Bank.

Schweikert, A. E., L. Nield, E. Otto, and M. Deinert. 2019. Resilience and critical power system infrastructure: Lessons learned from natural disasters and future research needs. Background paper for this report, World Bank, Washington, DC.

Wender, B.A., M.G. Morgan, and K.J. Holmes. 2017. Enhancing the resilience of electricity systems. *Engineering* 3 (5): 580–582.

WB, ESMAP, SE4ALL. 2017. Overview: State of electricity access report. Washington, DC.

Williamson, J. 2004. From the Washington consensus towards a new global governance, Barcelona, September 24–25, 2004. https://www.piie.com/pub lications/papers/williamson0904-2.pdf.

World Bank. 2019. *World development report 2020: Trading for development in the age of global value chains (English)*. Washington, DC: World Bank Group.

Zhang, F. 2019. *In the dark: How much do power sector distortions cost South Asia?* South Asia Development Forum. Washington, DC: World Bank Group. https://doi.org/10.1596/978-1-4648-1154-8.

CHAPTER 8

Islamic Financial Product Development in the Context of Education and Health

With expanding business volumes and demand from Muslim communities, the Islamic finance industry has embarked on product development to grapple with the request coming from markets and to keep up with conventional financial institutions. In the process, newly developed Islamic finance products may not end up being *Shariah* compliant.[1] To address this problem, Muda and Jalil (2007) proposed a matrix approach for product development: *Maqasid Al Shariah* as the first axis and *Maslaha* as the second to frame product development. As they did in their approach, a classical interpretation of *Maqasid Al Shariah* and pretext of *Maslaha* opens up doors for controversial products. Indeed, even if those products are stamped as being *Shariah* compliant, the products cannot avoid criticism, as new products launched lead to similar side effects of conventional finance. Habib (2011) names such products, conforming to legal form but not serving social needs, as "Pseudo-Islamic" products. Amine (2015), in his work focusing on *Sukuk*, categorizes the problems with *Sukuk* into macro-*Maqasid* and micro-*Maqasid*. He made a categorization to highlight the distinction between *Shariah* jurisprudence for transactions (*Shariah* compliance/micro-*Maqasid*) and wider economic

---

[1] Muda and Jalil (2007).

A. T. Diallo and A. S. Gundogdu, *Sustainable Development and Infrastructure*, Palgrave Studies in Islamic Banking, Finance, and Economics, https://doi.org/10.1007/978-3-030-67094-8_8

well-being (*Maqasid Al Shariah*/macro-*Maqasid*). The purpose of micro-*Maqasid* is to reach macro-*Maqasid*. That is, *Shariah* compliance is a tool to reach *Maqasid Al Shariah*. Relying on *Maslaha* leeway for *Shariah* compliance would not fulfill macro-*Maqasid*, more formally known as *Maqasid Al Shariah*. The literature clearly indicates that it is inevitable to center the product development methodology in Islamic finance on *Maqasid Al Shariah* rather than the perfunctory *Shariah* compliance checklist deconsecrated by *Maslaha*.

8.1   Setting the Stage for *Maqasid*

The *Maqasid* is a concept related to how we understand the gist of holy revelation: the purpose of divine rules. Although traditional understanding of *Maqasid Al Shariah* is based on Ghazali's interpretation, there is much more to say.[2] There are other components of *Maqasid* as indicated in the Quran and Hadith. The ultimate goal of Islam is human well-being and blessing for all humanity. This is the aim of all societies and not peculiar to Islam alone.[3] However, there is something that is peculiar to Islam: Islam proposes a detailed to-do and not-to do list concerning issues related to economics and finance. A conducive economic and financial environment is a must to achieving human well-being, according to Islamic understanding. The framework of *Maqasid* is derived from the Quran and Hadith, yet contemporary issues are addressed with *Fatwa* of scholars within this framework. However, the phenomenon of "*Fatwa* shopping" has strong potential to derail Islamic finance, since most of the controversial Islamic finance structures are able to get *Fatwa* in exchange for a service fee paid to some scholars who are ready to issue any verdict. Islamic financial institutions are not very willing to accept a central authority. Hence, anyone can present him or herself as an authority and give *Fatwa*.[4] This trend, as it undermines *Maqasid Al Shariah*, gives rise to debate on product development in Islamic finance.

The major debate concerning product development in Islamic finance revolves around *Sukuk* and modern *Murabaha*. Unlike the most of the

---

[2] Ghazali based *Maqasid* understanding on safeguarding the five pillars: faith (*Dīn*), the human self (*Nafs*), intellect (*'Aql*), posterity (*Nasl*), and wealth (*Māl*).

[3] Chapra (2008).

[4] Gundogdu (2019a).

existing Sukuk, prevalent modern *Murabaha* is *Shariah* compliant, yet
there is strife regarding its acceptability because, similar to *Riba*-based
loans, it increases the debt level in society.[5] Particularly if used for
household consumption finance, it gives rise to side effects similar to
those associated with conventional finance: squander, inflation created by
temporary bubble demand through a credit mechanism, and a vicious
circle of wealth inequality, thus *Fasad*. *Murabaha* credit cards lead to
household bankruptcy similar to interest-based ones.[6] Although developed as an alternative to non-*Shariah* compliant organized *Tawarruq*
or *Bay Al-Inah* based alternatives, *Murabaha* credit cards, in the same
fashion, can be an instrument of cash borrowing. In financial distress,
cardholders can purchase precious metals from jewelers and cash in the
precious metals. Product development should consider such side effects,
and it should be designed for the well-being of society in the long run:
it should bring sustainable solutions. Islamic finance should contribute
to sustainable development rather than merely fulfilling *Shariah* rules to
facilitate the profitmaking whims of the Islamic finance industry.

Focusing on *Maqasid Al Shariah* in the product development process
is expected to entail sound *Shariah* compliance and in many instances
better risk management results. The methodology indicated in Fig. 4.1
suggests that, in addition to *Shariah* compliance and risk management,
the factoring of operational efficiency and the compliance with local rules
and regulations is also essential to form a purposive table that requires all
four pillars – and no fewer – to stand. The four pillars should support and
fit the top of the table, which is the ultimate goal: *Maqasid Al Shariah*.

From the contemporary literature, two-step *Murabaha* product development for financing merchandise imports is a good example of innovation in Islamic finance product development. The product two-step
Murabaha was developed to replace the traditional line of financing
in pursuit of operational efficiency with the purpose of finalizing trade
transactions expeditiously. Either line of financing or two-step *Murabaha*
financing greases the wheel by facilitating the purchase of intermediary
goods for industrial production, thus fulfilling *Maqasid Al Shariah*. Both
products are *Shariah* compliant. From a local rules and regulations point
of view, there are some adjustments needed for the wider use of both

---

[5] Roslyn and Sanusi (1999) and Yousef (2004).

[6] Dariyoushi and Nazimah (2016).

products since they require local banks to sign a contract stipulating the purchase of goods, which is only allowed for investment and development banks, but not deposit collecting banks due to regulations. Unlike line of financing, which requires months to make a payment, two-step *Murabaha* ensures payments to supplier on the same day with the payment request of the client. Indeed, line of financing fulfills all requirements of product development, but lacks operational efficiency; thus, it is doomed to bungle. The pitfall makes line of financing nugatory for international trade finance, in which financing needs to be availed in a couple of days, if not on the same day, but at the time ships arrive to the port of discharge. Any delay in payment would translate into payment of expensive demurrage charges for keeping the ship waiting in the port.[7]

The case sermonizes that being *Shariah* compliant and fulfilling *Maqasid Al Shariah* is not adequate for product development. The product should be efficient enough to be implemented smoothly and timely to satisfy, in the long run, customers and executers. Besides, newly developed products that do not abide by local rules and regulations cannot operate in practice. For example, if local rules and regulations do not allow banks to buy and sell goods, *Murabaha* could not be a way to finance merchandise trade through local banks. In the same fashion, the product should come up with sound risk management practices since a high propensity to default products would eventually be shelved, no matter how instrumental they are. A good example would be the experience of *Murabaha* credit cards. As highlighted previously, customers who are desperately in need of money may use the cards to buy gold and subsequently sell it for cash. The result would be skyrocketing default rates. A highly efficient product would end up being discarded because of risk management deficiency.[8]

The experience of *Murabaha* credit cards substantiates the proposition that *Maqasid Al Shariah* flaws in product development sprout *Shariah* compliance and risk management problems. In the case of *Murabaha* cards, during implementation and in case of defaults, Islamic banks

---

[7] Gundogdu (2009).

[8] Refers to the authors work experience and Proceedings of the 2nd International Congress on Islamic Commercial Law, October 15–18, 2015, Konya, Turkey.

started to charge so-called "profit deprivation charges."[9] Unlike the name suggests, a "profit deprivation charge" is a mere default interest. The episode set in by getting delay charges up to inflation rate or pegging the debt amount to foreign currency. When foreign currency prices went down instead of going up, Islamic banks requested *Shariah* boards to pave the way for a profit deprivation verdict. The issue of charging up to the inflation rate is also problematic because it would require Islamic banks to pay the defaulted debtor, should the inflation rate become negative.[10]

The key question relates to debt creation with *Murabaha* transactions. Is it not the case that Islamic banks' finance is needed for household consumption such as for home appliances? Islam is not against debt creation as long as debt is created for value addition through bona fide activities. For example, if a household does not have a refrigerator, it cannot store perishable foods, such as meat, and, in the end, the lack of refrigerator would cost the household more than the debt/financing cost of procuring a refrigerator.[11] Financial development creates wealth while it may give rise to inequality.[12] The Islamic view on financial inclusion, akin to the debate on international trade, is straightforward. It supports value-adding activities, without any hesitation, while advising to address the issue of inequality created in the process with a wealth redistribution mechanism: *Zakat*. The redistribution mechanism in the form of *Zakat* to compensate for the side effects of debt creating Islamic financial products is much needed.[13] So long as there is no wealth distribution mechanism in a society, any debt-creating instrument, Islamic or conventional, may lead to similar unpleasant consequences.

Nevertheless, it is important to make the distinction between necessary needs and consumerism. Unlike the assumptions of classical economic views, Islamic philosophy teaches that "there are enough resources to

---

[9] Late payment charges are acceptable in Islamic finance as long as funds received from late payments by no means get into balance sheet of the bank. The separation will include use of these funds for PR or marketing campaigns in the name of so-called charity.

[10] Refers to the authors work experience and Proceedings of the 2nd International Congress on Islamic Commercial Law, October 15–18, 2015, Konya, Turkey.

[11] In addition to value addition requirement for debt creation, the rights and obligation of parties in a debt contract should clearly be stipulated in order to dismiss *Gharar*.

[12] Beck et al. (2007).

[13] Amine (2015).

fulfill necessary needs of all humans on earth."[14] Unlike capitalism, it makes a distinction between necessary needs for contentment as opposed to dissipation. The way that the lending rate and default interest rate are factored into consumer loans strongly contradicts Islamic views.[15] Assuming human beings as being merely a statistical error is a big problem in itself since a percentage of default rates lead to deteriorated social conditions. Besides, in the long run, the infectious effect of debt on wealth distribution and unsustainable demand gather for increased default rates, causing the stumbling of the financial system. Corsettin et al. (2006) analyzed the trade-off between official liquidity provision by central banks and the issue of moral hazards in financial crises. Central banks as a lender of last resort, stepping in to save debt-fueling financial institutions, create an even bigger bubble for the next cycle. The bill of recurring failures in the financial system is paid by the public at the end through central banks' interventions and deposit insurance provided by governments. Islamic finance products should not give rise to such systematic risks in the economy. Newly developed products should ignite productivity increase, support sustainable job creation, and create wealth with value addition in order to achieve *Maqasid Al Shariah*.

The introduction of modern *Murabaha* in merchandise trade and two-step *Murabaha* as a resource mobilization extension can apparently serve *Maqasid Al Shariah*, as long as certain precautions are observed. Given the successful example of *Murabaha*, can we finance health and education services in Islamic finance? The question deserves serious attention, since Islamic banks can finance services with organized *Tawarruq*-based commodity *Murabaha*. Such an implementation of organized *Tawarruq* opens the doors for further expanding the controversial treasury department products as well as loan restructuring, which are unacceptable from a *Shariah* point of view.[16] It is clear that organized *Tawarruq* is not a solution for financing services. How about *Murabaha* contracts? Can we

---

[14] Surat Al-Isra, Verse 30: "Verily thy Lord doth provide sustenance in abundance for whom He pleaseth, and He provideth in a just measure. For He doth know and regard all His servants."

[15] Financial institutions calculate interest rates of credit cards by adding statistical default rates on top of their cost of capital and expected real return. For instance, if the cost of capital is 5 percent, expected real return is 3 percent and observed default rate is 3 percent, they would determine the lending rate at 11 percent.

[16] Gundogdu (2014).

design acceptable Islamic finance products with reference to recent literature, which proposed an alternative use of *Murabaha* as a solution for protracted debate, or should we avoid financing such services for the sake of *Maqasid Al Shariah*?

8.2   From Merchandise Trade Finance to Financing Trade in Services

Islamic financial institutions have traditionally been very active in merchandise trade financing. The main reason is its compatibility with the basic principles of Islamic finance and the prevalence of *Murabaha* (profit sale) contracts, which constitute the bulk of overall Islamic finance transactions. In order to comply with Islamic finance principles, a transaction needs to be bona fide among independent parties. There are several modes of Islamic finance contracts, yet a *Murabaha* transaction, which requires three independent parties (supplier, buyer, and financier), is the most popular mode of financing. Putting the requirements of bona fide transaction and a *Murabaha* sale together, international trade is a perfect fit for Islamic financial institutions. The payment methods of international trade (documentary credit [L/C], cash against documents [CAD], and cash against goods [CAG], as well as INCOTERMS for delivery) assure bona fide transactions. Converting a traditional trade finance department of a bank to being Islamic is a mere change in the financing contract signed between a bank and a loan seeker. In practice, the main difference would be the content of the contract between the bank and the loan seeker to incorporate deferred sale features and clauses pertaining to late payment charges; in a *Murabaha* sale, an Islamic bank sells the goods financed with predetermined tenor and sale prices that cannot be changed afterwards, even if the repayment is delayed. It is suggested that not only trade but also many conventional transactions can be converted to Islamic finance by stark changes in financing contracts.[17] This may be particularly appropriate when it comes to areas where Islamic finance and conventional finance converge the most: trade finance and leasing transactions. As long as conventional finance emerges out of a need for facilitating value-adding economic activities, such similarity with Islamic finance is anticipated. However, Islamic finance would totally differ, at

---

[17] Beck et al. (2010).

least in theory, in certain areas from conventional finance in *Riba*, *Maysir*, and *Gharar*. Most importantly, Islamic finance observes a wider vision of *Maqasid Al Shariah*: Human well-being.

Although Islamic finance has been very active in trade finance, particularly in import financing, there has been relatively little progress in the areas of export financing and financing services. As highlighted in ch. 6 the main problem with export finance has been executing *Murabaha* sales, as in import financing – where Islamic financial institutions establish a contractual obligation on an importer, which is buyer as well as debtor – both the bank and the importer are in the same country. In the case of export financing, however, the buyer and the Islamic financial institutions would be in different countries; this would make it difficult to establish contractual obligation. Due to risk management difficulties, Islamic financial institutions introduced Islamic discounting schemes with the clauses of recourse to their clients, the seller, in case of non-payment. Once implemented, this scheme was not deemed to be different from the debt-trading factoring transaction, *Bay Al-Dayn*, of conventional finance, so it was reprimanded. Due to this dissatisfaction, new products, based on *Murabaha* contract, were proposed for Islamic export financing.[18]

In 2016, a new Islamic export finance product was introduced, as an alternative to controversial discounting practices.[19] The structure of this new product is unique as it uses export declaration forms to assure bona fide transactions. The general tendency in Islamic finance sector used to avoid financing services. More recently, a new trend has emerged: use faulty organized *Tawarruq* based on commodity *Murabaha* to finance services. For services, assuring a bona fide transaction would, from an Islamic Shariah perspective, be problematic as similarly observed in export financing.[20]

---

[18] Gundogdu (2016b).

[19] Gundogdu (2016b).

[20] WTO categorization of trade in service:

(a) from the territory of one member into the territory of any other member;
(b) in the territory of one member to the service consumer of any other member;
(c) by a service supplier of one member, through commercial presence in the territory of any other member;
(d) by a service supplier of one member, through presence of natural persons of a member in the territory of any other member.

Using invoices alone, which can be cancelled by the issuer after financing, would not suffice, as delivery needs to be observed in Islamic finance. Imposing the use of export declaration type of documents for services might be considered for paving the way for Islamic finance industry, as the exporter of services would then be officially bound in a bona fide transaction. The cancellation of export declaration forms from customs authorities is not as easy as cancellation of invoices issued by companies. Islamic finance requires certainty pertaining to the nature of the item financed – including price, quality in the form of product specification, quantity, buyer, and seller. In the case of merchandise trade, such information is readily available in customs declaration forms; the nature of merchandise is identified with "Harmonized Commodity Description and Coding System," HS Codes. The scope of the WTO's General Agreement on Trade in Services (GATS) might be detailed in such categorization, akin to HS system, to fit Islamic finance contracts. The course to record trade in services through export/import declaration forms can support the endeavors toward obtaining precise statistics, since classification similar to the HS system would reflect a clear picture of international trade in services flows.[21] The principles of Islamic finance require protocols similar to those that have long been available in merchandise trade, such as UCP, INCOTERMS, UCR, customs declaration forms, etc. Since Islamic financial intuitions need to pay suppliers of the service, such protocols at least for official custom declaration forms could open up doors for engagement of Islamic finance with trade in services. However, such documents are only specific to cross-border trade. Besides, intangible aspect of services cannot be handled with such an arrangement. Nevertheless, use of such documents for trade in services has other benefits such as the provision of sound statistics relating to cross-border trade in services.

In practice, modern *Murabaha* is almost on the red light between Islamic finance and conventional finance. The *Murabaha*-based export finance is at the edge. From the experience of export financing, *Murabaha* contracts cannot be a solution to financing trade in services.

---

[21] Such discourse might have not been feasible at the initial stage of GATS. But rapid diffusion and development in Information and Communication Technology afterwards and widespread use of Single Windows in customs by many countries as a consequence can make such option reasonable; today customs declaration forms can be completed online through Single Window applications of customs and excise departments.

8.3   ISLAMIC DISCOURAGEMENT OF FINANCING
SERVICES: HEALTH AND EDUCATION

Although replacing faulty organized *Tawarruq* with *Murabaha* contracts, akin to those of Islamic export financing, may at first glance appear to be a solution, the proposal is better evaluated from a *Maqasid Al Shariah* perspective with the systematic methodology indicated in Fig. 4.1: a table with four underpinnings. Unfortunately, experience has shown that financial innovation in services financing can be rather vain if not maleficent. The novelty of student loans and insurance coverage for medical care can be put forward as two precedents. Student loans instigated soaring college tuition fees and caused desolation for youngsters. Although there is no evidence for increased salaries for lecturers or cost of educating people, access to loans by students allow education providers to ask higher prices based on affordability, but not the cost of education. In the same fashion, the existence of insurance might be the reason for flourishing medical businesses with increased treatment fees that cripple public finance in many countries. The intangible aspect of services appears to lead to unjustified price bubbles if services are supported with a financing scheme.[22]

Indeed, before exploring ways of financing services such as health and education, it is better to examine the repercussions with commodification of these services, as provided in Case Box 8.1.

Case Box 8.1 Commodification of Health care, Lesotho Hospital PPP
Visitors to the Queen Mamohato Memorial Hospital in Maseru, Lesotho's small capital city, enter a building unlike any other in this impoverished country of 2 million people surrounded by South Africa. Built at a cost of at least US$100 million and operated under an 18-year contract between the Lesotho Ministry of Health and a consortium assembled by Netcare, the largest operator of private hospitals in South Africa and the UK, the 425-bed facility is an outpost of stylish architectural functionalism in threadbare Maseru. Like Netcare's hospitals in South Africa, the Queen Mamohato, which opened in 2011, is a spacious clinical oasis furnished with technologically advanced care units and patient-friendly lounges and

---

[22] Gundogdu (2019a).

wards. The Mamohato hospital project was presented as a model for public–private partnership (PPP) as government operated Queen Elizabeth hospital failed.

In 2012, under the terms of the PPP contract, Lesotho's public learned, the consortium was to be paid a $32·6 million index-linked annual unitary charge for up to a maximum of 20,000 in-patient admissions and 310,000 outpatient attendances (or about a third of Lesotho's total hospital demand). Beyond this cap, the consortium can bill extra for each additional patient. Extra patient numbers should be very high for such a stylish hospital as alternative for people is not there.

In April, 2014, Oxfam released a report charging that the hospital contract granted Netcare and its consortium partners substantial profits while creating "a dangerous diversion of scarce public funds from primary healthcare services in rural areas, where three-quarters of the population live."

Even before the Queen Mamohato contract was signed, Oxfam observed, health spending in Lesotho was already skewed toward urban-based tertiary care. The contract "dramatically exacerbated this inequitable trend by absorbing over half of the Ministry of Health's budget in 2013/14, up from 28 per cent for the old public hospital in 2006/7," Oxfam reported.

Source Webster (2015)

A similar pattern can be observed with education sector. Neither public ownership nor PPP business models work. Examples of real-life events can depict the problem more than an explanation of a thousand words. The moral hazard with charter schools are immense and some examples are presented in Case Box 8.2.

Case Box 8.2 A News Paper Report on Charter School Scandals in a Year[23]

1. **A3 Education: Eleven are indicted over their involvement in a charter scheme that defrauded California taxpayers of more than $50 million.**

---

[23] The full story is available at: https://www.washingtonpost.com/education/2020/01/27/5-most-serious-charter-school-scandals-2019-why-they-matter/.

In May, the California Superior Court for the County of San Diego indicted 11 people on charges that they helped defraud California taxpayers out of $50 million via an elaborate scheme to create phony attendance records to increase revenue to an online charter chain known as A3.

2. **IDEA Charter Chain: Board approves a private jet lease for nearly $2 million a year and then reverses the approval when that vote becomes public.**

   In December, the Houston Chronicle reported that the IDEA Charter Schools Board voted to lease a private jet at an annual cost of $1.92 million. That story was quickly replaced with an update when the deal was canceled within hours after it was exposed in the news media. Two months earlier, the Texas Monitor revealed the use of first-class tickets for IDEA top employees, along with paying for their families to travel.

3. **Today's Fresh Start Charter School: A Los Angeles couple makes millions from self-dealing with their charter schools.**

   In March, the Los Angeles Times ran an exposé on how Clark and Jeanette Parker of Beverly Hills made millions from their Today's Fresh Start charter schools by renting property they own to their schools. The charter schools pay Clark Parker as a consultant. It was reported that the couple also used their private child-care business to provide food to their charter schools and sent most of the funding from a half-million-dollar state grant to an unaccredited university that Jeanette Parker founded.

4. **A nonprofit operator of migrant shelters, Southwest Key, coordinated with its for-profit organizations to bleed its charter schools into rat-infested classrooms.**

   A Texas charter school named East Austin College Prep made national news in 2019 when the New York Times reported complaints of raccoons and rats invading classrooms, rain pouring in through a leaky roof, and furniture occasionally falling through rickety floors. Yet, according to the story, the charter high school pays almost $900,000 in annual rent to its landlord, Southwest Key Programs.

5. **The North Jersey Record uncovered hundreds of millions in taxpayer funds going to buildings owned by private interests, with charter schools paying inflated rents that far exceed building debt.**

A 2019 five-part series written by a team of reporters from the North Jersey Record exposed the shady dealings hidden from the public eye that allow developers to cash in on public money and tax breaks by providing real estate to charter schools. The reporters found that information was buried so deeply in documents, it was difficult in many cases to find out who was making the profit.

Source From the report by Valerie Strauss, *Washington Post*

Neither traditional infrastructure development nor financialization of these services with health insurance and student loans do any good for poverty; indeed, they exacerbate the problem. Assuming widespread implementation of *Murabaha*-based new products for financing services, the availability of access to financing should expect to inflate the prices of services and impoverish people directly and/or indirectly through:

1. financial burden of loans received and
2. increased commodified-services prices.

Widespread financing trade in services has a strong potential to create a vicious economic circle. Is this the case for financing tangible assets? Referring to the product development table with four underpinnings, the product development issue should be the subject of a wider question of *Maqasid Al Shariah* – e.g., is it permissible to commodify education and healthcare to enable financial institutions, whether Islamic or non-Islamic, to prey in the name of *Shariah* compliance or financial intermediation? For *Murabaha*-based products to finance trade in services, a similar deficiency relating to *Maqasid Al Shariah* will be observed. If there is a mismatch with *Maqasid*, the product will manifest this into Shariah compliance or product specific or systematic risk. The abovementioned deformity with *Murabaha* for trade in services is expected to manifest itself subtly in *Shariah* compliance.

Financing trade in services with *Murabaha* would not be *Shariah* compliant. Unlike tangible assets financed in the example of two-step *Murabaha* for merchandise financing, the possibility of assuming ownership is unclear in the case of trade in services. A bank may claim contractually assuming ownership of merchandise traded. This is not the case for services. For example, a bank cannot claim to acquire a tailor-made hospital treatment, such as tailor-made heart surgery, and sell it to its customers. It violates the principle of "Sell not what is not with you." Companies in financial stress can issue fictitious invoices for purported services to access financing, much easier than they can for goods. Such incidences give rise to systematic risk. Saying that, in the case of project financing, there is a possibility of financing consultancy work, which is key to the success of the infrastructure project. However, the present practice of a service *Ijara* or a service *Murabaha* agreement is also problematic as it stipulates sales of services. In the case of consultancy service financing, *Shariah* acceptability appears, since such consultancy work is key to the success of project finance, and the involvement of Islamic banks is encouraged from the *Maqasid* perspective. Unlike service *Ijara and Murabaha* agreements, consultancy services are the part of the *Istisna* contracts as services are integral to create assets for infrastructure projects. However, Istisna contracts bring certain responsibilities for the financiers as financiers are clearly indicated as being manufacturers. In cases of environmental and social safeguard issues, Istisna contracts make them responsible. This is not the case with conventional infrastructure finance contracts. Dividing Istisna agreement, to downgrade a financier's involvement to a simple *Murabaha* sale, to avoid such responsibility is Shariah circumvention.

As proposed with the four legged table methodology, ignoring *Maqasid Al Shariah* is expected to spur subtle issues in *Shariah* compliance in transactions as well as systematic risk. These defects increase the conflict with *Maqasid Al Shariah,* creating a vicious circle through linked mechanisms within the economy. Primarily, it is vital to start Islamic finance product development with a spotlight on *Maqasid Al Shariah.* The case of trade in services merits this approach. Although it appeared viable to replace organized *Tawarruq* with *Murabaha* to finance trade in services, both contracts give rise to similar dissonance with *Maqasid Al Shariah.* Islamic financial institutions should not be in a position to cater to all request from the market, neither do they need to replicate all products of conventional banks. None can give a *Fatwa,* which allows a Muslim to sell non-permissible items in his/her grocery shop with the pretext of competing with other grocery shops. The same holds for Islamic banks, which are no different to grocery shops, both being commercial enterprises. Islamic banks should observe "to do" lists and "not to do" lists as per *Maqasid Al Shariah* in order to serve the necessary, but not boundless, needs of humans. The *Maslaha* approach to allow Islamic banks to provide products contradicting *Maqasid* undermines the well-being of society, and it delays the implementation of proper Islamic solutions to address issues. Besides, if there is no solution, as is the case with public goods of health and education, there should be a good reason not to finance such activities. The Islamic perspective clearly indicates that public goods should not be financed. It is not a coincidence that Islam proposes *Waqf* business model for health and education. To avoid subtle exploitation, social infrastructure should be provided with a *Waqf* model, with breakeven pricing strategy. The same holds for the water sector, as in the case of irrigation and drainage, which is discussed from infrastructure development perspective in the next chapter.

REFERENCES

Amine, M.B. 2015. Product development and *Maqasid* in Islamic finance: Towards a balanced methodology. *Islamic Economic Studies* 23(1).

Beck, T., A. Demirgüç-Kunt, and R. Levine. 2007. Finance, inequality, and the poor. *Journal of Economic Growth* 12(1): 27–49.

Beck, T., A. Demirgüç-Kunt, and O. Merrouche. 2010 Islamic vs. conventional banking: business model, efficiency and stability. World Bank Policy Research Working Paper No. 5446.Washington, DC.

Chapra, M.U. 2008. *The Islamic vision of development in the light of Maqasid Al Shariah*. London: Cromwell Press.

Corsettia, G., B. Guimarãesb, and N. Roubini. 2006. International lending of last resort and moral hazard: A model of IMF's catalytic finance. *Journal of Monetary Economics* 53(3): 441–471.

Dariyoushi, J., and H. Nazimah. 2016. Forecasting patronage factors of Islamic credit card as a new e-commerce banking service: An integration of TAM with perceived religiosity and trust. *Journal of Islamic Marketing* 7(4): 378–404.

Gundogdu, A.S. 2009. Two-Step Murabaha as an alternative resource mobilization tool for Islamic banks in the context of international trade. *International Journal of Monetary Economics and Finance* 2(3/4).

Gundogdu, A.S. 2014. Two-step Murabaha in stock exchange as an alternative to commodity Murabaha for liquidity management. *International Journal of Financial Services Management* 7(3/4).

Gundogdu, A.S. 2016. Exploring novel Islamic finance methods in support of OIC exports. *Journal of Islamic Accounting and Business Research* 7(2).

Gundogdu, A.S. 2019. *A modern perspective of Islamic economics and finance*. Bingley, UK: Emeralds Publishing.

Habib, A. 2011. *Product development in Islamic banks*. Edinburgh: Edinburgh University Press.

Muda, M., and A. Jalil. 2007. Research and development: The bridge between ideals and realities. Paper presented at IIUM International Conference on Islamic Banking and Finance.

Rosly, S.A., and M.M. Sanusi. 1999. The application of Bay' Al-'Inah and Bay' Al-Dayn in Malaysian Islamic bonds: An Islamic analysis. *International Journal of Islamic Financial Services* 1(2).

Webster, P. 2015. Lesotho's controversial public–private partnership project. *The Lancet* 386(14): 1929–1931.

Yousef, T.M. 2004. The murabaha syndrome in Islamic finance: Laws, institutions and politics. In *The Politics of Islamic* Finance, ed. R. Wilson, 63–80. Edinburgh: Edinburgh University Press.

CHAPTER 9

Irrigation and Drainage

Irrigation is at the forefront in the international development agenda in the context of rural development and poverty alleviation. Irrigated farming is presented as a solution toward meeting global food and fodder demand, thus enabling food security. Of the total global food and fodder produced, 40 percent is grown on irrigated areas that cover only 6.5 percent of worldwide cultivated land. Since higher value crops are produced in irrigated lands, a 40 percent share in production jumps to 55 percent in gross value. For rural poverty alleviation, the adoption of irrigation infrastructure development is a strategic priority.[1] Nonetheless, rural poverty persists, and urban poverty is exacerbated as evidenced by the continued migration from rural to urban and developed countries. This alone suggests that the existing strategy – which is described as "increasing agricultural production with irrigation abates rural poverty" – is based on unfulfilling assumptions.

[1] Molden (2007).

© The Author(s), under exclusive license to Springer Nature Switzerland AG 2021
A. T. Diallo and A. S. Gundogdu, *Sustainable Development and Infrastructure*, Palgrave Studies in Islamic Banking, Finance, and Economics, https://doi.org/10.1007/978-3-030-67094-8_9

9.1   TRIO OF PERFORMANCE AREAS: WATER SERVICE DELIVERY, ORGANIZATIONAL RESOURCES, AND GOVERNANCE

The traditional sector solutions have been engineered to equip the irrigation area for full control irrigation: lowland areas and flood-spate.[2] Initial performance areas were more engineering-based and aimed at "water service delivery" to address the adequacy parameter: plant-water stress, an occasion when irrigation plus rainfall is less than crop-water demand. They also focused on engineering sustainability with proper drainage to avoid waterlogging (in case irrigation plus rainfall is more than crop-water demand), have stable table water, and prevent soil salinization. Contemporary approaches have emerged to address operation and maintenance (O&M) assurances in the form of O&M institution building, tariff collection, the timing of invoicing for water use such as post-harvest tariff collection, and assuring allocation of an O&M budget. These approaches formed "organizational resources" parameters – financial sustainability, asset management, technical operations management, organizational management, fiduciary management, and strategy and processes – and pinpointed the importance of other water service delivery parameters for organizational resources apart from adequacy alone, such as:

- Reliability to avoid crop risk. In the case of unreliable water supply farmers switch to less sensitive lower value crops, resort to groundwater supply, and have buffer storages.[3]
- Equity as the parameter of a fair supply of irrigation water.[4]

The emergence of advanced farming practices, which use much less water and other inputs, such as the System of Rice Intensification (SRC), increased the performance requirement of flexibility, in addition to reliability, in water service delivery. The dissatisfaction of water users with multifaceted of water service delivery leads to low tariff collection and

---

[2] Oweis et al. (2004).

[3] Renault and Vehmeyer (1999).

[4] Fan et al. (2018).

independent water supply solutions in a way to feed the build-neglect-rehabilitate circle since organizational resources are negatively affected. The performance evaluation of the service providers has now evolved to encompass not only water service delivery and organizational resources but also governance.[5]

The worldwide land equipped for irrigation was double the area in 1960.[6] Massive irrigation investment enabled such progress. However, today most of the irrigation and drainage infrastructure projects have the "rehabilitation of irrigation and drainage" phrase in their name. Regardless of engineering perfection for irrigation and drainage infrastructure development, existing infrastructure requires additional investment to continue the service. And this suggests that it is the business model, not the engineering design, that is the root cause of the problem. In the irrigation sector, the main challenge has now been identified as being organizational resources in particular, but also poor management and maintenance of the I&D system vis-à-vis tariff collection. The build-neglect-rehabilitate vicious circle has urged policymakers toward "doing right things" rather than "doing things rightly in engineering."

The PPP business model has been championed as a solution with its strong asset management and maintenance features. Although public–private partnership has emerged as a viable business model, the involvement of the private sector and PPPs as a new trend since the 1990s has, nevertheless, presented varied and destructive outcomes in I&D sector.[7] Given that irrigated lands are agriculturally profitable in a way that favors big farmers and leads to elite capture, the tariff collection problem with smallholders indicates a more convoluted problem in the context of rural development and poverty alleviation. The nature of the business model in the form of centralized big infrastructure and favoring big farmers and cronyism in centralized big infrastructure management – which is common in both the I&D government agencies' models and the PPP business model – requires attention vis-à-vis governance parameters. Rent-seeking in large-scale schemes and investment have caused strife between rival bureaucracy cronies.[8] In the irrigation sector, corruption is

---

[5] Bos et al. (1994). Details are provided in Appendix B.

[6] Lankford et al. (2016).

[7] Obertreis et al. (2016).

[8] Molle et al. (2009).

systematic in a way that illegal payment to "higher-ups" is not a choice but an obligation for keeping employment and promotion.[9] The larger the scheme, the more the obligation toward "higher-ups" emerges.

The purpose of this chapter is to evaluate the reemerging PPP business model for irrigation and drainage infrastructure development in the context of traditional state agency approaches and to come up with an Islamic proposition. Section 9.2 elaborates on the root causes of the challenge in the wider context of rural poverty alleviation. Section 9.3 evaluates the emerging irrigation PPP business model. Section 9.4 compares PPP, government agency, and proposed Islamic *Waqf* alternative models in a modified assessment, with the addition of an affordability performance area to Bos et al.'s (1994) Trio of Performance Areas: water service delivery, organizational resources, and governance.

Affordability, which is the long-term ability of the irrigator to pay, has been the missing parameter. Given the defining importance of affordability, it was added to Trio Performance Areas to make up Four Performance areas. Detailed descriptions for these areas, including affordability parameters, as introduced herewith, are provided in the Appendix B.

9.2   ROOT CAUSES

Large-scale engineering-centered I&D infrastructure schemes globally were proliferated by national agencies funded through government budgets and development banks' finance in the last century.[10] These agencies also assumed the role of management, operations, and maintenance (MOM) roles with their engineering backgrounds, putting emphasis on the more technical aspects without enhanced expertise on management and service delivery.[11] Root causes were viewed as technical rather than organizational and/or social, hence maintenance and operating costs of I&D schemes with declined service delivery quality became an unsustainable burden on government fiscal space.[12] Such water insecurity shifted farmer preferences from water-dependent high-value crops

---

[9] Butterworth and de la Harpe (2009a, b) and Zinnbauer and Dobson (2008).

[10] Obertreis et al. (2016).

[11] Suhardiman and Giordano (2014).

[12] Darghouth et al. (2007).

to low-risk crops that meant low cash return to pay water fees. Moreover, this paved the way for further infrastructure neglect, due to lack of financial resources for maintenance, and a rehabilitation investment wave.

The build-neglect-rehabilitate cycle suggests ownership problems in project formulation with I&D infrastructure development. The policy discourse of Irrigation and Management Transfer (IMT) to irrigators/WUAs in order to enhance the feeling of ownership within communities has also been unsuccessful.[13] Neither the government agency nor IMT discourse has inhibited the build-neglect-rehabilitate cycle. Having management, operations, and maintenance (MOM) by government agencies or IMT has been repeatedly tried for large-scale I&D schemes. Perhaps the very presence of large-scale, heavily centralized infrastructure itself is the root cause of the entire problem concerning the build-neglect-rehabilitate vicious cycle.

Farmers today prefer to invest in their wells and pumps because large-scale irrigation distribution networks are not efficient enough to meet the farmers' needs. Farmers prefer an independent water supply that requires initial investment over the tariffing of a centralized irrigation infrastructure.[14] Electricity subsidies and emerging PV solar technologies enable such trends.[15] Groundwater irrigation, more so than canal irrigation, brings about flexibility for irrigation, and it is reliable. Thirty-eight percent of the world's irrigated land uses groundwater supplies.[16] Nevertheless, groundwater irrigation leads to sustainability issues, such as the depletion of shared aquifer and saline intrusion into coastal aquifers, with excess water abstraction higher than the recharge rate.[17] The individualistic approach to irrigation is a new trend and might be deemed as another extreme position in the spectrum, opposing strongly centralized irrigation infrastructure. Such an extreme position is also not viable in the long run should the farmer's coordination and joint ownership enforce precautionary measures: to enforce efficient water use with new drop technologies to avoid salinization and protect water level in aquifer.

---

[13] North (1990).
[14] Shah (2018).
[15] Shah (2014).
[16] Siebert et al. (2010).
[17] Wada et al. (2012).

The example of IMT suggests that such coordination and joint owner-ship is not a simple task for the existing large-scale infrastructure. Due to MOM concerns, centralized irrigation schemes have evolved to become co-managed schemes, by which management responsibilities of irriga-tion infrastructure has transferred from a public sector agency to Water Users Associations (WUAa), irrigator groups, for medium-to-large-scale schemes under Irrigation and Management Transfer (IMT) initiatives.[18] Co-managed schemes, as the rehabilitation programs indicate, also suffer from operations and maintenance (O&M) deficiency. Usually, Water Users Associations (WUAs) cannot handle large infrastructures. Hence, the transfer of O&M responsibilities to the community is not a viable solution in the case of large infrastructure. However, unlike IMT of large-scale schemes, small irrigation schemes such as village-owned schemes operated by voluntary farmer labor without government agency presence have proven to be operationally sustainable and successful.[19] The perfor-mance and sustainability of smaller irrigation schemes are higher than that of larger schemes due to the technical simplicity of smaller infras-tructure and stronger social cohesion and ownership in smaller groups of irrigators.[20]

Lack of market orientation toward irrigation can be presented as another root cause because on large-scale public irrigation schemes government crop selection might not be market-oriented and the govern-ment may not able to continue heavy subsidy for management, opera-tions, and maintenance of deteriorating infrastructure for which farmers are not willing or able to pay.[21] Irrigation projects once again attained popularity with governments after the 2008 financial crisis as a tool for food security challenges faced by developing countries. The major assumptions during project formulation of this new irrigation project wave were:

1. Irrigation would allow off-season cultivation and enhance overall yield.

---

[18] Lankford et al. (2016).

[19] Suhardiman and Giordano (2014).

[20] Inocencio et al. (2007), Lankford et al. (2016), and Shah (2018).

[21] Burton (2010) and Lankford et al. (2016).

2. Shifting to staple crops, such as rice, cultivation would enable food security as cash crops commodity prices and foreign currency fluctuation have made countries vulnerable in food security during the 2008 financial crisis.

The government preferences are based on the above assumption while the smallholders' preference is toward low-risk crops: short-cycle, easy to produce/obtain inputs, and easy to sell crops. Indeed, the new wave project formulation rightly identified the key role of irrigation as input, yet the issue of smallholders' preference and other inputs, such as fertilizers and seeds, need further attention for the next generation of I&D project formulation. Input dependency is to be blamed for exacerbating the balance of payments of the countries, not crop selection. Once the cash crop prices drop, the farmers are not able to purchase inputs for the next season during a crisis. For instance, West African countries started to focus more on rice compared to cotton or groundnuts, yet local rice prices are much higher than international prices and trade barriers constituted for import substitution.[22] Such a distorted market would precipitate wealth transfer from the urban population to the rural population assuming that the overall rural population exploits the import substitution but that not few local traders will take advantage of financially strained farmers.[23]

Elite capture of irrigated agricultural land happens due to the lack of agricultural input provision and post-harvest unfair markets that do not ring-fence smallholders from local traders. Hence, I&D infrastructure development can lead to more rural poverty with elite capture, particularly in the case of unfair input and output markets which explain the reason for enhanced agricultural production with irrigation while unstoppable rural poverty and mass migration still continues.[24] These aspects of input and output markets and crop selection constitute affordability parameters and this parameter needs to be added to Trio of Performance Areas.

---

[22] Refers to the author's work experience.

[23] Gundogdu (2018b).

[24] Houdret (2012).

A more holistic approach is key to achieve desired outcomes: poverty alleviation and food security. Otherwise, irrigation and drainage infrastructure investment can make poverty alleviation and food security worse by favoring few with overall public resources or public debt from development banks. Root causes revolve around centralized policy orientation with centralized large-scale infrastructure schemes that favor economies of scale farming, yet they do not factor in the preferences of smallholders communities and their trends. Nevertheless, smallholders' preference alone cannot solve the problem as coordination is needed to assure the sustainability of aquifers and carry out affordability measures. Although economies of scale are more associated with larger farm sizes, the new trends and peculiarities enable smaller farm sizes so far as smallholders are ring-fenced against exploitation in input and output markets. Family labor and proximity to the field facilitate better husbandry and lower production costs.[25] Successful interventions for I&D schemes are not about one-size-fits-all engineering and project finance; instead, they require responsive to the context of natural resource management, agro-socioeconomics, service delivery, and inclusiveness.[26]

9.3   PUBLIC–PRIVATE PARTNERSHIP FOR IRRIGATION

Irrigation services are provided across a spectrum from the public to private. At the one end of the spectrum are state irrigation agencies that suffer from MOM problems, and their business model has failed. In the middle are water user organizations – that is, communal irrigation management – and this business model has been practiced throughout history. At the other end of the spectrum is the private sector, such as canal companies that build and operate the irrigation assets by borrowing money.[27] Indeed, this spectrum should also factor in the farmers with their wells and pumps as an irrigation business model. Nevertheless, this individualistic approach is mostly ignored in seeking remedies for the problems of large-scale infrastructure business models due to aquifer sustainability concerns.

---

[25] Van Rooyen and Nene (1996).

[26] Ostrom (1992).

[27] Svendsen (2005) and de Fraiture et al. (2007).

Recurring rehabilitation needs, water stress vis-à-vis population growth, and limited government fiscal space to fulfill investment need burgeons the idea of resourcing private resources via the PPP business model.[28] It is proposed that the private sector, with its management competencies, technical capacities, and financial resources, should be involved in the provision of I&D agency irrigation services, which suffer from low performance, poor asset management, and maintenance, to release immense public fiscal burden.[29] There exist mainly two types of irrigation PPPs: "service contracts" to the private sector to operate existing public CAPEX for water service delivery and "public service delegation" which requires CAPEX investment from the private sector.[30] The PPP business model is defined as "a long-term contract between a private party and a government entity, for providing a public asset or service, in which the private party bears significant risk and management responsibility, and remuneration is linked to performance."[31] There is a tendency to propose the PPP business model as an innovative way to address the build-neglect-rehabilitate cycle. Nevertheless, the PPP business model is not a novelty for the irrigation sector should one follow this definition with reference to canal companies.[32]

The main interest of governments is about appeasing their inefficiency and responsibilities while for the private sector it is mainly about profit from either investment or I&D service delivery. The inclusion of the private sector in I&D is not only about increasing efficiency in water service delivery and organizational resources performance areas but also the desire to attract additional funds to the sector. The PPP business model is supposed to bring value-for-money – not get rid of public service delivery – for governments in a way to ensure improved irrigation service quality and to improve maintenance of assets with better service fees

---

[28] Lankford et al. (2016).

[29] Darghouth et al. (2007) and Meinzen-Dick (2007).

[30] Darghouth et al. (2007).

[31] World Bank definition for public–private partnership.

[32] Irrigation canal companies (for example, Société du Canal de Provence in France) were established under corporate law and borrowed money to build and operate the canal to provide an irrigation service.

collection from irrigators. The government is freed from CAPEX investment needed but operation and maintenance function is separated from government policy and regulation function.[33]

Regardless of all the merits, in theory, there are severe challenges for irrigation PPPs.[34] First, the profit objective of the project sponsor is difficult to align with the priorities of rural development. Because long-tenor financing is required, most of the PPP projects are financed with FX funds that necessitate FX scaling of fees. This suggests that the government would have a preference for cash crops to enhance FX earning capacity for repayment. Unlike the government, farmers have a preference for low-risk crops. Cash crops for export is a risky business due to high commodity price volatility in the international market as well as standard and conformity assessment test and phytosanitary requirements that may cause refusal in cross-bordering. Cash crops for the export business model can also lead to import dependency for agricultural inputs. In an adverse year, farmers may end up selling their crops at very low prices, leaving them short of funds to purchase inputs to get ready for the next season – as abruptly happened during the 2008 crisis. At least once during the PPP concession, even if farmers are willing to pay, there would be affordability problems due to the following factors: the risk of refusal due to phytosanitary requirements, and a standard and conformity assessment; import dependency for inputs; and commodity price volatility. Unlike regular repayment requirements for FX funded projects, regularity is not attainable in the agricultural sector across a long-tenor. Hence, PPP presents weak potential in the I&D sector for affordability. Unlike PPP, local currency funded government agency and *Waqf* models are less likely to manipulate farmers for high-risk crops and put them in peril of unaffordability.

When evaluating the PPP business model, it is important to note that PPPs lead to a higher water-use fee in most of the cases.[35] The Senyera scheme in Spain proved that community-owned irrigation systems outperform the PPP business model. The outcomes of Senyera PPP indicated the exploitation of farmers and proved that collective action irrigation is more efficient and more affordable in practice, unlike the neoliberal

---

[33] Mandri-Perrot and Bisbey (2016).

[34] Bernier and Meinzen-Dick (2015).

[35] Molle and Berkoff (2007).

theory that assumes private ownership would have a trickle-down effect resulting in lower prices and higher-quality services.[36] The other show-case example for irrigation PPP is El Guerdane scheme in Morocco as presented in Case Box 9.1.

Case Box 9.1 El Guerdane Irrigation PPP, Morocco[37]

Recurring and persistent droughts force Moroccan farmers to rely heavily on irrigation. In the southern part of the country, citrus farmers on the Guerdane perimeter have long been dependent on water from an underground aquifer. However, the years of inten-sive agricultural practices have seriously diminished groundwater levels. The government looked to attract private investment in an irrigation network that could channel water to the perimeter from a distant dam complex. The concession—the world's first public-private partnership irrigation project—was awarded in July 2004. A consortium led by Omnium Nord-African (ONA), a Moroccan industrial conglomerate, won the 30-year concession. Other members included Morocco's Fond Igrane and Infrastructure Development and Management (Infra Man), an Austrian firm. By providing half the water needed by the citrus farmers, the Guerdane project reduced the risk of depleting underground water resources and safeguarded an agricultural industry that provides a living for an estimated 100,000 people.

The transaction is structured as a 30-year concession to build, co-finance, and manage an irrigation network to channel water from the dam complex and distribute it to farmers in El Guerdane. At the end of the concession, the infrastructure will be returned to the government. The concession grants exclusivity to channel and distribute irrigation water in the perimeter while allocating operational, commercial, and financial risks among the various stake-holders. The construction (time and costs) and the collection risk are transferred to the concessionaire. The government is responsible for ensuring water security. The demand/payment risk was mitigated by carrying out an initial subscription campaign whereby farmers paid an initial fee covering the average cost of on-farm connection. The

---

[36] Sanchis-Ibor et al. (2017).

concessionaire's construction obligation did not begin until subscriptions were received for 80 percent of the water available. The risk related to water shortage was allocated among the concessionaire (up to a consequential revenue loss capped at 15 percent), the farmers (via the application of a tariff surcharge in case of drought leading to a shortage of water, capped at 10 percent of the tariff), and the Government (sustaining the risk of more significant water shortage through a financial compensation to the concessionaire). The unique selection criteria was the lowest water tariff, in support of the government's goal of making surface water accessible and affordable to the largest number of farmers possible. **The public subsidy was designed to maintain water tariffs equivalent to current pumping costs, making them affordable to farmers.** The winning bidder provided a tariff significantly lower than the price that citrus farmers in El Guerdane had typically paid for irrigated groundwater supplies.

Source World Bank

In the case of El Guerdane, it is suggested that farmers received better and more sustainable I&D services after PPP with the same service fees they used to pay. Because better services are being offered, many rich people have been attracted into the farming sector and they have ended up buying land from smallholders, who have become marginalized in the process.[38] Keeping in mind that the major motivation behind I&D infrastructure development is rural development and poverty alleviation, there is no excuse to ignore the fact that applying PPPs in the irrigation sector has a substantial role in land and water grabbing.[39]

9.4   Islamic Approach with *Waqf* Development

The methodology used in the assessment of the PPP business model, Bos et al.'s (1994) Trio of Performance Areas, categorizes performance assessment according to "water service delivery", "organizational structure," and "governance." Such assessment for the PPP business model yields promising results vis-à-vis government agency business

---

[37] World Bank. Available at http://documents.worldbank.org/curated/en/873481468 190767800/pdf/103551-BRI-PUBLIC-PPPStories-Morocco-GuerdaneIrrigation.pdf.

[38] Houdret (2012).

[39] von Braun and Meinzen-Dick (2009).

models. PPPs should outperform government agencies in "water service delivery" (adequacy, reliability, equity, flexibility, multiple-use service, productivity, and operability) and "organizational resources" (financial sustainability, asset management, technical operations management, organizational management, fiduciary management, strategy, and process). Nevertheless, PPP does not provide much better "governance, enforcement, and conflict management" habitat due to the lack of water user engagement. Although PPP appears to offer better accountability to avoid favoritism with the government agency business model, it lacks customer inclusive representation. The PPP business model is inclined to favor project sponsors and big farmers while leaving behind smallholders. Hence, the PPP business model has a flaw that makes it unsustainable regardless of the merits it brings for water service delivery and operational resources themes.

In the case of irrigation, if individual users act independently, assuming that their free-riding is insignificant, it would lead to the depletion of common sources, and such uncoordinated action would work against a common good for all.[40] In this regard, the Islamic proposition for the water sector in general, which is a social infrastructure, is a *Waqf* business model. Water is not classified as a commodity belonging to anyone but as a public good in Islam. As a result, it is rendered with a *Waqf* business model similar to other public services, such as health and education, in a decentralized manner in the Islamic world for long period of time.[41] *Waqf*'s business model has embedded qualities for "governance, enforcement, and conflict management" by assuring social cohesion in the provision of social goods. It indicates that all infrastructure formulation should be devised for social cohesion as a priority and infrastructure design should be amended accordingly.

Table 9.1 provides a systematic comparison of three business models across four performance areas. It is necessary to have one that can perform well in all four areas in order to find a remedy for the build-neglect-rehabilitate circle. PPPs outperform *Waqf* in "organizational resource" themes for large-scale infrastructure due to the low technical capacity of rural communities to handle complicated assets and related financial, fiduciary, and technical operational management. Government agencies

---

[40] Tang (1992) and Ostrom (1990).

[41] Kuran (2001).

Table 9.1 Performance area comparison of different business models

	Government agency business model	PPP business model	Waqf business model
Water service delivery	Weak	Strong	Strong with small scale schemes
Operational resources	Weak	Strong	Strong with small scale schemes
Governance	Weak	Weak	Strong
Affordability for Smallholders	Strong	Weak	Strong

Source The authors

have proved to be unsuccessful in all three-performance areas. PPPs have very strong potential for "water service delivery" and "organizational resources", yet negative effects with "governance, enforcement, and conflict management" would lead to turmoil in rural development and poverty alleviation efforts. The only remaining solution is community ownership with *Waqf*, which can be successful with decentralized, smaller-scale, and flexible I&D infrastructure. Looking at the subject from the point of view of trying to select the right business model for I&D reveals that having large-scale centralized infrastructures is the root cause of the build-neglect-rehabilitate vicious circle. The Islamic proposition for the water sector, whether for rural I&D or urban water and sanitation, is the *Waqf* business model wherever possible. As long as the project formulation adopted for smaller-scale infrastructures provides for the realities of *Waqf*, the build-neglect-rehabilitate circle can be avoided.

The traditional I&D performance assessments have a relatively narrow perspective because irrigation is also about collective action and is a prong of agricultural production such as fertilizing practices, seed quality, and assuring fair prices in agricultural input procurement and post-harvest crops sale for the farmers. Any I&D infrastructure project for rural development should come up with a holistic approach for comprehensive intervention. Providing reliable water services alone would not yield any result for farmers if a viable solution for other inputs is not provided. And, more importantly, the focus should be on fair price formation for inputs and post-harvest crop sale. Otherwise, input providers and local traders during post-harvest continue to take advantage of the vulnerable rural population. It is not enough to have a solution based on the evaluation of the three-performance assessment areas to assure the desired outcomes of poverty alleviation and rural development; affordability parameters should also be factored in.

In this regard, the PPP business model is more on water service delivery and can turn into massive wealth transfer due to the vulnerability of smallholders since it does not fulfill affordability parameters. Eighty-four percent of farmers hold less than 2 hectares of land but cover only 12 percent of the farmland.[42] They are not directly integrated into the global value chain and rely on localized input and output markets. Hence, they are inflicted by price and quality disadvantage as a result of limited financial means for bulk purchase and organizational skill for crop.[43] The economic empowerment of farmers – by which they get economies of scale in buying inputs and selling post-harvest crops with fair prices – is key to attain affordability to yield the desired outcomes and to inhibit elite capture of irrigated lands. There is a need to fairly integrate small-holders to the global value chain and decrease market uncertainties in order to lower exposure to risk and vulnerability to livelihood socks.[44] And this is possible with a *Waqf* business model by which farmers not only get organized to engage with economic empowerment microfinance to assure reliable and fair input and post-harvest crop prices but also carry out MOM responsibilities of I&D infrastructure. *Waqf* can deliver MOM services for decentralized, small, and flexible infrastructure.

Waqf participation should be based on the sharing of the same aquifer and watershed. The inclusion of downstream water users should also be evaluated should they have a potential negative impact from upstream arrangements. Those using the same aquifer and watershed, with the possible inclusion of downstream water users, should form a *Waqf* not only for the sustainable use of aquifer and watershed water resources but also to collectively engage in economic empowerment through micro-finance programs. Hence, I&D schemes should be accompanied by economic empowerment microfinance solutions to factor ring-fencing.

[42] Lowder et al. (2016).

[43] Sale: Christen and Anderson (2013), Deininger and Byerlee (2011), and Sur et al. (2014).

[44] Ellis (1998).

Otherwise, carrying out irrigation infrastructure investment without tackling the affordability issues has the potential to make rural poverty worse by attracting elites to irrigated land that was not profitable beforehand.[45]

When it comes to the water sector, the best Islamic business model fit is *Waqf* due to the Islamic understanding of water as a public good. Conventionally, water ownership is defined as "the right acquired to the user under government regulation or water law for the abstraction, diversion, and use of water."[46] Since the right acquisition refers to the government, the conventional proposition for water delivery would be a government I&D agency or government PPP concession to the private sector. The Islamic definition of water ownership is different; it is not a commodity that can be traded, but a public good. Allah who sends water in due measure, makes it lodge underground and drain for the common good of communities.

> And We send down from the sky water in measure, and We give it lodging in the earth, and lo! We are able to withdraw it.
>   Quran 23:18

According to the Quran, it is not to establish large-scale infrastructure to subdue nature but to focus on a governance structure to ensure the common good of communities. The verse hints that the duty of policymakers should be:

- to ensure fairness in water use and agricultural input and output markets;
- to select crops based on water and soil realities of the geography, and not to change the geography with big infrastructure to have fantasy crops such as rice in drought-inflicted lands.

So long as fairness is sustained in and among communities and water and soil peculiarities of the land are factored for agriculture, Allah promises to sustain water provision in measure. An Islamic approach for a sustainable result is to make sure infrastructure is designed in harmony with, but not as mastery of, nature.

---

[45] Smallholders may be defined as farmers holding less than two hectares of land and relying on localized inputs and output markets.

[46] World Bank (2002) definition.

The focus of I&D infrastructure should shift from large-scale, centralized schemes to smaller, more flexible schemes to be operated by community *Waqf*. Other alternatives cannot provide a sustainable service delivery and there is no logic in continuing to try the same business models, either government agency or PPP, and await for a different result this time. A *Waqf* business model for the management, operations, and maintenance of smaller-scale and flexible I&D appears as a viable redress based on centuries of experience. Hence, the I&D infrastructure finance business should transform into smaller and flexible I&D *Waqf* development business models for communities. Irrigation and drainage should not be evaluated as a standalone element, but embedded into a wider context of agricultural input provision and sale of post-harvest crops. In this regard, economic empowerment microfinance schemes should accompany I&D infrastructure *Waqf* development to ring-fence the rural population, against elite capture, and input providers and post-harvest traders, by providing scale and finance for input purchase and fair post-harvest prices for crops.

References

Bernier, Q., and R.S. Meinzen-Dick. 2015. *Public–private partnerships for irrigation: Expanding access or increasing inequality.* Washington, DC: International Food Policy Research Institute.

Bos, M.G., D.H. Murray-Rust, D.J. Merry, H.G. Johnson, and W.B. Snellen. 1994. Methodologies for assessing performance of irrigation and drainage management. *Irrigation and Drainage Systems* 7: 231–261.

Burton, M. 2010. *Irrigation management: Principles and practices.* Wallingford, UK: CAB International Publishing.

Butterworth, J., and J. de la Harpe. 2009a. Grand designs: Corruption risks in major water infrastructure projects. U4Brief No. 27, CMI and U4, Anti-Corruption Resource Centre, Bergen, Norway.

Butterworth, J., and J. de la Harpe. 2009b. Not so petty: Corruption risks in payment and licensing systems for water. U4Brief No. 26, CMI and U4, Anti-Corruption Resource Centre, Bergen, Norway.

Christen, R.P., and J. Anderson. 2013. Segmentation of smallholder households: Meeting the range of financial needs in agricultural families. CGAP Focus Note No. 85. Washington, DC: World Bank.

Darghouth, S., H. Tardieu, B. Préfol, A. Vidal, J. Plantey, and S. Fernandez. 2007. Emerging public–private partnerships in irrigation development and management. Water Sector Board Discussion Paper Series 10, World Bank, Washington, DC.

De Fraiture, C., D. Wichelns, J. Rockström, and E. Kemp-Benedict. 2007. Looking ahead to 2050: Scenarios of alternative investment approaches. In *Water for food, water for life: A comprehensive assessment of water management in agriculture*, ed. D. Molden, 91–145. London: Earthscan, and Colombo: International Water Management Institute.

Deininger, K., and D. Byerlee. 2011. *Rising global interest in farmland. Can it yield sustainable and equitable benefits?* Washington, DC: World Bank.

Ellis, F. 1998. Household strategies and rural livelihood diversification. *The Journal of Development Studies* 35(1): 1–38.

Fan, Y., Z. Gao, S. Wang, H. Chen, and J. Liu. 2018. Evaluation of the water allocation and delivery performance of Jiamakou Irrigation Scheme, Shanxi, China. *Water* 10: 654. FAO (Food and Agricultural Organization).

Gundogdu, A.S. 2018b. An inquiry into Islamic finance from the perspective of sustainable development goals. *European Journal of Sustainable Development* 7(4).

Houdret, A. 2012. The water connection: Irrigation and politics in southern Morocco. *Water Alternatives* 5(2): 284–303.

Inocencio, A., M. Kikuchi, M. Tonosaki, A. Maruyama, D. Merrey, H. Sally, and I. de Jong. 2007. Costs and Performance of Irrigation Projects: A Comparison of Sub-Saharan Africa and Other Developing Regions. IWMI Report 109. Colombo, Sri Lanka: International Water Management Institute.

Kuran, T. 2001. The provision of public goods under Islamic law: Origins, impact, and limitations of the *waqf* system. *Law & Society Review* 35(4): 841–898.

Lankford, B.A., I. Makin, N. Matthews, A. Noble, P.G. McCornick, and T. Shah. 2016. A compact to revitalise large-scale irrigation systems using a leadership-partnership-ownership "theory of change." *Water Alternatives* 9(1): 1–32.

Lowder, S.K., J. Skoet, and T. Raney. 2016. The number, size, and distribution of farms, smallholder farms, and family farms worldwide. *World Development* 87: 16–29.

Mandri-Perrott, C., and J. Bisbey. 2016. *How to develop sustainable irrigation projects with private sector participation*. Washington, DC: World Bank.

Meinzen-Dick, R. 2007. Beyond panaceas in water institutions. *Proceedings of the National Academy of Sciences* 104(39): 15200–15205.

Molden, D.J. 2007. Summary for decision-makers. In *Water for food, water for life: A comprehensive assessment of water management in agriculture*, ed. D. Molden, 1–37. London: Earthscan, and Colombo: International Water Management Institute.

Molle, F., and J. Berkoff (eds.). 2007. *Irrigation water pricing: The gap between theory and practice*. Wallingford, UK: CAB International Publishing.

Molle, F., P.P. Mollinga, and P. Wester. 2009. Hydraulic bureaucracies and the hydraulic mission: Flows of water, flows of power. *Water Alternatives* 2(3): 328–349.

North, D. 1990. *Institutions, institutional change, and economic performance.* Cambridge: Cambridge University.

Obertreis, J., T. Moss, P. Mollinga, and C. Bichsel. 2016. Water, infrastructure, and political rule: Introduction to the special issue. *Water Alternatives* 9(2): 168–181.

Ostrom, E. 1990. *Governing the commons: The evolution of institutions for collective action.* Cambridge: Cambridge University Press.

Ostrom, E. 1992. *Crafting institutions for self-governing irrigation systems.* Oakland, CA: Institute for Contemporary Studies Press.

Oweis, T., A. Hachum, and A. Bruggeman (eds.). 2004. *Indigenous water-harvesting systems in West Asia and North Africa.* Aleppo, Syria: International Center for Agricultural Research in the Dry Areas.

Renault, D., and P.W. Vehmeyer. 1999. *On reliability in irrigation service preliminary concepts and application.* Colombo, Sri Lanka: International Irrigation Management Institute.

Sanchis-Ibor, C., R. Boelens, and M. García-Mollá. 2017. Collective irrigation reloaded: Recollection and re-moralization of water management after privatization in Spain. *Geoforum* 87: 38–47.

Shah, T. 2014. Accelerating smallholder irrigation in Sub-Saharan Africa: Lessons from South Asia's groundwater revolution. In *Proceedings of the workshop on irrigation in West Africa: Current status and a view to the future.* Ouagadougou, Burkina Faso, December 1–2, 2010. Ed. R.E. Namara and H. Sally, 373. Colombo, Sri Lanka: International Water Management Institute (IWMI). https://doi.org/10.5337/2014.218.

Shah, T. 2018. Institutional patterns in farmer-led irrigation: Global trends and their relevance to Sub-Saharan Africa. Unpublished Report, World Bank, Washington, DC.

Siebert, S., J. Burke, J.M. Faures, K. Frenken, J. Hoogeveen, P. Döll, and F.T. Portmann. 2010. Groundwater use for irrigation: A global inventory. *Hydrology and Earth System Sciences* 14: 1863–1880. https://doi.org/10.5194/hess-14-1863-2010.

Suhardiman, D., and M. Giordano. 2014. Is there an alternative for irrigation reform? *World Development* 57(C): 91–100.

Sur, M., D. Larson, E. Kucheriavenko, and K. Masylkanova. 2014. Facilitating smallholder access to markets. Prepared for Standing Committee for Economic and Commercial Cooperation of the Organization of Islamic Cooperation (COMCEC).

Svendsen, M. (ed.). 2005. *Irrigation and river basin management: Options for governance and institutions.* Wallingford, UK: CAB International Publishing.

Tang, S. 1992. *Institutions and collective action: Self-governance in irrigation.* San Francisco, CA: ICS Press.

Van Rooyen, C.J., and S. Nene. 1996. What can we learn from previous small farmer development strategies in South Africa. *Agrekon* 35(4): 325–331.

Von Braun, J., and R. Meinzen-Dick. 2009. *"Land grabbing" by foreign investors in developing countries: Risks and opportunities.* IFPRI Policy Brief No. 13. Washington, DC: International Food Policy Research Institute.

Wada Y., L.P.H. van Beek, and M.F.P Bierkens. 2012. Nonsustainable groundwater sustaining irrigation: A global assessment. *Water Resources Research* 48(6): W00L06.

Zinnbauer, D., and R. Dobson (eds.). 2008. *Global corruption report 2008: Corruption in the water sector.* Cambridge: Cambridge University Press.

CHAPTER 10

Identifying Equitable and Fitting Business Models for Infrastructure Projects

The claim is that there is a large shortfall of infrastructure investment to achieve SDGs. Yet, regardless of a massive infrastructure investment by public resources, Multilateral Development Banks (MDBs), PPPs, parameters related to SDGs have not to improve in the last century. The assumption that infrastructure projects bring about an economic growth that then trickles down for development is questionable. At least, the way infrastructure has developed as-is does not contribute to sustainable development. There are mainly three types of traditional infrastructure project financing: public procurement based on tax resources, Multilateral Development Banks procurement based on funds provided by the other countries, and lastly public–private partnership (PPP) procurement based on resources mobilized from financial markets. There is enough stocktaking for each method, which suggests that the way infrastructure project are formulated is not equitable. A one-size-fits-all approach yields mixed results. Neither public, nor MDB and PPP procurement should be implemented across all infrastructure sectors. From a historical perspective, constraints and difficulties of projects developed solely with public procurement, leading to the emergence of MDB financing, are listed below:

© The Author(s), under exclusive license to Springer Nature Switzerland AG 2021
A. T. Diallo and A. S. Gundogdu, *Sustainable Development and Infrastructure*, Palgrave Studies in Islamic Banking, Finance, and Economics, https://doi.org/10.1007/978-3-030-67094-8_10

1. Wealth Transfer: There exists mass-scale corruption and rent-seeking/distribution with public procurement. Large-scale infrastructure development turns into massive wealth transfer from household to a few contractors close to government. Resources belong to the public but most of the benefits of the large-scale infrastructure are confined to project-area residents or certain segments of the population, in addition to contractors. For example, mass-scale urban infrastructure development is a wealth transfer from rural to urban populations.
2. FX Constrain: The required procurement of goods and services from abroad leads to FX difficulties.
3. Sustainability: Project assets go to rack and ruin after project completion. In certain cases infrastructures are either not properly built or are deficient from the beginning. In the long run, there is no proper management, operations, and maintenance to ensure quality service delivery after project completion.

10.1   Sustainability

In order to address the FX problem, countries resort to bilateral loans. However, unpredictable politics makes lending countries shun from developing countries due to the long-term nature of infrastructure projects. Newly formed governments can rescind or obscure previous deals with the pretext of unfairness, imperfections, and corruption, as they were not part of the deal set up by their predecessors. One solution was the introduction of an international arbitration mechanism. The other was a change in the business model to convert bilateral loans to multilateral loans via MDBs. MDBs' involvement is a good omen to impede contract breach and abate the level of corruption in procurement of civil works, goods, and services under infrastructure projects. Although MDB financing brought about improvement for the provision of FX resources with containment of corruption as much as possible by employing procurement and project financial management guidelines, it is still far from perfect. The issue of wealth transfer with large-scale infrastructure is still there. The issue of wealth transfer effects of FX resources of MDBs for infrastructure development should be accounted for vis-à-vis sustainability issues. Sustainability weakness in infrastructure projects is common across all MDB projects, which are not superior to public resources financed projects, in account of this aspect. Project assets, in both cases, are at rack and ruin. In the case of MDB loans, the problem is even worse due to FX repayment obligations, yet governments are still eager for the following reasons.

1. FX Loans disbursed help the balance of payments. It facilitates importation of consumer goods.
2. Large-scale infrastructure creates employment for workers.
3. Large corporations get business opportunities.
4. Government officials' popularity increases with media news on a booming economy.

Assuming that government officials do not have a say in procurement in MDB projects, even without rent distribution capabilities, large-scale infrastructure projects are very appealing for governments. Sustainability is not a concern as in democracies government post are short to medium term, and there are two alternatives for incumbents:

1. To serve the country and/or themselves as much as possible during the short period of time; or
2. Encounter freedom fighters and/or revolutionists who are also eager to serve the country and/or themselves.

The problems spurs, however, in the long term. In most of the cases, project assets end up in a state of rack and ruin, and hence they cannot generate economic benefits to repay loans back. The issue of sustainability entered into the agenda of MDBs for these reasons to ensure that loans are used for their intended purpose. The reaction to the sustainability issue was a move toward the PPP business model. PPP offers superior results with the management, operations, and maintenance of infrastructure assets. Hence, regardless of its higher financing cost, the model is a viable solution since the higher financing cost for countries is compensated by the savings gained from the sustainability of project assets. This is defined as value-for-money since the same or superior quality of public services can be delivered with lower cost accounted during the lifetime of the project assets with the PPP alternative.

However, PPPs should be considered a panacea as they sometimes yield mixed result when it comes to developmental impact. For many instances, FX loans are not invested in infrastructure to enhance FX earning capacity of the country. Rather, PPPs are used to allow government to spread needed investment over time due to lack of physical space. PPPs have a low developmental impact in the health, education, and water sectors, in relation to prices to be paid by households, particularly for the most vulnerable who do not have resources to pay for services. PPPs works better with the transport sector (roads, railroads, airports, ports, the first-mile ICT).

As presented in Fig. 10.1, the Islamic proposition is to provide economic infrastructure with fewer PPPs and more SMEs as much as possible based on the technological realities, and to provide social infrastructure with community *Waqf*. There is no one-size-fit-all intervention of Islamic economics and finance. Economic infrastructure services should be commercially priced while social infrastructure services should not be commodified. In the case of economic infrastructure the focus should be on fair price formation. PPPs with large infrastructure and monopolistic characteristics can turn into exploitation if necessary measures are not taken by governments. This also suggests the importance of economic policy imposition to assure fairness; infrastructure development alone would not yield sustainable results without proper economic policy. However, adaptation of proper economic policy is difficult with large-scale infrastructure due to the lobbying power of project sponsors. The ideal situation is to provide economic infrastructure services with SMEs

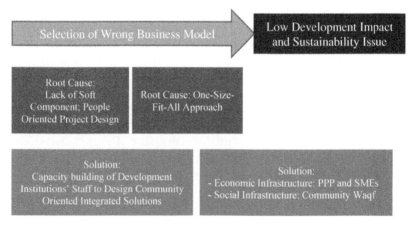

Fig. 10.1 Project formulation and sustainability. (*Source* The authors)

if the technology allows such provision, i.e., PV panels for energy. Until technological progress is in place to make such discourse viable – such as levitation technologies for transport – PPPs can be used for transport projects (airports, port, railways, mass transit, roads, and first-mile ICT).

10.2 RESOURCE MOBILIZATION FOR SCALE-UP

In addition to existing public and MDB funds, further funds need to be mobilized by the involvement of the private sector and by tapping into capital markets. Islamic finance is more constrained from a resource mobilization aspect than conventional finance. As presented in Fig. 10.2, time overrun feeds into cost overrun and low disbursement with Islamic project finance. Due to such weak performance, investors are hesitant to participate in projects as low disbursement means low profitability. The reason time overrun is more of a problem with Islamic finance has to do with Islamic restriction in financing contracts. Upfront fees and commitment fees are disallowed in Islamic finance. Conventional project finance resorts to such fees to counterbalance the negative effect of land acquisition, counterpart funds, and executing agency capacity impediment in large infrastructure projects. The peculiarities of large-scale infrastructure, such as land appropriation, necessitate counter measures to impede

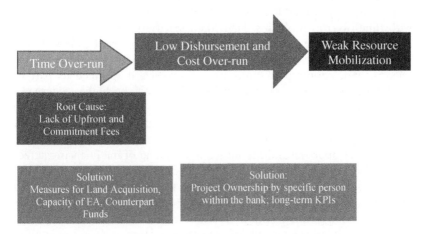

Fig. 10.2 Link between project implementation and resource mobilization. (*Source* The authors)

time overrun. Although the ideal case would be the provision of services without large-scale infrastructure, present technological boundaries still make large-scale infrastructure a necessity, particularly in the transport sector.

Nothing can be done about the fee restriction of Islamic finance. They are not allowed – and that fact is clearcut. Fee restrictions not only protect the borrower, but are also handy for lenders in some circumstances. In the case of conventional finance, once the upfront fee and commitment fee have been acquired, it is very difficult to cancel the project even if the project is not relevant anymore. In Islamic finance, since there are no locking fees, project cancellation is more possible. The issue of time overrun can be handled with enhanced project ownership within the bank and alignment of KPIs to long-tenure realities of infrastructure projects. It is important to mention the devastating side effects of irrelevant KPI setting in present development practice. Infrastructure projects are long-term interventions with project implementation taking up to five or six years. Repayment and project results, such as financial/economic outcomes and environmental impact, are observed in up to thirty years. In most cases, myriads of people get involved in the project, and this leads to lack of project ownership. Annual KPI setting does not help to carry out superb projects with long-term accountability. Aligned long-term KPI setting would be a solution to tackle the problems of time overruns.

In addition, Islamic lenders can take necessary covenants to grapple with time overrun problems. First, the capacity of the executing agency (EA) is key for the timely implementation of projects. Lenders should influence the EA selection process with an EA capacity assessment exercise. Second, counterpart funds from borrower, if specified as part of the financing requirement, should be locked with the highest degree of approval authorities, such as parliament. Development institutions require counterpart funds to assure that government has a stake in the project and such measures enhance the success of the project. The process starts with the loan approval and the subsequent signing of the financing agreement. The process continues with the declaration of effectiveness with the provision of necessary documents by the borrower, and ends with first disbursement with the start of the project. Nevertheless, these are all about "doing things rightly," but it is not right for development institutions to engage in all infrastructure sectors with a single tool: either classical sovereign lending or PPP. There should be different business models for sectors based on sector peculiarities. Hence, the focus should be on "doing right things" while minding the repercussions of having too much power in the hands of MDB staff. Scale-up should start after matching the right business model, based on realities of sectors, with the right resource mobilization tools. Scaling up using the wrong project approaches would not contribute toward sustainable development; it would make things worse. And this is what has been happening, as evidence suggests that infrastructure projects do not help in ending hunger, alleviating poverty, and abating income inequality. Pro-economic growth's simplistic approach favors the privileged minority at the expense of the unfortunate masses. Economic growth with intermediation of project finance, SME finance, and consumer loan model, which is based on trickling down assumptions, does not work. The Islamic approach is focused on framing financial intermediation with checks and balances, as well as strict restrictions, based on peculiarities of intervention areas. Besides, Islamic finance has different approaches based on the realities of intervention area.

10.3   Economic Infrastructure and Resource Mobilization

The provision of economic infrastructure should be commercially priced based on the motivation of profit maximization, while also observing competition law to inhibit unfair price setting with monopoly, oligopoly, or cartel, with the involvement of private sector. It is better to define economic infrastructure first. Economic infrastructure can be defined as infrastructure, the provision of which directly contributes toward economic growth. This suggests that such projects should be evaluated based on economic and financial calculations in the form of return prospects, such as internal rate of return or economic internal rate of return. If the numbers do not support the return prospects, such infrastructure should not be developed, and this can be the line between economic infrastructure and social infrastructure. Social infrastructure should be developed as much as possible with concessional resources even if Net Present Value (NPV), Internal Rate of Return (IRR), or Economic Internal Rate of Return (EIRR) does not support such infrastructure development. On the other hand, economic infrastructure should be developed only with commercially priced resources and should be assessed using NPV and IRR, while social infrastructure should be assessed based on EIRR. Based on these lines two economic infrastructure sectors can be defined:

1. Transport: Airports, port, railways, mass transit, roads, and ICT first-mile subsectors.
2. Energy: Electricity generation, electricity distribution and transmission, district heating and cooling subsectors.

The renewable alternatives of solar and wind trend would not only dismiss the electricity transmission and distribution subsector but also allow valuable natural gas resources to be used for better purposes. Electricity generation can be done with PV panels and wind power. SMEs can play substantial role in provision, operation, and maintenance of small infrastructure assets such as in the case of decentralized electrification. By using renewable energy, such as solar and wind, this process can also provide streetlighting for neighborhoods, which can help decrease crime rate and increase the chances of attaining SDGs.

Unlike the energy sector, the transport sector does not allow small and flexible infrastructure, at least for now, until the emergence of new technologies such as levitation vehicles. Presently, the most suitable business model for the transport sector is PPP, which allows concessions or availability payment to the private sector in exchange for the provision of services. The ideal case is concession PPPs, but in some cases governments can accept availability payments or provide minimum guarantees. The PPP business model is a good fit for the transport sector with its robust sustainability measures. Nevertheless, governments should take necessary precautions to ensure value-for-money in project selection. Value-for-money is the difference between the total life cycle cost of a public procurement project and the same for an alternative PPP procurement in the provision of the same level of service quality.

Based on an appropriate business model for energy and transport, projects can be scaled up with resource mobilization. For the energy sector, SMEs finance resources can be mobilized with *Musharaka* and two-step *Murabaha* platforms of commercial banks in way a similar to crowdfunding. As for transport PPP projects, upon the start of repayment, *Sukuk* can be used for resource mobilization. Development Banks should carry out preparation of bankable projects. The project should be securitized with *Sukuk* for capital markets only after project completion. Such asset-backed PPP *Sukuk* would provide very valuable liquidity management means for Islamic banks.

10.4   SOCIAL INFRASTRUCTURE AND RESOURCE MOBILIZATION

Apart from transportation and energy, the infrastructure for the remaining sectors of

- water and sewage – W&S (water utility; water treatment)
- solid waste management (collection and transport; treatment and disposal)
- Irrigation and drainage – I&D
- health
- education

would fall under social infrastructure development. The development institution role of being financing arranger for PPPs or SME developer for economic infrastructure should be expected to continue for some time; however, in the case of social infrastructure their business model needs to change. Unlike with economic infrastructure, the provision of social infrastructure should be based on breaking even – for sustainable provision of public goods, factoring is needed for additional investment and maintenance. This suggests a transformation of development banks' sovereign lending and PPP intervention for social infrastructure into a *Waqf* development business model.

Directing public resources for the education sector with either public procurement or MDB sovereign debt is very problematic. Public resources should be directed to address the misery of those at the bottom in terms of poverty levels. Education investment should not be directed in a way to supply the market with a workforce for big corporations; instead, it should enhance consciousness in the society. It should enhance capacity of the public to handle their sustenance rather than being dependent on the government or big corporations. Education should empower them so they become literate and able to integrate into the global value chain with enhanced basic IT literacy. In this regard, focus should be on sensible and relevant curriculum development with a focus on basic skills: literacy,

ICT, and foreign language. Physical assets in the form of schools should be the subject of community *Waqf* development. The same holds for the health sector.

Hospitals are instruments of intergenerational wealth transfer. Public resources for hospitals mainly serve the elderly while the tax burden, or FX loan burden, is on the shoulder of youngsters. Indeed, healthcare services should not just focus on tertiary services but take into account the importance of primary healthcare for the benefit of young people who are the productive asset of the society. For the health sector, the focus of development intervention should be on the following.

- Targeting vulnerable and poor populations
- Strengthening public health prevention
- *Waqf* development support for tertiary care and specialized hospitals
- Supporting national health initiatives
- Improving capacity building for sector staff with global research, not only for achieving new frontiers but also for enhancing existing practices.

Indeed, the factors that are relevant for the health sector, as listed above, are also relevant for the education sector. The public goods of health, education, and water should not be commodified or backed with insurance and/or financing mechanisms in order to impede intergenerational and rural/urban wealth transfer as well as price bubbles. From an Islamic perspective, it is clear that health, education, and water services should be provided with a *Waqf* business model. Bearing in mind the realities of the water sector (I&D and W&S), the *Waqf* model also presents itself as the best fit for solid waste management (SWM). These three sectors – I&D, W&S, SWM – have common characteristics beyond being public services.

1. They are immediately connected to another public service: Health. Proper management of these three sectors would substantially increase public health.
2. They have a high-risk factor for the environment, and hence for the community. If there were to be a leakage from facilities, the environment around the facility and the community would be heavily affected.

Building a water treatment facility or solid waste treatment facility has adverse effect on the neighborhood. It not only decreases the value of assets around the facility but also leads to health problems for the neighborhood – even though it enhances the health condition of the public. Very often affluent neighborhoods exert their influence to have such facilities relocated to areas where the poorer people live.

Making funding decisions with public money in the selection of location, contractors to build such infrastructure, and maintenance is not equitable. With the same amount of funds being collected from taxes, communities are more likely to choose the best location and contractors to ensure they receive value-for-money. Carrying out large-scale infrastructure projects with general public resources is not equitable. The situation with I&D, W&S, and SWM is more acute due to health and environmental concerns. Grouping SWM with the other two water sectors (I&D and SWM) also hints toward a community definition. In the case of I&D, community *Waqf* should be formed based on watershed, aquifer, and downstream. The same logic holds for W&S as well as for SWM. Environmental risk is high in W&S and SWM infrastructure for water. Grouping should be based on watershed to address the risk.

In the case of basic human necessities such as health, it is observed that using financing makes such services less affordable. Based on realities of the sector, it is advisable not to finance certain sectors at all. Financing such peculiar sectors can exacerbate the financial well-being of people. The housing sector is in the same category. Although affordable housing is on the agenda of public housing development and MDBs, such programs end up with elite capture and rent distribution to contractors. Availing mortgages also makes thing adverse. There is a negative correlation between housing affordability and the percentage of mortgage in a house purchase.[1] Availing more loans for house purchase increases the amount that is bid and inflates real estate prices. Hence, the best alternative is not to provide financing for real estate purchase. This is the way to enhance affordability, not social housing projects of banks' mortgage loans.

Resource for the provision of these public goods can be mobilized from (1) complementary currency investment as implemented in economic

---

[1] Gundogdu (2019).

empowerment microfinance programs or (2) cash *Waqf* and cash *Waqf Sukuk* type of concessional loans.[2]

10.5   Infrastructure Projects, SDGs, and Global Value Chain

SDGs can play an important role in sustainable development, but with some fine-tuning based on Islamic philosophy. SDGs should be aligned to the definition of Islamic economics and finance. For example, the definition of poverty by SDGs is not acceptable from an Islamic point of view. Islam seeks the harmony of people having different attributes with fairness. The alternative of everybody being equal may turn into some being more equal than others, and equality in being slaves, as humanity has experienced in the name of different systems.

The way SDGs define key terminology as-is may not be conducive for sustainable development. Regardless of the decades of infrastructure investment by MDB, also with public procurement, poverty is a formidable issue, still. Development institutions' business model should transform into *Waqf* development for social infrastructure. As for economic infrastructures, for now development institutions should continue to play a role in the transport sector (including first-mile ICT), but it should be borne in mind that for new technologies the stage should be left for SMEs. The energy sector trend for SME is already there. In this regard, SME financing will become increasingly important in the future, and the existing deposit banking business model cannot fill the bill for such a trend. Similar to development institutions, banks are very valuable for sustainable development but their business model should be transformed so that they become mediators between those with access to funds and those who are looking for funds for viable business opportunities. In this regard, the deposit banking business model should be reformed based on the crowdfunding business model to be suitable for SME financing in pursuit of the provision of economic infrastructure. The involvement of SMEs in infrastructure provision and maintenance of infrastructure would contribute to decent work and economic growth (SDG-8).

Using the wrong infrastructure model can exacerbate poverty. Poverty should be contained in rural areas through economic empowerment

---

[2] Gundogdu (2018, 2019).

of communities and sustainable provision of the needed infrastructure. Developing sustainable cities also requires the provision of social infrastructure with community-owned *Waqf*. Cities should not be rendered with public funds in a way to transfer wealth from rural to urban areas. All the reflection on infrastructure development hints at massive wealth transfer toward urban elitism. Not only the present monetary system but also the infrastructure development approach works at the expense of rural population, forcing them to migrate to urban areas to get some access to the wealth transferred there. Although a certain level of elitism is needed to select talented people so they can serve society, the way elitism works in modern society is more to do with multifaceted, rural–urban, intergenerational exploitation. The mechanism works in a way to disintegrate our societies.

No matter what we do, there will be some form of wealth transfer with infrastructure development; at least some will benefit more than others. This does not mean that infrastructure development should be halted due; instead, the issues should be addressed. The Islamic proposition to address the imperfections is to minimize them as much as possible with equitable and fitting business models and embed wealth redistribution mechanism with *Zakat* as a counterbalancing mechanism to spur the remnants of unfairness out of wealth transfer.

Similar to as with SDGs, GVC should be taken with a pinch of salt. GVC can exacerbate poverty and fuel inequality in an unjust manner. In the past feudal lords and empire states used to invest in railroads and ports to bring natural resources of exploited lands to the markets under their control. The way GVC is implemented can be even worse since it proposes public procurement or MDB sovereign loans/PPPs to make this investment for the same outcome. The focus of GVC should be on smallholder farmers and SMEs. Having GVCs provide an enabling environment for big corporations would work against poverty alleviation and sustainable development. The focus should be on providing market access to smallholders and SMEs, not only with tariff concessions but also by implementing a phytosanitary standard through the issue of standard and conformity assessment tests. This requires investment for capacity enhancement in standard and conformity assessment test laboratories of the least-developed countries. The issue of lack of export capacity and connectivity of least-developed countries should be addressed via the provision of economic infrastructure (roads, ports, airports, etc.) as well as using SME development programs and loans.

References

Gundogdu, A.S. 2018. An inquiry into Islamic finance from the perspective of sustainable development goals. *European Journal of Sustainable Development* 7(4).

Gundogdu, A.S. 2019. *A modern perspective of Islamic economics and finance.* Bingley, UK: Emeralds Publishing.

Appendix A: Transaction Scheme for the Case of Unlocking Energy Access Finance Through Crowdfunding

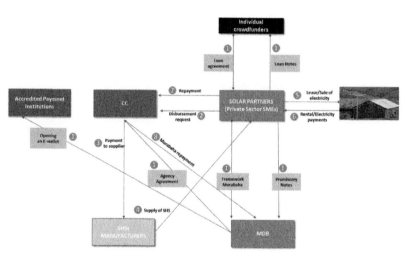

Source Product developed by Bandar Alhoweish, Khalid Ismaili Idrissi, and Hussain Mugaibel

© The Editor(s) (if applicable) and The Author(s), under exclusive license to Springer Nature Switzerland AG 2021
A. T. Diallo and A. S. Gundogdu, *Sustainable Development and Infrastructure*, Palgrave Studies in Islamic Banking, Finance, and Economics, https://doi.org/10.1007/978-3-030-67094-8

Appendix B: Irrigation and Drainage Water Management Performance Areas

1. Water service delivery	
Adequacy	1.1.1 Do the farmers receive enough flow, pressure (if applicable), and total quantity to meet their crop-water requirements and timeliness?
	1.1.2 Is excess irrigation water suitably drained from farmers' plots without causing damage to soil and crops?
	1.1.3 Is the biological and chemical quality of irrigation water supplied safe for users, crops, the environment, and livestock?
Reliability	1.2.1 For irrigation services based on irrigation scheduling: Does the farmer receive water according to the agreed-on schedule and with predictability?
	1.2.2 For on-demand service: Does the service provider ensure continuity of service at the delivery point (for example, hydrants or other)?
	1.2.3 For proportional distribution or spate irrigation: Does the farmer receive water according to agreement?
	1.2.4 For flood protection: Are the fields and other conveyance infrastructure protected against the design flood (of the relevant return period—for example, one in 50 years)?

(continued)

© The Editor(s) (if applicable) and The Author(s), under exclusive license to Springer Nature Switzerland AG 2021
A. T. Diallo and A. S. Gundogdu, *Sustainable Development and Infrastructure*, Palgrave Studies in Islamic Banking, Finance, and Economics, https://doi.org/10.1007/978-3-030-67094-8

(continued)

Equity	1.3.1 Is irrigation water distributed fairly across all users of the system? 1.3.2 Are drainage and flood protection services comparable across all users? 1.3.2 Are irrigation service parameters (adequacy, reliability, flexibility, quality) built into infrastructure that enables equitable distribution to all users? 1.3.4 If service varies within the irrigation scheme, are these variations reflected in the pricing policy?
Flexibility	1.4.1 Does the system allow farmers to vary their demand in response to changing needs at the farm level during the cropping cycle and over the seasons? 1.4.2 To what extent can farm decisions on cropping and irrigation methods be made independent of others in the same system, within the overall service agreement? 1.4.3 Can farmers make choices in relation to the services, which are then reflected in the price they pay (for example, increased flow rates at a higher price or formal and informal water trading between irrigators)?
Multiple-use services	1.5.1 Are the needs of other groups of water users or services recognized by **the Service Provider** (such as watershed management, flood protection, environment, ecological flow, hygiene, livestock, fisheries, domestic water, washing, tourism, recreation, groundwater recharge, and so on)? 1.5.2 Is there a pricing policy for other users adapted to their use?
Productivity	1.6.1 Is the irrigation service attuned to enabling sustainably maximized and diversified production (in terms of yield or return per unit of water, labor, inputs, and so on)? 1.6.2 Is the cost of service affordable compared to productivity gains, and is the invoicing done in relation to farmers' expected cash flow?
Operability	1.7.1 Is the physical design of the infrastructure (density of network, type of control structure, measurement capability) fit to deliver the required level of service required by farmers? 1.7.2 How sensitive is the service to flow fluctuations, breakdowns, and other variations and anomalies, and can service be maintained without high deployment of water, energy, and personal resources?

(continued)

(continued)

2. Organizational resources	
Financial sustainability	2.1.1 Are sufficient resources budgeted for and mobilized to manage, operate, maintain, and replace irrigation infrastructure to deliver quality irrigation and drainage services now and in future? 2.1.2 Do water users pay for irrigation services? (Is there effective fee setting, and are fee collection mechanisms enforced?) 2.1.3 Is there access to finance for scheme management from commercial sources such as private financial institutions (for example, banks), technology suppliers, and so on?
Asset management	2.2.1 Is there an asset management plan to maintain the condition of I&D assets and an optimum operating standard to provide a level of service to farmers that is consistent with cost effectiveness and sustainability objectives? 2.2.2 Is there an appropriate operation plan that rationalizes the type and costs of various operational requirements (to provide a suitable level of service to farmers consistent with cost effectiveness and sustainability objectives)?
Technical operations management	2.3.1 Is the organizational structure and decision-making clear and functional in terms of inclusiveness, hierarchy, functions, and reporting? 2.3.2 Is there a suitable inventory on main system and service parameters (users, land owners, irrigation network, irrigation rights, geography, crops) to support decisions? 2.3.3 Are there internal service standards and process workflows for common MOM functions, and are records on service levels maintained?
Organizational management (including HR)	2.4.1 Is the staffing composition adequate to fulfill the mission in terms of technical, financial, social, and management positions, skills, and capacities? 2.4.2 Is there an effective staffing plan, including training and development, performance management, adequate compensation, and learning opportunities? 2.4.3 Is there a transparent and merit-based staff performance and reward system in place to incentivize employees? 2.4.4 Are there outsourcing policies and practices for specific functions?

(continued)

(continued)

Fiduciary management	2.5.1 Is there effective expense control and cash flow management of the I&D agency based on accurate forecasting? 2.5.2 Are there performance standards for I&D services that are used as the basis for fund allocations, prioritization of activities, and monitoring improvements in service delivery?
Strategy and processes	2.6.1 Is the institutional vision, mission, and sector road map to support change management and improved service-delivery performance by **the Service Provider** aligned to water and agricultural policy? 2.6.2 Is there an appropriate investment strategy for development and sustainability of I&D infrastructure and services? 2.6.3 Is there appropriate due diligence on decision-making, including attention to issues of inclusiveness and to decision meetings with due process and record-keeping?

3. Governance, enforcement and conflict management

Transparency and customer orientation	3.1.1 Is management accountable to users, owners, and stakeholders, and are there performance assessment mechanisms? 3.1.2 Does management include staff and users in institutional improvement processes, and is there an effective communication strategy? 3.1.3 Is information on scheme operation and service delivery routinely and effectively measured (metered) and documented? 3.1.4 Is there an effective and responsive information management system to provide **the Service Provider**-related information on structure, people, and processes? 3.1.5 Are conflict management mechanisms in place to enable debate and resolve conflict regarding the service (either between users or between service providers and users)? 3.1.6 Is there adequate tracking of conflicts and analysis to overcome structural problems?
Enabling policies and associated legal instruments in place	3.2.1 Are there adequate policy and legal frameworks (including suitable legal instruments in place) to strengthen performance of irrigation service delivery? 3.2.2 Do the water and other relevant sectors demonstrate compatibility between policies?

(continued)

(continued)

Institutional/organizational coherence	3.3.1 Does the Service Provider have organizational autonomy (financial, political, and so on)?
	3.3.2 Are there suitable mechanisms defined for inter- and intra-Service Providers coordination?
	3.3.3 Is there clarification of tasks and responsibilities (spatially, functionally, hierarchically, and hydraulically) of the various service providers regarding delivery of irrigation and drainage services?
	3.3.4 Is the I&D service provider considered credible by the people it serves, financiers, and other stakeholders?
Accountability	3.4.1 Is provision of irrigation water regulated and licensed, and are these suitably enforced?
	3.4.2 Are there service agreements (formal or informal) between parties for the provision of services, and are these agreements enforced?
	3.4.3 Are there process management and performance monitoring systems within the organization that ensure adequate accountability to the management and to members, users, and customers?
	3.4.4 Are farmers and water users of I&D services engaged in the accountability of the Service Providers and other stakeholders responsible for service delivery?
	3.4.5 Is there effective communication within the organization and with its clients on the formulation, execution, and evaluation of service delivery activities?
Inclusive representation	3.5.1 Is there transparency, equity, and inclusiveness in the stakeholders associated with services delivery, including women, youth, and other marginalized groups, as well as the Service Provider?
	3.5.2 Is the level of representation of various stakeholders, including women, youth, and marginalized groups, suitably reflected in the composition of water user groups and the Service Provider?
	3.5.3 Are stakeholders, including women, youth, and marginalized groups, suitably empowered, included in dialogue, and involved in decision-making, including setting their agenda?

(continued)

(continued)

4. Affordability for smallholders vis-à-vis financing and funding realities of the service provider	
Crop selection	4.1.1 Are farmers encouraged to change their crop selection after the project to meet affordability requirements vis-à-vis financing and funding realities of the Service Provider?
	4.1.2 Does financing and funding FX denomination brings about the long-term burden on irrigators?
	4.1.3 Do crop preferences with the involvement of the Service Provider are sustainable for the region even if the project fails in the future?
	4.1.4 Does soil and water realities of irrigated land has a comparative advantage in the selected crop as compared to other regions and countries?
Inputs markets	4.2.1 Does new project lead to import dependency, FX burden, of inputs such as fertilizer and seed?
	4.2.2 Does the new project introduce soft elements of water and soil analysis for sustainable best use/type of inputs (not only water but also fertilizer and seed) in the local context?
	4.2.3 Do input markets competitive to assure fair prices for smallholders? Do smallholders have access to inputs with the same price comparable to big farmers?
	4.2.4 Do input prices comparable to those in peer countries?
	4.2.5 Is there any form of monopoly, oligopoly, or unfair price-setting mechanism in input markets?
Output markets	4.3.1 Does intervention comes up with a solution for phytosanitary and standard and conformity assessment test to enhance the marketability and attain higher price margins of crops in local, regional, and international markets?
	4.3.2 Do output price for farmers comparable to international prices?
	4.3.3 Do farmers left alone with unscrupulous local traders in the post-harvest phase?
	4.3.4 Do farmers have financial strength not to sell their products in a hurry during the post-harvest phase for unfair prices?

Note The Service Provider: Either of Government Agency, PPP or Community Waqf
Source Affordability performance area added to modified table of World Bank, 2019. *Governance in Irrigation and Drainage: Concepts, Cases, and Action-Oriented Approaches – A Practitioner's Resource* (English). Washington, DC: World Bank Group

Bibliography

Abdul-Aziz, A.R, and P.S. Jahn Kassim. 2011. Objectives, success and failure factors of housing public-private partnerships in Malaysia. *Habitat International* 35(1).

Abdullah, M.A., and S.K.A. Manan. 2011. Small and medium enterprises and their financing patterns: Evidence from Malaysia. *Journal of Economic Cooperation and Development* 32(2): 1–18.

Abdul-Rahman, Y. 1999. Islamic instruments for managing liquidity. *International Journal of Islamic Financial Services* 1(1): 1–7.

Abdulsaleh, A.M., and A.C. Worthington. 2013. Small and medium-sized enterprises financing: A review of literature. *International Journal of Business and Management* 8(14): 36–54.

Abor, J. 2007. Debt policy and performance of SMEs: Evidence from Ghanaian and South African firms. *The Journal of Risk Finance* 8(4): 364–379. https://doi.org/10.1108/15265940710777315.

Ahmed, O.B. 1997. Islamic financial instruments to manage short-term liquidity. Islamic Research and Training Institute, Islamic Development Bank, Research Paper 41, pp. 19–40.

Ahmed, Habib. 2004. *Role of zakat and awqaf in poverty alleviation*. Jeddah: Islamic Research and Training Institute, Islamic Development Bank Group.

Ahmed, H. 2011a. *Product development in Islamic banks*. Edinburgh: Edinburgh University Press.

Ahmed, H. 2011b. Waqf-based microfinance: Realizing the social role of Islamic finance. In *Essential readings in contemporary waqf issues*, ed. K. Monzer and M.M. Siti, 205239. Kuala Lumpur: CERT.

Ahmed, H., M. Mohieldin, J. Verbeek, and F. Aboulmagd. 2015a. *On the sustainable development goals and the role of Islamic finance.* Policy Research Working Paper No. 7266, World Bank, Washington, DC.

Ahmed, H., M. Mohieldin, J. Verbeek, and F. Aboulmagd. 2015b. On the sustainable development goals and the role of Islamic finance. World Bank Policy Research Working Paper No. 7266. Available at SSRN: https://ssrn.com/abstract=2606839.

Aijaz, A., and A. Abayomi. 2017. *Mobilizing Islamic finance for infrastructure public-private partnerships* (English). Washington, DC: World Bank Group. http://documents.worldbank.org/curated/en/898871513144724493/Mobilizing-Islamic-finance-for-infrastructure-public-private-partnerships. Accessed October 11, 2018.

Al-Qaradawi, Yusuf. 1994. *Fiqh al-Zakat.* Cairo: Maktabah Wahbah.

Altman, E.I., M. Esentato, and G. Sabato. 2020. Assessing the credit worthiness of Italian SMEs and mini-bond issuers. *Global Finance Journal* 43(February). https://doi.org/10.1016/j.gfj.2018.09.003.

Amine, M.B. 2015. Product development and *Maqasid* in Islamic finance: Towards a balanced methodology. *Islamic Economic Studies* 23(1).

Antras, Pol, and Alonso de Gortari. 2017. On the geography of global value chains. NBER Working Paper 23456 (May), National Bureau of Economic Research, Cambridge, MA.

Anwar, Muhammad. 1995. Financing socio-economic development with zakat funds. *Journal of Islamic Economics* 4: 15–32.

Ariffin, N.M., S. Archer, and R.A.A. Karim. 2009. Risks in Islamic banks: Evidence from empirical research. *Journal of Banking Regulation* 10(2).

Asian Development Bank. 2005. Special evaluation study: The role of project implementation units. https://www.oecd.org/derec/adb/35249987.pdf. Accessed January 13, 2020.

Asian Development Bank Procurement Guidelines, issued in April 2015. Available at: https://www.adb.org/sites/default/files/procurement-guidelines-april-2015.pdf. Accessed January 13, 2020.

Asian Development Bank Loan Disbursement Hand Book. 2017. https://www.adb.org/sites/default/files/adb-loan-disbursement-handbook-2017.pdf. Accessed January 13, 2020.

Asutay, Mehmet. 2007. Conceptualization of the second best solution in overcoming the social failure of Islamic finance: Examining the overpowering of homoislamicus by homoeconomicus. *IIUM Journal in Economics and Management* 15(2): 167–195.

Bacha, O.I. 1999. Financial derivatives: Some thoughts for reconsideration. *International Journal of Islamic Financial Services* 1(1): 12–28.

Bacha, O.I. 2020. Dana Gas Sukuk: The need for improved shariah governance. https://www.researchgate.net/publication/339165026_Dana_Gas_Sukuk_ The_Need_for_improved_Shariah_Governance.

Bacon, Robert W., and John Besant-Jones. 2001. Global electric power reform, privatization, and liberalization of the electric power industry in developing countries. *Annual Review of Energy and the Environment* 26(1): 331–359.

Bank Negara Malaysia. 2010. *Commodity murabahah programme.* http://iimm. bnm.gov.my/index.php?ch=4. Accessed April 23, 2014.

Baqar, D.M. 2005. Need for hedging instruments. *Capital Markets Review* 4 (March). Bahrain Monetary Agency, Bahrain.

Beck, T.H.L. 2007. *Financing constraints of SMEs in developing countries: Evidence, determinants and solutions.* In Financing innovation-oriented businesses to promote entrepreneurship: Unknown Publisher.

Beck, T., and R. Cull. 2014. SME finance in Africa. *Journal of African Economies* 23(5): 583–613.

Beck, T., A. Demirgüç-Kunt, and R. Levine. 2005. SMEs, growth, and poverty: Cross-country evidence. *Journal of Economic Growth* 10: 199–229. https:// doi.org/10.1007/s10887-005-3533-5.

Beck, T., A. Demirgüç-Kunt, and R. Levine. 2007. Finance, inequality, and the poor. *Journal of Economic Growth* 12(1): 27–49.

Beck, T., A. Demirgüç-Kunt, and O. Merrouche. 2010. Islamic vs. conventional banking: business model, efficiency and stability. World Bank Policy Research Working Paper No. 5446, Washington, DC.

Berger, A.N., and G.F. Udell. 1998. The economics of small business finance: The roles of private equity and debt markets in the financial growth cycle. *Journal of Banking & Finance* 22: 613–673.

Berger, A.N., and G.F. Udell. 2002. Small business credit availability and relationship lending: The importance of bank organisational structure. *The Economic Journal* 112(477).

Bernier, Q., and R.S. Meinzen-Dick. 2015. *Public–private partnerships for irrigation: Expanding access or increasing inequality.* Washington, DC: International Food Policy Research Institute.

Besant-Jones, John E. 2006. Reforming power markets in developing countries: What have we learned? Energy and Mining Sector Board Discussion Paper No. 19, World Bank, Washington, DC.

Bhattacharyna, A., J. Oppenheim, and N. Stern. 2015. *Driving sustainable development through better infrastructure: Key elements of a transformation program.* Global Working Paper, Brookings Institution, Washington, DC.

Black, A., H. Esmaeili, and N. Hosen. 2013. *Modern Perspectives on Islamic Law.* Cheltenham: Edward Elgar.

Bos, M.G., D.H. Murray-Rust, D.J. Merry, H.G. Johnson, and W.B. Snellen. 1994. Methodologies for assessing performance of irrigation and drainage management. *Irrigation and Drainage Systems* 7: 231–261.

Burton, M. 2010. *Irrigation management: Principles and practices.* Wallingford, UK: CAB International Publishing.

Butterworth, J., and J. de la Harpe. 2009a. Grand designs: Corruption risks in major water infrastructure projects. U4Brief No. 27, CMI and U4, Anti-Corruption Resource Centre, Bergen, Norway.

Butterworth, J., and J. de la Harpe. 2009b. Not so petty: Corruption risks in payment and licensing systems for water. U4Brief No. 26, CMI and U4, Anti-Corruption Resource Centre, Bergen, Norway.

Cassar, G. 2004. The Financing of Business Start-Ups. *Journal of Business Venturing* 19(2): 261–283.

Central Bank of Malaysia. 2014. *Shariah Issues in Islamic Finance.* Kuala Lumpur: Central Bank of Malaysia.

Chapra, M.U. 2008a. *The Islamic vision of development in the light of Maqasid Al Shariah.* London: Cromwell Press.

Chapra, M.U. 2008b. *The Islamic vision of development in the light of Maqasid Al-Shariah.* London: Cromwell Press.

Chapra, M.U., and T. Khan. 2000. *Regulation and supervision of Islamic banks.* Occasional Paper No. 6, Islamic Research and Training Center, Islamic Development Bank, Jeddah.

Christen, R.P., and J. Anderson. 2013. Segmentation of Smallholder Households: Meeting the Range of Financial Needs in Agricultural Families. CGAP Focus Note No. 85. Washington, DC: World Bank.

Choi, Jieun, Emiko Fukase, and Albert Zeufack. 2019. Global value chain (GVC) participation, competition, and markup: Firm-level evidence from Ethiopia. Background paper, World Bank, Washington, DC.

Cizakca, Murat. 2000. *History of Philanthropic Foundations.* Istanbul: Bogazici University Press.

Cizakca, M. 2004. Cash waqf as alternative to NBFIs Bank. Paper presented at the International Seminar on Nonbank Financial Institutions: Islamic Alternatives, jointly organized by Islamic Research and Training Institute, Islamic Development Bank, and Islamic Banking and Finance Institute Malaysia, Kuala Lumpur, March 1–3.

Collier, P. 2009. Rethinking finance for Africa's small firms. *Private Sector & Development, Proparco's Magazine* 1: 3–4.

Constantinescu, Cristina, Aaditya Mattoo, and Michele Ruta. 2019. Does vertical specialization increase productivity? *World Economy.* Published electronically April 10. https://doi.org/10.1111/twec.12801.

Corsettia, G., B. Guimarãesb, and N. Roubini. 2006. International lending of last resort and moral hazard: A model of IMF's catalytic finance. *Journal of Monetary Economics* 53(3): 441–471.

Cressy, R. 2002. Funding gaps: A symposium. *The Economic Journal* 11(2): 1–27.

Cross, C.G., C.R. Nethercott, H. Rai, and M.A. Al-Sheikh. 2012. *Islamic project finance*. Latham & Watkins LLP. Practical Law Company. https://www.lw.com/thoughtLeadership/islamic-project-finance. Accessed October 11, 2018.

Darghouth, S., H. Tardieu, B. Préfol, A. Vidal, J. Plantey, and S. Fernandez. 2007. Emerging public–private partnerships in irrigation development and management. Water Sector Board Discussion Paper Series 10, World Bank, Washington, DC.

Dariyoushi, J., and H. Nazimah. 2016. Forecasting patronage factors of Islamic credit card as a new e-commerce banking service: An integration of TAM with perceived religiosity and trust. *Journal of Islamic Marketing* 7(4): 378–404.

De Fraiture, C., D. Wichelns, J. Rockström, and E. Kemp-Benedict. 2007. Looking ahead to 2050: Scenarios of alternative investment approaches. In *Water for food, water for life: A comprehensive assessment of water management in agriculture*, ed. D. Molden, 91–145. London and Colombo: Earthscan, International Water Management Institute.

Deininger, K., and D. Byerlee. 2011. *Rising global interest in farmland. Can it yield sustainable and equitable benefits?* Washington, DC: World Bank.

Dong, Y., and C. Men. 2014. SME financing in emerging markets: Firm characteristics, banking structure and institutions. *Emerging Markets Finance and Trade* 50(1): 120–149. https://doi.org/10.2753/REE1540-496X500107.

Dusuki, A.W. 2007. Commodity Murabahah Programme (CMP): An innovative approach to liquidity management. *Journal of Islamic Economics, Banking and Finance* 3(1): 1–23.

Ebrahim, M.S., and S. Rehman. 2005. On the Pareto-optimality of futures contracts over Islamic forward contracts: Implications for the emerging Muslim economies. *Journal of Economic Behaviour and Organization* 56(2, February): 273–295.

Ellis, F. 1998. Household strategies and rural livelihood diversification. *The Journal of Development Studies* 35(1): 1–38.

Eniola, A., and H. Entebang. 2015. Small and medium business management-financial sources and difficulties. *International Letters of Social and Humanistic Sciences* 58: 49–57.

Esho, Ebes, and Grietjie Verhoef. 2018. The Funding Gap and the Financing of Small and Medium Businesses: An Integrated Literature Review and an Agenda. MPRA Paper No. 90153.

Fan, Y., Z. Gao, S. Wang, H. Chen, and J. Liu. 2018. Evaluation of the water allocation and delivery performance of Jiamakou Irrigation Scheme, Shanxi, China. *Water* 10: 654.

FAO (Food and Agricultural Organization). Financial Accounting Standard No. 2 (FAS 2). 1997. *Murabaha to the purchase orderer*. Bahrain: AAOIFI.

Foster, V., S. Witte, S.G. Banerjee, and A. Moreno. 2017. Charting the diffusion of power sector reforms across the developing world. Policy Research Working Paper 8235, World Bank, Washington, DC.

Goldthau, A. 2014. Rethinking the governance of energy infrastructure: Scale, decentralization and polycentrism. *Energy Research & Social Science* 1 (March): 134–140.

Granado, F.J.A., D. Coady, and R. Gillingham. 2012. The unequal benefits of fuel subsidies: A review of evidence for developing countries. *World development* 40(11).

Gratwick, Katharine N., and Anton Eberhard. 2008. Demise of the standard model of power sector reform and the emergence of hybrid power markets. *Energy Policy* 36(10): 3948–3960.

Gundogdu, A.S. 2009. Two-Step Murabaha as an alternative resource mobilization tool for Islamic banks in the context of international trade. *International Journal of Monetary Economics and Finance* 2(3/4).

Gundogdu, A.S. 2010. Islamic structured trade finance: A case of cotton production in West Africa. *International Journal of Islamic and Middle Eastern Finance and Management* 3(1): 20–35. https://doi.org/10.1108/175383 91011033843.

Gundogdu, A.S. 2012. Developing Islamic finance opportunities for trade financing: Essays on Islamic trade vis-à-vis the OIC ten-year programme of action. PhD dissertation, Durham University, UK.

Gundogdu A.S. 2014. Margin call in Islamic finance. *International Journal of Economics and Finance* 6(8).

Gundogdu, A.S. 2016a. Risk management in Islamic trade finance. *Bogazici Journal* 30(2): 64–82. https://doi.org/10.21773/boun.30.2.4.

Gundogdu, A.S. 2016b. Exploring novel Islamic finance methods in support of OIC exports. *Journal of Islamic Accounting and Business Research* 7(2).

Gundogdu, A.S. 2016c. Islamic electronic trading platform on organized exchange. *Borsa Istanbul Review* 16(4).

Gundogdu, A.S. 2018a. The rise of Islamic finance: Two-Step Murabaha. *Asia-Pacific Management Accounting Journal* 13(1).

Gundogdu, A.S. 2018b. An inquiry into Islamic finance from the perspective of sustainable development goals. *European Journal of Sustainable Development* 7(4).

Gundogdu, A.S. 2018c. How different is Islamic finance? Abstract Book ISEFE 2018 Fall Symposium.

Gundogdu, A.S. 2019a. *A modern perspective of Islamic economics and finance.* Bingley, UK: Emeralds Publishing.

Gundogdu, A.S. 2019b. Determinants of success in Islamic public–private partnership projects (PPPs) in the context of SDGs. *Turkish Journal of Islamic Economics* 6(2).

Gundogdu, A.S. 2019c. Poverty, hunger and inequality in the context of zakat and waqf. *Darulfunun Ilahiyat* 30(1): 49–64.

Habib, A. 2011. *Product development in Islamic banks.* Edinburgh: Edinburgh University Press.

Hafidhuddin, Didin, and Syauqi Beik. 2010. Zakat development: Indonesia's experience. *Jurnal Ekonomi Islam al Infaq* 1: 40–52.

Hallegatte, Stephane, Jun Rentschler, and Julie Rozenberg. 2019. *Lifelines: The resilient infrastructure opportunity. Sustainable infrastructure.* Washington, DC: World Bank.

Hanedar, E.Y., Y. Altunbas, and F. Bazzana. 2014. Why do SMEs use informal credit? A comparison between countries. *Journal of Financial Management, Markets, and Institutions* 2(1): 65–86.

Haneef, M.A., A.H. Pramanik, M.O. Mohammed, M.F.B. Amin, and A.D. Muhammad. 2015. Integration of waqf-Islamic microfinance model for poverty reduction: The case of Bangladesh. *International Journal of Islamic and Middle Eastern Finance and Management* 8(2): 246–270. https://doi.org/10.1108/IMEFM-03-2014-0029.

Harrison, R.T., and R. Baldock. 2015. Financing SME growth in the UK: Meeting the challenges the global financial crisis. *Venture Capital* 17(1–2): 1–6.

Harwood, A., and T. Konidaris. 2015. SME exchanges in emerging market economies: A stocktaking of development practices. World Bank Publications. https://elibrary.worldbank.org/doi/abs/10.1596/1813-9450-7160.

Hashim, M.A. 2010. The Corporate Waqaf: A Malaysian experience in building sustainable business capacity. Paper delivered at Dubai International Conference on Endowments, February 16–17, 2010, Dubai, United Arab Emirates. https://www.unescwa.org/events/dubai-international-conference-endowments-innovative-sources-finance-small-and-medium-sized. Accessed 13 January 2019.

Hassan, M.K. 2010. An integrated poverty alleviation model combining zakat, awqaf and micro-finance. Seventh International Conference: The Tawhidi Epistemology: Zakat and Waqf Economy, January 6–7, 2010, Bangi, Malaysia. http://www.ukm.my/hadhari/publication/proceedings-of-seventh-international-conference-the-tawhidi-epistemology-zakat-and-waqf-economy. Accessed January 13, 2019.

Heck, Paul. 2018. *Taxation in Encyclopaedia of the Qurʾān.* Washington, DC: Georgetown University Press.

Heyneman, Stephen. 2004. *Islam and Social Policy*. Nashville: Vanderbilt University Press.

Houdret, A. 2012. The water connection: Irrigation and politics in southern Morocco. *Water Alternatives* 5(2): 284–303.

Ibrahim, B.A. 2003. Poverty alleviation via Islamic banking finance to micro-enterprises in Sudan: Some lessons for poor countries. Institute for World Economics and International Management (IWIM), Sudan Economy Research Group, Discussion Paper, University of Bremen.

IMF (International Monetary Fund). 2019. Corporate taxation in the global economy. Policy Paper 19/007 (March 10), IMF, Washington, DC.

Inocencio, A., M. Kikuchi, M. Tonosaki, A. Maruyama, D. Merrey, H. Sally, and I. de Jong. 2007. Costs and Performance of Irrigation Projects: A Comparison of Sub-Saharan Africa and Other Developing Regions. IWMI Report 109, International Water Management Institute, Colombo, Sri Lanka.

International Energy Agency; International Renewable Energy Agency; United Nations Statistics Division; World Bank; World Health Organization. 2019. *Tracking SDG 7: The Energy Progress Report 2019: Main Report* (English). Washington, DC: World Bank Group.

Iqbal, Zamir. 1999. Financial Engineering in Islamic Finance. *Thunderbird International Business Review* 41(4/5): 541–560.

Iqbal, Z., and M.K. Lewis. 2014. Zakat and the economy. In *Handbook on Islam and Economic Life*, ed. M. Kabir Hassan and Mervyn K. Lewis, ch. 23, 453–475. Cheltenham, UK and Northampton, MA: Edward Elgar Publishing.

Iqbal, Z., and A. Mirakhor. 2007. Qard hasan microfinance (QHMF). http://www.newhorizonislamicbanking.com/index.cfm?section=academicarticles&action=view&id=10461. Accessed April 2, 2009.

Islamic Development Bank Disbursement Manual. http://www.tagtenders.com/UploadFiles/Disbursement%20Manual.pdf. Accessed January 13, 2020.

Islamic Development Bank Guidelines for Procurement of Goods and Works under Islamic Development Bank Financing. Issued April 2019. https://www.isdb.org/sites/default/files/media/documents/2019-06/IsDB_Official_Guidelines_Procurement_of_GoodsNWorks_ENG.pdf. Accessed January 13, 2020.

Kahf, Monzer. 1989. Zakat: Unresolved issues in the contemporary fiqh. *IIUM Journal of Economics and Management* 2: 1–23.

Kahf, M. 1999. Zakah: Performance in theory and practice. Paper presented at the International Conference on Islamic Economics Towards the 21st Century, Kuala Lumpur, August.

Kahf, M. 2000. *al Waqf al Islami, Tatawwuruh, Idaratuh, Tanmiyatuh* (Islamic waqf, its growth, management and development). Damascus: Dar al Fikr.

Kahf, M. 2004. Shari'ah and historical aspects of zakat and awqaf. Background paper prepared for the Islamic Research and Training Institute, Islamic Development Bank.

Kayed, N.K., and M.K. Hassan. 2013. *Islamic Entrepreneurship*. London, UK: Routledge.

Kemal, A.R. 2001. Debt accumulation and its implications for growth and poverty. *Pakistan Development Review* 40(4).

Kersten, R., J. Harms, K. Liket, and K. Maas. 2017. Small firms, large impact? A systematic review of the SME Finance Literature. *World Development* 97(September): 330–348.

Khan, S. 2015. Impact of sources of finance on the growth of SMEs: Evidence from Pakistan. *Decision* 42(1): 3–10.

Khan, T., and H. Ahmed. 2001. Risk management: an analysis of issues in Islamic financial industry. Occasional Paper No. 5 of Islamic Research and Training Institute.

Kister, Meir Jacob. 1965. The parket of the Prophet. *Journal of the Economic and Social History of the Orient* 8: 272–276.

Kuran, T. 2001. The provision of public goods under Islamic law: Origins, impact, and limitations of the *waqf* system. *Law & Society Review* 35(4): 841–898.

Lankford, B.A., I. Makin, N. Matthews, A. Noble, P.G. McCornick, and T. Shah. 2016. A compact to revitalise large-scale irrigation systems using a leadership-partnership-ownership "theory of change". *Water Alternatives* 9(1): 1–32.

Lawless, M., B. O'Connell, and C. O'Toole. 2015. Financial structure and diversification of European firms. *Applied Economics* 47(23): 2379–2398.

Lima, P.F.D., M. Crema, and C. Verbano. 2020. Risk management in SMEs: A systematic literature review and future directions. *European Management Journal* 38(1): 78–94. https://doi.org/10.1016/j.emj.2019.06.005.

Loan Agreement between ADB and Kingdom of Thailand for Greater Mekong Subregion Highway Expansion Phase 2 Project. Available at: https://www.adb.org/projects/documents/tha-41682-039-lna. Accessed January 13, 2020.

Loan Agreement between World Bank and Empresa Municipal De Agua Potable Y Alcantarillado De Guayaquil, EP Emapag EP for Guayaquil Wastewater Management Project. Available at: http://documents.worldbank.org/curated/en/799591468249013159/pdf/RAD1122628120.pdf. Accessed January 13, 2020.

Lowder, S.K., J. Skoet, and T. Raney. 2016. The number, size, and distribution of farms, smallholder farms, and family farms worldwide. *World Development* 87: 16–29.

Maghrebi, N., and A. Mirakhor. 2015. Risk sharing and shared prosperity in Islamic finance. *Islamic Economic Studies* 23(2).

Maizaitulaidawati, M., and Haron Razali. 2019. Financial sustainability of SMEs through Islamic crowdfunding. In *Handbook of research on theory and practice of global Islamic finance*, ed. Abdul Rafay. Hershey, PA: IGI Global.

Mandri-Perrott, C., and J. Bisbey. 2016. *How to develop sustainable irrigation projects with private sector participation*. Washington, DC: World Bank.

Marcus, J., and S.E. Chen. 2004. Identifying risk factors of boot procurement: A case study of stadium Australia. *Construction Economics and Building* 4(1).

Meinzen-Dick, R. 2007. Beyond panaceas in water institutions. *Proceedings of the National Academy of Sciences* 104(39): 15200–15205.

Molden, D.J. 2007. Summary for decision-makers. In *Water for food, water for life: A comprehensive assessment of water management in agriculture*, ed. D. Molden, 1–37. London and Colombo: Earthscan, International Water Management Institute.

Molle, F., and J. Berkoff. 2006. *Cities versus agriculture: Revisiting intersectoral water transfers, potential gains and conflicts*. Comprehensive Assessment of Water Management in Agriculture Research Report 10, International Water Management Institute, Colombo, Sri Lanka.

Molle, F., and J. Berkoff (eds.). 2007. *Irrigation water pricing: The gap between theory and practice*. Wallingford, UK: CAB International Publishing.

Molle, F., P.P. Mollinga, and P. Wester. 2009. Hydraulic bureaucracies and the hydraulic mission: Flows of water, flows of power". *Water Alternatives* 2(3): 328–349.

Moritz, A., J.H. Block, and A. Heinz. 2016. Financing patterns of European SMEs: An empirical taxonomy. *Venture Capital* 18(2): 115–148.

Muda M., and A. Jalil. 2007. Research and development: The bridge between ideals and realities. Paper presented at IIUM International Conference on Islamic Banking and Finance.

Muhtada, Dani. 2008. The role of zakat organization in empowering the peasantry: A case study of the Rumah Zakat Yogyakarta Indonesia. In *Islamic finance for micro and medium enterprises*, ed. Mohammed Obaidullah and Salma Abdullateef. IRTI, Islamic Development Bank: Jeddah.

North, D. 1990. *Institutions, institutional change, and economic performance*. Cambridge: Cambridge University.

Nguyen, N., and N. Luu. 2013. Determinants of financing pattern and access to formal-informal credit: The case of small and medium sized enterprises in Vietnam. *Journal of Management Research* 5(2): 240–258.

Obaidullah, Mohammed. 2013. *Awqaf development and management*. Jeddah: Islamic Research and Training Institute, Islamic Development Bank.

Obaidullah, Mohammed. 2016a. Revisiting estimation methods of business zakat and related tax incentives. *Journal of Islamic Accounting and Business Research* 7: 349–364.

Obaidullah, Mohammed. 2016b. *Zakat management for poverty alleviation.* Jeddah: Islamic Research and Training Institute.

Obaidullah, Mohammed, and Salma Abdullateef. 2011. *Islamic finance for micro and medium enterprises.* Jeddah: IRTI, Islamic Development Bank.

Obertreis, J., T. Moss, P. Mollinga, and C. Bichsel. 2016. Water, infrastructure, and political rule: Introduction to the special issue. *Water Alternatives* 9(2): 168–181.

OECD. 2016. *OECD DAC blended finance principles for unlocking commercial finance for the sustainable development goals.* Paris: OECD. http://www.oecd.org/dac/financing-sustainable-development/development-finance-topics/OECD-Blended-Finance-Principles.pdf. Accessed February 6, 2020.

OECD. 2018. Public–Private Partnerships: In pursuit of risk sharing and value for money. Paris: OECD. http://www.oecd.org/gov/budgeting/public-privatepartnershipsinpursuitofrisksharingandvalueformoney.htm#B3. Accessed November 11, 2018.

Ong, H.C., and D. Lenard. 2002. Can private finance be applied in the provision of housing? Book of Proceedings FIG XXII International Congress.

Ono, A., and I. Uesugi. 2014. SME financing in Japan during the global financial crisi: Evience from firm surveys. *International Review of Entrepreneurship* 12(4): 191–218.

Osei-Kyei, R., and A. Chan. 2017. Implementing public–private partnership (PPP) policy for public construction projects in Ghana: critical success factors and policy implications. *International Journal of Construction Management* 17(2).

Oseni, U.A., M.K. Hassan, and D. Matri. 2013. An Islamic finance model for the small and medium-sized enterprises in France. *JKAU: Islamic Economics* 26(2): 151–179.

Ostrom, E. 1990. *Governing the Commons: The Evolution of Institutions for Collective Action.* Cambridge: Cambridge University Press.

Ostrom, E. 1992. *Crafting institutions for self-governing irrigation systems.* Oakland, CA: Institute for Contemporary Studies Press.

Oweis, T., A. Hachum, and A. Bruggeman (eds.). 2004. *Indigenous water-harvesting systems in West Asia and North Africa.* Aleppo, Syria: International Center for Agricultural Research in the Dry Areas.

Panteli, M., and P. Mancarella. 2015. Influence of extreme weather and climate change on the resilience of power systems: Impacts and possible mitigation strategies. *Electric Power Systems Research* 127 (October): 259–270.

Pasha, Shaheen. 2010b. *Islamic finance needs regulation: experts.* Reuters. http://www.reuters.com/article/idUSTRE61H3AT20100218. Accessed April 23, 2014.

Pasha, Shaheen 2010c. Sharia boards face scrutiny amid crisis. Reuters. http://www.reuters.com/article/idUSLDE62A0J420100311. Accessed April 23, 2014.

Paul, J. 2020. SCOPE framework for SMEs: A new theoretical lens for success and internationalization. *European Management Journal* 38(2): 219–230. https://doi.org/10.1016/j.emj.2020.02.001.

Peria, M.S.M. 2009. Bank financing to SMEs: What are Africa's specificities? Private Sector & Development. *Proparco's Magazine* 1: 5–7.

Pervez, I.A. 2000. Liquidity Requirements of Islamic Banks. In *Anthology of Islamic Banking*, ed. A. Siddiqi. London: Institute of Islamic Banking and Insurance.

Predkiewicz, K. 2012. Is it possible to measure a funding gap? Research Papers of the Wroclaw University of Economics, No. 271.

Qaradhawi, Yusuf. 1995. *Fiqh Al-Zakah*. Trans. Monzer Kahf. Jeddah: Center for Research in Islamic Economics, King Abdulaziz University.

Quartey, P. 2003. Financing small and medium enterprises (SMEs) in Ghana. *Journal of African Business* 4(1): 37–55.

Renault, D., and P.W. Vehmeyer. 1999. *On reliability in irrigation service preliminary concepts and application*. Colombo, Sri Lanka: International Irrigation Management Institute.

Rentschler, J., M. Kornejew, S. Hallegatte, M. Obolensky, and J. Braese. 2019a. Underutilized potential: The business costs of unreliable infrastructure in developing countries. Background paper for this report, World Bank, Washington, DC.

Rentschler, J., M. Obolensky, and M. Kornejew. 2019b. Candle in the wind? Energy system resilience to natural shocks. Background paper for this report, World Bank, Washington, DC.

Revest, V., and A. Sapio. 2013. Does the alternative investment market nurture growth? A comparison between listed and private companies. *Industrial and Corporate Change* 22(4): 953–979.

Rosly, S.A., and M.M. Sanusi. 1999. The application of Bay' Al-'Inah and Bay' Al-Dayn in Malaysian Islamic bonds: AN Islamic analysis. *International Journal of Islamic Financial Services* 1(2).

Rozenberg, J., and M. Fay. 2019. *Beyond the gap: How countries can afford the infrastructure they need while protecting the planet*. Washington, DC: World Bank.

Salehi, Djavad. 2017. Poverty and income inequality in the Islamic Republic of Iran. *Revue Internationale des Etudes du Développement* 1: 113–136.

Salti, N., and J. Chaaban. 2010. On the poverty and equity implications of a rise in the value added tax. *Middle East Development Journal* 2(1).

Sacerdoti, E. 2009. Credit to the private sector in Sub-Saharan Africa: Developments and issues. *Private Sector & Development, Proparco's Magazine* 1: 8–12.

Sanchis-Ibor, C., R. Boelens, and M. García-Mollá. 2017. Collective irrigation reloaded: Recollection and re-moralization of water management after privatization in Spain. *Geoforum* 87: 38–47.

Schweikert, A. E., L. Nield, E. Otto, and M. Deinert. 2019. Resilience and critical power system infrastructure: Lessons learned from natural disasters and future research needs. Background paper for this report, World Bank, Washington, DC.

Sestanovic, A. 2015. *SME stock exchanges: Should they have a greater role?* Zagreb, Croatia: EFFECTUS—College of Finance and Law.

Shah, T. 2014. Accelerating smallholder irrigation in Sub-Saharan Africa: Lessons from South Asia's groundwater revolution. In *Proceedings of the workshop on irrigation in West Africa: Current status and a view to the future.* Ouagadougou, Burkina Faso, December 1–2, 2010. Ed. R.E. Namara and H. Sally, 373. Colombo, Sri Lanka: International Water Management Institute (IWMI), p. 373. https://doi.org/10.5337/2014.218.

Shah, T. 2018. Institutional patterns in farmer-led irrigation: Global trends and their relevance to Sub-Saharan Africa. Unpublished Report, World Bank, Washington, DC.

Shirazi, N.S., M.F.B. Amin, and T. Anwar. 2009. Poverty elimination through potential zakat collection in the OIC-member countries: revisited. *The Pakistan Development Review* 48(4): 739–754.

Siddiqui, Abdur Rashid. 2008. *Qur'anic Key Words.* Markfield: The Islamic Foundation.

Siebert, S., J. Burke, J.M. Faures, K. Frenken, J. Hoogeveen, P. Döll, and F.T. Portmann. 2010. Groundwater use for irrigation: A global inventory. *Hydrology and Earth System Sciences* 14: 1863–1880. https://doi.org/10.5194/hess-14-1863-2010.

Sinclair, H. 2012. *Confessions of a microfinance heretic: How microlending lost its way and betrayed the poor.* San Francisco, CA: Berrett Koehler Publishers.

Songco, J.A. 2002. *Do rural infrastructure investments benefit the poor? Evaluating linkages: A global view, A focus on Vietnam.* Policy Research Working Paper, World Bank, Washington DC.

Stiglitz, J.E., and A. Weiss. 1981. Credit rationing in markets with imperfect information. *American Economic Review* 71(3): 393–410.

Suhardiman, D., and M. Giordano. 2014. Is there an alternative for irrigation reform? *World Development* 57(C): 91–100.

Sur, M., D. Larson, E. Kucheriavenko, and K. Masylkanova. 2014. Facilitating smallholder access to markets. Prepared for Standing Committee for

Economic and Commercial Cooperation of the Organization of Islamic Cooperation (COMCEC).

Svendsen, M. (ed.). 2005. *Irrigation and river basin management: Options for governance and institutions.* Wallingford, UK: CAB International Publishing.

Tang, S. 1992. *Institutions and collective action: Self-governance in irrigation.* San Francisco, CA: ICS Press.

Usman, A., I. Yusnidah, and A. Arpah. 2018. Malaysian public private partnership. *Academy of Accounting and Financial Studies Journal* 22(Special Issue).

Usmani, M.T. 2008. *Sukuk and their contemporary application.* South Africa: Mujlisul Ulama of South Africa.

Van Rooyen, C.J., and S. Nene. 1996. What can we learn from previous small farmer development strategies in South Africa. *Agrekon* 35(4): 325–331.

Vasilescu, L.G. 2010. Financing gap for SMEs and the mezzanine capital. *Ekonomska Istrazivanja* 23(3): 57–67.

Vermoesen, V., M. Deloof, and E. Laveren. 2013. Long-term debt maturity and financing constraints of SMEs during the global financial crisis. *Small Business Economics* 41: 433–448.

Vijil, Mariana, and Laurent Wagner. 2012. Does aid for trade enhance export performance? Investigating the infrastructure channel. *World Economy* 35(7).

Von Braun, J., and R. Meinzen-Dick. 2009. *"Land grabbing" by foreign investors in developing countries: Risks and opportunities.* IFPRI Policy Brief No. 13. Washington, DC: International Food Policy Research Institute.

Wada, Y., L.P.H. van Beek, and M.F.P Bierkens. 2012. Nonsustainable groundwater sustaining irrigation: A global assessment. *Water Resources Research* 48(6): W00L06.

Wagenvoort, R. 2003. Are finance constraints hindering the growth of SMEs in Europe? EIB Papers, ISSN 0257-7755, European Investment Bank (EIB), Luxembourg, 8(2): 23–50.

WB, ESMAP, SE4ALL. 2017. Overview: State of electricity access report. Washington, DC.

Webster, P. 2015. Lesotho's controversial public–private partnership project. *The Lancet* 386(14): 1929–1931. https://www.thelancet.com/journals/lancet/article/PIIS0140-6736(15)00959-9/fulltext.

Wehinger, G. 2012. Bank deleveraging, the move from bank to market-based financing, and SME financing. *OECD Journal: Financial Market Trends* 1: 65–79.

Wender, B.A., M.G. Morgan, and K.J. Holmes. 2017. Enhancing the resilience of electricity systems. *Engineering* 3(5): 580–582.

Williamson, J. 2004. From the Washington consensus towards a new global governance, Barcelona, September 24–25, 2004. https://www.piie.com/publications/papers/williamson0904-2.pdf.

Wilson, R. 2007. Making development assistance sustainable through Islamic microfinance. *IIUM Journal of Economics and Management* 15(2): 197–217.

Woetzel, J., N. Garemo, J. Mischke, M. Hjerpe, and R. Palter. 2016. *Bridging global infrastructure gaps*. McKinsey Global Institute, McKinsey & Company.

World Bank. 2015a. *From billions to trillions: transforming development finance post-2015 financing for development: multilateral development finance* (in English). Washington, DC: World Bank Group. http://siteresources.wor ldbank.org/DEVCOMMINT/Documentation/23659446/DC2015-0002% 28E%29FinancingforDevelopment.pdf. Accessed October 28, 2018.

World Bank. 2015b. *World Bank Group support to Public-Private Partnerships; lessons from experience in client countries, FY02-12*. Washington, DC: World Bank Group. http://documents.worldbank.org/curated/en/405891 468334813110/pdf/93629-REVISED-Box394822B-PUBLIC.pdf. Accessed November 11, 2018.

World Bank. 2019a. *World development report 2020: Trading for development in the age of global value chains (English)*. Washington, DC: World Bank Group.

World Bank. 2019b. *Governance in irrigation and drainage: Concepts, cases, and action-oriented approaches—A practitioner's resource (English)*. Washington, DC: World Bank Group.

World Bank Disbursement Guidelines for Projects, issued in May 2006. Available at: http://documents.worldbank.org/curated/en/410851468161639013/ pdf/385750ENGLISH01ement0Guide01PUBLIC1.pdf. Accessed January 13, 2020.

World Bank Group Guidelines for Procurement of Goods, Works, and Non-consulting Services Under IBRD Loans and IDA Credits & Grants by World Bank Borrowers, issued in January 2001 and revised in July 2014. http://pubdocs.worldbank.org/en/492221459454433323/Pro curement-GuidelinesEnglishJuly12014.pdf. Accessed January 13, 2020.

Xiao, L. 2011. Financing high-tech SMEs in China: A three-stage model of business development. *Entrepreneurship & Regional Development* 23(3–4): 217–234.

Yousef, T.M. 2004. The murabaha syndrome in Islamic finance: Laws, institutions and politics. In *The Politics of Islamic Finance*, ed. R. Wilson, 63–80. Edinburgh: Edinburgh University Press.

Zarrouk, J. 2015. The role of Islamic finance in achieving sustainable development. *Development Finance Agenda* 1(3): 4–5.

Zhang, F. 2019. *In the dark: How much do power sector distortions cost South Asia?* South Asia Development Forum. Washington, DC: World Bank Group. https://doi.org/doi:10.1596/978-1-4648-1154-8.

Zinnbauer, D., and R. Dobson (eds.). 2008. *Global Corruption Report 2008: Corruption in the Water Sector*. Cambridge: Cambridge University Press.

FURTHER READING

Abdul-Rahman, Y. 1999. Islamic instruments for managing liquidity. *International Journal of Islamic Financial Services* 1(1): 1–7.

Ahmed, H. 2011. *Product development in Islamic banks*. Edinburgh: Edinburgh University Press.

Ahmed, O.B. 1997. Islamic financial instruments to manage short-term liquidity. Islamic Research and Training Institute, Islamic Development Bank, Research Paper 41, pp. 19–40.

Asian Development Bank Procurement Guidelines, issued in April 2015. Available at: https://www.adb.org/sites/default/files/procurement-guidelines-april-2015.pdf. Accessed January 13, 2020.

Asian Development Bank Loan Disbursement Hand Book. 2017. https://www.adb.org/sites/default/files/adb-loan-disbursement-handbook-2017.pdf. Accessed January 13, 2020.

Asian Development Bank. 2005. Special evaluation study: The role of project implementation units. https://www.oecd.org/derec/adb/35249987.pdf. Accessed January 13, 2020.

Bank Negara Malaysia. 2010. *Commodity murabahah programme*. http://iimm.bnm.gov.my/index.php?ch=4. Accessed April 23, 2014.

Baqar, D.M. 2005. Need for hedging instruments. *Capital Markets Review* 4 (March). Bahrain Monetary Agency, Bahrain.

Black, A., H. Esmaeili, and N. Hosen. 2013. *Modern perspectives on Islamic law*. Cheltenham: Edward Elgar.

Central Bank of Malaysia. 2014. *Shariah issues in Islamic finance*. Kuala Lumpur: Central Bank of Malaysia.

Chapra, M.U., and T. Khan. 2000. *Regulation and supervision of Islamic banks.* Occasional Paper No. 6, Islamic Research and Training Center, Islamic Development Bank, Jeddah.

Dusuki, A.W. 2007. Commodity murabahah programme (CMP): An innovative approach to liquidity management. *Journal of Islamic Economics, Banking and Finance* 3(1): 1–23.

Ebrahim, M.S., and S. Rehman. 2005. On the Pareto-optimality of futures contracts over Islamic forward contracts: Implications for the emerging Muslim economies. *Journal of Economic Behaviour and Organization* 56(2) (February): 273–295.

Financial Accounting Standard No. 2 (FAS 2). 1997. *Murabaha to the purchase orderer.* Bahrain: AAOIFI.

Gundogdu, A.S. 2012. Developing Islamic finance opportunities for trade financing: Essays on Islamic trade vis-à-vis the OIC ten-year programme of action. PhD dissertation, Durham University, UK.

Goldthau, A. 2014. Rethinking the governance of energy infrastructure: Scale, decentralization and polycentrism. *Energy Research & Social Science* 1(March): 134–140.

Iqbal, Zamir. 1999. Financial Engineering in Islamic Finance. *Thunderbird International Business Review* 41(4/5): 541–560.

Islamic Development Bank Disbursement Manual. http://www.tagtenders.com/UploadFiles/Disbursement%20Manual.pdf. Accessed January 13, 2020.

Islamic Development Bank Guidelines for Procurement of Goods and Works under Islamic Development Bank Financing. Issued April 2019. https://www.isdb.org/sites/default/files/media/documents/2019-06/IsDB_Official_Guidelines_Procurement_of_GoodsNWorks_ENG.pdf. Accessed January 13, 2020.

Khan, T., and H. Ahmed. 2001. Risk management: An analysis of issues in Islamic financial industry. Occasional Paper No. 5 of Islamic Research and Training Institute.

Loan Agreement between ADB and Kingdom of Thailand for Greater Mekong Subregion Highway Expansion Phase 2 Project. Available at: https://www.adb.org/projects/documents/tha-41682-039-lna. Accessed January 13, 2020.

Loan Agreement between World Bank and Empresa Municipal De Agua Potable Y Alcantarillado De Guayaquil, EP Emapag EP for Guayaquil Wastewater Management Project. Available at: http://documents.worldbank.org/curated/en/799591468249013159/pdf/RAD1122628120.pdf. Accessed January 13, 2020.

Molle, F., and J. Berkoff. 2006. *Cities versus agriculture: Revisiting intersectoral water transfers, potential gains and conflicts.* Comprehensive Assessment of

Water Management in Agriculture Research Report 10. Colombo, Sri Lanka: International Water Management Institute.

Pasha, Shaheen. 2010a. Islamic finance needs regulation: Experts. *Reuters.* http://www.reuters.com/article/idUSTRE61H3AT20100218. Accessed April 23, 2014.

Pasha, Shaheen 2010b. Sharia boards face scrutiny amid crisis. *Reuters.* http://www.reuters.com/article/idUSLDE62A0J420100311. Accessed April 23, 2014.

Pervez, I.A. 2000. Liquidity requirements of Islamic banks. In *Anthology of Islamic banking*, ed. A. Siddiqi. London: Institute of Islamic Banking and Insurance.

Usman, A., I. Yusnidah, and A. Arpah. 2018. Malaysian public private partnership. *Academy of Accounting and Financial Studies Journal* 22(Special Issue).

World Bank Disbursement Guidelines for Projects, issued in May 2006. Available at: http://documents.worldbank.org/curated/en/410851468161639013/pdf/385750ENGLISH01ement0Guide01PUBLIC1.pdf. Accessed January 13, 2020.

World Bank Group Guidelines for Procurement of Goods, Works, and Nonconsulting Services Under IBRD Loans and IDA Credits & Grants by World Bank Borrowers, issued in January 2001 and revised in July 2014. http://pubdocs.worldbank.org/en/492221459454433323/Procurement-GuidelinesEnglishJuly12014.pdf. Accessed January 13, 2020.

Index

Printed by Printforce, the Netherlands